P9-CDZ-596

# AMERICAN REFORMERS

ALSO BY RONALD G. WALTERS

*A Black Woman's Odyssey: The Narrative of Nancy Prince* (editor)
*The Antislavery Appeal: American Abolitionism after 1830*
*Primers for Prudery: Sexual Advice to Victorian America* (editor)

# AMERICAN REFORMERS 1815-1860

*REVISED EDITION*

## RONALD G. WALTERS

*CONSULTING EDITOR*

## ERIC FONER

HILL AND WANG

*A DIVISION OF FARRAR, STRAUS AND GIROUX*

*NEW YORK*

Hill and Wang
A division of Farrar, Straus and Giroux
19 Union Square West, New York 10003

Copyright © 1978, 1997 by Ronald G. Walters
All rights reserved
Distributed in Canada by Douglas & McIntyre Ltd.
Printed in the United States of America
First edition, 1978
Revised edition, 1997

LIBRARY OF CONGRESS CATALOGING-IN-PUBLICATION DATA
Walters, Ronald G.
   American reformers, 1815–1860 / Ronald G. Walters ; consulting
editor, Eric Foner. — Rev. ed.
      p.   cm.
   Includes bibliographical references and index.
            ISBN-13: 978-0-8090-1588-7
            ISBN-10: 0-8090-1588-9
   1. Social reformers—United States—History.   I. Foner, Eric.
II. Title.
HN64.W2136   1997
303.48'4'092—dc20                                    96-31399
                                                           CIP

Designed by Jonathan D. Lippincott

www.fsgbooks.com

P1

To Nathaniel Walters
*who grew from child to man*
*over the life of the first edition*

# CONTENTS

Author's Note to the Revised Edition    ix

Preface    xiii

Introduction: Patterns and Changes    3

ONE    The Missionary Impulse    21

TWO    Heaven on Earth    39

THREE    Earth as Heaven    61

FOUR    Antislavery    77

FIVE    Women and a World without War    103

SIX    Strong Drink    125

SEVEN    The Body and Beyond    147

EIGHT    Dangerous Classes    175

NINE    Institutions and Uplift    197

Afterword: A Matter of Time    219

Bibliographical Essay    223

Index    237

# Author's Note to
# the Revised Edition

The first edition of *American Reformers* appeared at a time when I was trying to come to terms with 1960s student radicalism and its aftermath, which I witnessed mostly as a participant-observer at the University of California, Berkeley. As a result of that experience, several things troubled and intrigued me about reform and radicalism in America and, especially, about how scholars and political commentators represent them.

Most conventional interpretations of antebellum reform at the time I was writing *American Reformers* seemed either self-evident or defective in some important respect, a matter to which I briefly return in the Preface. Some scholars dismissed reformers and radicals as cranks; others presented them as noble, farseeing men and women; still others saw them as resolving their own "status anxiety" by engaging in reform. In all of these cases, it seemed—and it still seems—inadequate to me to reduce reform and radicalism to the character and motivation, good or bad, of reformers and radicals. Still other scholars presented antebellum reform as the product of evangelical Protestantism, a view that persists and has merit. The problem with these interpretations, as far as I was concerned, was their failure to explain the existence of non-evangelical reformers, of anti-reform evangelicals, and of reformers who moved away from their evangelical heritage over the course

of their careers. Finally, there were scholars who saw antebellum reform as "social control" on the part of elites bent on making working-
class and ethnic "others" conform to their code of morality and accept
the discipline of an emerging capitalist order. The social-control theory
struck me as less wrong than self-evident. Of course reformers and
radicals want others to conform to their beliefs; it is hard to imagine a
reform or radical movement based on anything else. The question for
me, then, was what else is there to reform and radical movements?

My own view came closest to that of a group of scholars whose work
lay on the horizon when *American Reformers* appeared in 1978. Reform
for us was part of a complicated process of class formation out of which
middle-class identity, and particular sorts of male and female roles,
emerged in the first half of the nineteenth century. This interpretation
certainly does not allow comprehension of everything about antebellum reform, including tensions and differences within it, but I continue to believe it ties together more aspects of the period than any
other view. Behind it, however, was an independent set of questions
running through both editions of *American Reformers*: Why does reform
appear more strongly at certain periods, with little apparent carry-over
from one period to the next? What connects the individual reformer
emotionally, culturally, and intellectually to the larger cause? What
connects one cause (such as antislavery) to another quite different one
(such as health reform)? What roles do radicalism and reform play in
American life—do they change the system, make it run better, serve
the interests of particular groups, help reformers make sense out of
their own lives, or simply provide a harmless safety valve for discontent?

In addition to those questions, I wanted to understand the relationship between antebellum reform and the emergence of new communications technologies (an appropriate issue for someone who saw the
fifties and sixties on television) and to understand why certain kinds
of language, symbol, and metaphor were persuasive.

In the end, however, what I most wanted was to write *American
Reformers* in a way that would emphasize the importance of history. I
hope it shows that the terms "radical" and "reformer" have meaning

only within particular historical contexts, and that we can understand our own positions, and the alternatives available to us, only in relation to other positions, including those of the past.

Because I have not entirely answered the questions I dealt with or laid my concerns to rest, I welcomed the opportunity to do a revised edition of *American Reformers*. It was a chance for me, and I hope for readers as well, to continue the process of coming to terms with the role of reform and radical movements in American life.

I want to renew my thanks to those who helped with the first edition and to friends, students, and readers who have commented on the book since then. The revisions also owe an enormous debt to the extraordinary volume and quality of scholarship that appeared after the first edition, particularly on such topics as women's activism, temperance, utopianism, what I call "body" reforms, and institution-building. A special note of appreciation goes to two people. The first is Arthur Wang, the kind of publisher and friend authors hope to have and seldom deserve. The second is Gayle Mowbray Walters, without whose help and support this, and much else, would remain undone.

There is, finally, an irony to the timing of a revised edition of *American Reformers*. Much like the first edition, it appears at a moment when the nation has taken a turn to the political right and when it is fashionable to attack a liberal tradition that stretches from Progressivism through the New Deal and Lyndon Johnson's Great Society of the 1960s. Elements of this conservative offensive against twentieth-century liberalism recall some of the antebellum reformers whom readers will meet on the following pages, especially those characterized by religious zeal, disgust with politics and politicians, and hostility to government. Although antebellum reformers were far from united under those banners, the recurrence of old patterns in new guises is a further reminder that we are all embedded in history, that human actions and beliefs have unintended and unanticipated consequences, and that what is progressive in one period may be the opposite, or even the subject of reform, in another.

# Preface

Reminiscing about the 1840s, Thomas Wentworth Higginson recalled that "there prevailed then a phrase, 'the Sisterhood of Reforms.' " It referred to "a variety of social and physiological theories of which one was expected to accept all, if any." The phrase was apt. There was an incredible proliferation of reforms in the pre–Civil War years, and it was a rare person who engaged in only one of them. Higginson himself was primarily involved with antislavery, yet he also worked for temperance, women's rights, and health reform. The causes he had in mind were at high tide in the 1840s, but the majority were ten or more years old by then. As early as 1815 Americans had begun to generate what would be one of the most fervent and diverse outbursts of reform energy in their history.

American reform has come in waves, with a decade or more of intense activity followed by periods of relative apathy about social problems. Arising after the War of 1812, antebellum reform crested in the 1830s and 1840s, declined in the 1850s, and seemed almost quaint by the 1870s. It had little influence on Progressivism, the next great collection of reforms. The Progressive era (roughly 1890–1920) emerged after a period of corruption in the late nineteenth century and nearly disappeared in the 1920s. It left a legacy to the 1930s, but a surprisingly small one. Reformers, radicals, and New Dealers of the 1930s, in turn, found themselves denounced or forgotten by youthful rebels in the 1960s. This lack of continuity is one of the chief characteristics of American reform: a failure, or inability, to build traditions and institutions able to survive from generation to generation.

In most instances, war played a major role in destroying reform impulses—the Civil War, World War I, and World War II. (Radicalism in the 1960s was killed by peace, but that is another story.) Wars lead to great social change and to the fulfillment of some reform objectives: the Civil War ended slavery, and World War I helped bring about Prohibition and voting rights for women. But wars also stifle reform. They channel moral energy into service to the nation, either drawing social critics into the war effort, silencing them, or making them appear selfish, unpatriotic, or simply irrelevant. At war's end, Americans have often fallen into moral exhaustion. Yet even in peacetime and under the most favorable circumstances a reform commitment is difficult to make and maintain. The majority of reformers, as well as many radicals, have come from the middle classes, and America offers such men and women more profitable and comfortable alternatives than spending a life in the service of reform.

Some reforms deal with new and disturbing situations. Certainly what reformers and radicals did in the 1930s was largely a response to the Depression. In other cases, however, it is hard to find direct connections between periods of reform and the social and economic conditions of the day. For example, the quality of life probably was no worse during the Progressive years, when many men and women tried to improve it, than it had been between 1870 and 1890, when most people had done less about it. Similarly, antebellum reformers attacked evils that had been around for generations. Slavery was two hundred years old before abolitionists raised the banner of immediate emancipation in 1831. Drunkenness, war, and sexual discrimination were old problems by the time the temperance, peace, and women's rights crusades got under way. Most reform and radical movements, past and present, have addressed real problems, but it takes something more than the existence of real problems to create reform and radical movements. Finding that something is the historian's job.

•   •   •

There are several ways of going about it. One is to try to explain
reform in terms of the moral character of reformers. Sympathetic historians have pictured them as noble idealists who saw wrongdoing and
tried to stop it—which begs the question of how people become idealists and why idealists appear, or are effective, only at certain moments in history. Unsympathetic historians have dismissed reformers
as irresponsible fanatics or as neurotics and malcontents, a view which
ignores the possibility that there might be genuine problems in the
world and that it might be reasonable to want to solve them.

A variation on the latter approach likewise emphasizes motivation
while avoiding making obvious judgments on the rightness or wrong-
ness of reform objectives. It consists of searching for sociological or
psychological factors that characterize reformers and of which they may
have been unaware. At one time the most prominent studies of this
type argued that antebellum crusaders tended to come from social
groups of declining status. Presumably reform was a mechanism to
preserve their social influence and to resolve their "status anxieties."
While I do not accept that interpretation, it helped focus attention on
the social characteristics of reformers. In general (and with many exceptions), they tended to have been evangelical Protestants from New
England families, and their strength was greatest in New England and
its cultural provinces, particularly in areas swept by revivalism and
economic change. (The prime examples of the latter were the Western
Reserve of Ohio and the "Burned-Over District," a portion of western
New York transformed by the Erie Canal.)

Although it has been helpful for historians to examine the family,
regional, class, religious, and psychological backgrounds of reformers,
it is a risky business to generalize about what caused people to participate in the antebellum crusades. For one thing, we know much more
about leaders than about the rank and file. For another, linkages between a particular kind of background and a moral commitment are
not always clear or consistent. There are, indeed, almost as many exceptions as rules—evangelical Protestants, young people, New Englanders, and people of declining status who were not reformers; and

non-evangelicals, old people, Southerners, and men on the make who
were. Most likely, people became reformers out of quite diverse motives and their commitments satisfied a great range of personal, social,
and cultural needs. At the moment, the best we can do is say that
reformers tended to be of such-and-such a background and admit that
we usually do not know, with absolute certainty, why particular individuals committed themselves to particular causes and crusades.

Fortunately, there is more to reform movements than the psyches,
motives, and sociological characteristics of their members. Reform
starts when a few men and women declare that something is evil and
they know the cure for it. What they say and do not say—their concerns, images, and metaphors—are worth examining carefully. What
do reformers claim is wrong with what they attack? Why do they feel
it is evil? The answers seldom prove to be obvious. There were, for
example, hundreds of objections that could have been made against
slavery, but abolitionists made only a handful of them. Why those and
not others? That question, in turn, leads to another approach to reform,
which involves exploring the social and cultural conditions that *permitted* (not *caused*) reformers to see reality as they did. To put it that
way leaves open the issue of what motivated individuals and places
emphasis on the relationship between reform rhetoric and why it made
sense at particular historical moments. My preference for such an approach is clear and this book owes much to it, even though I firmly
believe we can learn more about the sociology of reform and radicalism. But rather than agonize over who American reformers were, I have
devoted most of my energies to finding out what they said and why
it was reasonable and emotionally compelling for them to say it.

It is time to face up to a serious difficulty in terminology. It concerns
the words "radicals" and "reformers." By "radicals" I mean those who
wish to change the structure of society. By "reformers" I mean those
who wish to improve individuals or existing social, economic, and political arrangements. In theory, there is an important distinction here.
Radicals seek to overturn the present order, while successful reformers
may actually strengthen it by making it work better. In practice,

though, the distinction frequently breaks down. Some people are radical from one perspective but not from others. In the 1950s, for instance, civil rights activists demanded an end to segregation. That was radical in the context of American race relations of the day. Yet most civil rights workers did not ask for a change in the basic American political or economic structure. They just wanted to open it up for black people. Do we judge them as radicals for being integrationist in the 1950s or as reformers because they did not seek a total alteration of American society? My answer is "reformers," but it is a fine and debatable matter.

Activists themselves do much to obscure the difference between radicals and reformers through their own actions and rhetoric. It is common for people to take extreme (or "radical") stands in order to gain concessions that are, in effect, reforms. A final complication is the fact that "radical" and "reform" have meaning only in particular historical contexts. What is progressive at one time may be reactionary in another. In the antebellum period, for instance, reformers and radicals frequently argued for what reformers and radicals in the 1960s rejected as sexual repression. Similarly, in the antebellum period, evangelical Protestantism was a driving force behind reform; for much of the twentieth century it has been politically conservative.

Perhaps the difficulty in defining "reform" and "radical" is appropriate. Above all, radicals and reformers are committed to causes and they have no obligation to live up to abstract definitions of themselves. They do what they think needs doing and say what they think needs saying, even though that may require shifting between what we see as reform and radicalism, a flexibility that puts them at risk of being repudiated by the next generation of reformers and radicals.

The difficulties do not end with separating radicals from reformers. There is the further problem of deciding what is a legitimate reform. Some scholars try to draw a line between genuine reformers, whom they see as wanting change to move in new directions, and reactionaries, whom they see as wanting change to move backward, toward old ways of doing things. There are times when that distinction is helpful, but antebellum reformers (and I think American reformers

generally) mingled old and new in complicated ways. They often
adapted traditional values to new situations and believed they could
restore an old order by building new structures. When that happened,
the boundary between reformers and reactionaries begins to look
vague. The course of least confusion is not to agonize over the distinction but simply to define a reform movement as I do here: as any
collective, organized effort to improve society or individuals by achieving a well-articulated goal.

Even so, from a present-day perspective many of the causes discussed in this book do not look much like reforms. Even though alcohol is still a problem, as it was in the nineteenth century, few of us
think the world would be a better place if we banned it (we did that
once and the world was not a better place). Far fewer of us would
agree with phrenologists that analyzing the shapes of skulls is the key
to human progress. And yet temperance and phrenology both figure
in the story of antebellum reform. They do so because people who
believed in them presented them as instruments of social and individual uplift and created an institutional structure to proclaim the
message.

So it comes down, in part, to taking the reformer's word that what
he or she is doing is really a reform. That is not completely satisfactory,
given the ability of people to misjudge and misrepresent themselves;
but the alternative is worse. If we relied entirely on our own standards
to decide whether a cause was a reform, we would put history at the
mercy of present-day politics and lose sight of the meaning past crusades had for the people caught up in them. I am not saying we must
suspend moral judgments altogether and let past generations determine their own place in history. The implications of this position are,
nonetheless, sometimes unpleasant. The Ku Klux Klan of the 1860s
and '70s, for example, had an institutional structure and a goal; its
leaders, moreover, portrayed it as a means of "improving" the South.
It therefore meets my definition of a reform. My inclination is thus to
accept the Klan as reformers of a specific kind for purposes of analysis,
and yet to state clearly that it was also racist, violent, and life-denying.
No one has to believe that all reforms are good.

Words like "reform" and "radical" are necessary abstractions. They have to be used and they ought to be explained. But this is not a book about abstractions. It is about vigorous, often flamboyant men and women and their strange, wonderful, and occasionally heroic causes, fads, and crusades. It is about the "Sisterhood of Reforms" that transformed Thomas Wentworth Higginson's life and the lives of thousands of other antebellum Americans. I hope that this revised edition will also shed light on the lives of subsequent generations of Americans who, like my antebellum reformers, have the courage and imagination to decry the mean-spiritedness of their own times and imagine a better future.

# AMERICAN REFORMERS

# Introduction:
# Patterns and Changes

Several things came together to produce antebellum reform, including important changes in what Americans believed. By 1814—the year the War of 1812 ended—a combination of theological and economic developments led many men and women to assume that the world did not have to be the way it was and that individual effort mattered. Such notions are not terribly ancient; nor are they universal among human societies. They were, however, articles of faith for middle-class nineteenth-century Americans, with their confidence in progress and human will. The religious revivalism of the 1820s encouraged this optimistic and activist spirit by teaching that good deeds were the mark of godliness and that the millennium was near. Other significant new ideas, attitudes, and systems of thought jostled around in the public press and likewise encouraged reform. Some of these beliefs were scientific, a few were daring, many were foolish, and all helped nineteenth-century people think of novel solutions to ancient evils, as well as discover sins that their ancestors never imagined.

Although antebellum reform emerged out of that cultural ferment, its moving force was a broad transformation of American society after 1814. Historians and economists grope for the correct term to describe what happened—"takeoff," "industrialization," and "modernization" have all been used. Scholars also endlessly debate how and why such dramatic changes occur. But the changes themselves touched the furthest corners of economic, social, and political life. They created the material conditions reform movements needed in order to exist, and they jarred thousands of people into thinking about what had to be done to ensure the future glory of America and Americans.

The most easily measured changes were in territory and population. In 1815 there were eighteen states in the Union, none farther west than Louisiana; in 1860 there were thirty-three, including two, California and Oregon, on the Pacific Coast. The land area of the United States in 1815 totaled around 1.7 million square miles. By 1860 the United States had reached its present continental limits, adding about 1.2 million square miles. Population growth more than kept up with territorial expansion: in 1814 there were 8,400,000 Americans; on the eve of the Civil War there were 31,443,321 of them, a rate of growth averaging more than 33 percent per decade. Quite remarkably, Americans increased and multiplied enough to expand urban areas while simultaneously settling an agricultural frontier: about 38 percent of the population in 1860 lived in the newer states and territories of the Midwest and West.

The manner in which the population grew had as many implications for reform as did growth itself. Reproduction, as usual, played the major role. But the antebellum birth rate, although high by present-day standards, declined steadily after 1800. That trend coincided with subtle but substantial alterations in family patterns, a matter of significance for understanding why reformers were so concerned about home life and why so many of them were women.

After 1820 increasing immigration, primarily from Germany, Ireland, and England, kept population growth high despite the downturn in birth rate. During the 1830s around 600,000 people came to the United States, a fourfold increase over the 1820s. In the next decade the figure rose to 1,700,000 and then to 2,600,000 in the decade of the 1850s. The census of 1860 revealed that there were slightly more foreign-born residents—4,138,697—than there were slaves, a rise of nearly 2,000,000 since 1850. Many of these new Americans were hostile to reform crusades, particularly to temperance, and a large number of them were Catholic. For reformers, these hordes of poor, religiously suspect aliens were one of several indications that America was changing rapidly and that decent men and women had to act quickly to keep it on a morally true course.

Even more spectacular evidence of change came from the performance of the American economy after 1814. Precise figures are impossible to give, but it is clear that the standard of living for most free Americans was improving and that the scale and location of industry were changing dramatically. The proportion of the workforce in agriculture declined while that in manufacturing and commerce rose. Much of the production of goods moved out of the household and into shops and factories using water or steam power. New cities sprang up and old ones boomed after 1820. In 1810 there were 46 "urban areas" (defined as places with 2,500 or more population). In 1860 there were 393, including two cities, New York and Philadelphia, with over half a million residents. At the close of the War of 1812 transportation was relatively slow and difficult. On land it was by paved turnpike at best, rutted trail at worst. On water it generally was easier—although occasionally risky to life and limb—thanks to the steamboat, then making its appearance on the rivers of the interior. An era of canal building would soon begin, the capstone of which would be New York's Erie Canal, started in 1817 and completed in 1825. Even so, in 1815 it was costly for most Americans to move themselves or their goods any distance, unless they were fortunate enough to be near a navigable waterway.

That soon changed. Generous amounts of public and private money went into "internal improvements" of all sorts, and in 1828 Americans began construction of the most crucial element in their transportation system, the railroad. By 1860 its tracks stretched across 31,000 miles of the countryside, taking people and products where canal barge and steamboat could not go. This "transportation revolution" diffused economic change throughout the United States as cities in the West such as Pittsburgh, Cincinnati, St. Louis, and Chicago used their locations on rivers (or, later, on railroad lines) to develop into important manufacturing and distributing centers.

Present-day economists quarrel over such difficult questions as rates of growth in per capita income or in "value added by commodity output" in the antebellum period, but anyone born in 1800 and still alive in 1860 would have been very certain that something had happened. Proof was no farther away than the whistle of a distant locomotive or the smoke of the nearest factory.

America's economic development provided reformers with problems in need of solutions. Troubled by the pains and dislocations of sudden expansion, cities were especially ripe for moral crusades. Reformers regarded them—with only a bit of exaggeration—as dismal swamps of vice, disease, and misery. Urbanization and industrialization also helped turn the attention of reformers toward slavery after 1830. As Northern and Southern ways of life became increasingly different, abolitionists saw the South's "peculiar institution" as a relic of barbarism and the North's mixture of farming, commerce, and industrial growth as the course of civilization and progress. Economic differences between the sections, from their point of view, reinforced moral judgments.

There were other, less direct, ways in which the transformation of the United States fostered antebellum reform. Prosperity meant that there were middle-class men and women with education, income, and leisure to devote to social causes. New technology put powerful weapons in the hands of such people. The same transportation revolution that brought goods to distant markets also carried lecturers to widely dispersed audiences they could not have reached a generation before. Innovations in printing reduced the cost of producing propaganda to the point where a person could make a living editing a reform newspaper or writing books and pamphlets for a limited but national readership. By the 1830s it was simpler in every respect to imagine moral connections between distant places, to cater to scattered groups of like-minded Americans, and to support oneself while doing it.

Change in the nature of politics had almost as much significance for antebellum reform as did the economic transformation of the United States. If nothing else served to indicate that there was political turmoil between 1815 and 1860, the ebb and flow of partisan organizations would tell the story. The War of 1812 was the deathblow to the Federalist Party, which had once claimed George Washington, John Adams, and Alexander Hamilton among its leaders. Even before 1812 it had virtually been reduced to a New England remnant, thanks to the rise of Thomas Jefferson and his supporters, called Republicans or Democratic-Republicans. For several years after the war, most national political conflict took place among Democratic-Republicans rather than between two distinct, well-identified parties. That changed after 1824, when John Quincy Adams, one of four Democratic-Republican presidential candidates, defeated Andrew Jackson. By 1828, when Jackson triumphed over Adams, the factions were becoming more sharply defined. Jackson, now under the Democratic label, had a superb ability to unite his supporters and create enemies. By the time he left office, his protégé and successor, Martin Van Buren, confronted a well-organized opposition, the Whig Party. Whigs and Democrats fought on fairly equal terms for more than a decade, but after 1848 the former disintegrated over the issue of slavery. The Democrats held together—often tenuously—until 1860, when they, too, split. After 1854, however, they faced a formidable challenge from the Republican Party, whose candidate, Abraham Lincoln, captured the Presidency in 1860. This brief catalogue of political flux, complicated though it may seem, leaves out ephemeral smaller parties: the Anti-Masonic, Liberty, Free-Soil, and Know-Nothing, some of which made respectable showings in local, state, and even national elections.

Reformers disagreed among themselves on political questions and could be found in every major and minor party, although more in the Whig and Republican than in the Democratic. Their ranks also included many men and women who rejected parties altogether. It was partisan conflict, rather than any particular political organization, that most influenced antebellum reform.

A new style of political warfare emerged after 1800, as politicians learned how to court an expanding electorate. By 1810 a majority of states had lowered franchise requirements to the point where most adult white males could vote. When Jackson made his first run for the

Presidency in 1824, only three states restricted suffrage for white men in any meaningful way and in many areas even recent immigrants found it easy to cast ballots. This may have been democracy, but it also permitted anyone, including the worst sort of rascals, to help select the nation's leaders. Reformers complained that a degraded and sinful majority, manipulated by political machines, had more of a voice in the nation's affairs than they, the godly minority, did.

Politicians confirmed reformers' dour view of them by seeking the electorate's lowest common denominator. No promise was too extreme, no spectacle too extravagant, if it got votes. The political system, reformers thought, rewarded those who appealed to the rabble and pretended to be common folk rather than risk appearing superior in morality and intellect. The results were horrifying to right-minded men and women: high office bestowed on the likes of Andrew Jackson, a duelist who married a divorcée, or Richard M. Johnson, Van Buren's Vice President, who lived in sin with a black mistress. All around them reformers saw a frightful decline from the days of the Founding Fathers, when great men walked the earth and wisdom and virtue had a place in government.

Yet reformers did not entirely reject politics. The Jacksonian political system itself made their propaganda effective by linking "public opinion" and governmental action. As reformers perceived, winning hearts and minds had become the essential first step toward political change, for better as well as for worse. Many reform crusades, moreover, explicitly sought political consequences. If everything worked according to plan, temperance, Sunday schools, and public education, for instance, would produce a morally responsible electorate. In even more direct ways reformers engaged in political action. Evangelical Protestants lobbied Congress in 1828 to stop postal employees from working on Sunday; and in the next decade abolitionists mounted a petition campaign urging Congress to take stands against slavery. An antislavery faction began to run its own candidates for office in 1840. Temperance workers likewise became involved in political campaigns, winning significant victories in the 1850s and making alcohol a major political issue for the next eighty years. When reformers went beyond the powers of persuasion and sought to use the government to make people behave, they dipped their toes, and sometimes a great deal more, into the muddy waters of democratic electioneering, despite their contempt for its excesses.

The ambivalence of reformers toward politics is revealing, even if it was not absolute. America was becoming a different place in the antebellum period, and partisan warfare symbolized the change just as surely as did territorial expansion, alterations in family patterns, and the appearance of immigrants, cities, and factories. But because politicians held out no promise of leading the transformation of the United States in a virtuous fashion, the task fell to reformers, or so they believed.

There were, naturally, many ways of responding to change besides becoming involved in a moral crusade. Although it may seem like a detour, examining some of the alternatives is worth while. Otherwise it would be easy to make the mistake of thinking that reform was disconnected from other kinds of social action. On the contrary, it was one of several means by which antebellum men and women attempted to impose moral direction on social, cultural, and economic turmoil.

In September 1826 a prisoner named William Morgan, who had planned to reveal the secrets of the Masonic lodge, was kidnapped from an upstate New York jail. Morgan was presumed murdered. His probable fate confirmed suspicions that a sinister conspiracy was afoot and precipitated a crusade against the Masons. In several states—New York, Pennsylvania, and Vermont, especially—Anti-Masonic parties became a significant force. Elsewhere in the Northeast anti-Masonry remained an issue, if not a political movement, for several years.

About the time it was declining, a professor at William and Mary, Thomas R. Dew, put pen to paper. In 1832 his *Review of the Debate in the Virginia Legislature of 1831 and 1832* defended slavery and sought to discredit the last shred of white Southern abolitionism, the idea of resettling all black people outside the United States. Dew's work was the beginning of a three-decade campaign of proslavery propaganda, pursued in periodicals and in lengthy treatises by Southern nationalists.

Two years after Dew's *Review* a mob gathered at a convent in

Charlestown, Massachusetts, and burned it to the ground. Mobs were not unusual in the 1830s—one scholar tabulated 157 of them between 1834 and 1837—but the target of this one deserves notice. It was Catholicism. From 1834 on, there would be acts of violence against Catholics and political campaigning against them and immigrants. The Irish, of course, were both. The high tide of nativism came between 1853 and 1855, when the Know-Nothing Party was the fastest-growing political organization in the land, running on its principle that "Americans must rule America."

What we have here are four things—anti-Masonry, proslavery, mobs, and nativism—more or less seeming to be unrelated to one another or to antebellum reform (although anti-Masonry and nativism attracted some reformers). Yet each of the four, in common with reform movements, represented an assessment of what was wrong with America and of what needed correcting. Each, also like reforms, focused upon a supposedly disruptive element in American society: Masons, the North, whoever angered rioters, and foreigners. Reformers, naturally, had different lists of villains—heathenism, the competitive impulse, slavery, war, alcohol, ignorance, and so forth. But the pattern of thought was the same: old values were being lost and whatever was at fault had to be eliminated or controlled if America was to fulfill its destiny.

Behind that reasoning was a suspicious mentality characteristic of many antebellum reformers, as well as non-reformers, that attributed the nation's troubles to conspiracies of one sort or another—by slaveholders, liquor dealers, Masons, the Catholic Church, or politicians and clergy serving special interests. Some historians describe that rhetoric as part of a witch-hunting "paranoid style" reappearing at certain periods in American politics. The label is overly melodramatic when applied to antebellum conspiracy theories. To believe that plotters were responsible for what was happening to the country was wrong; but it was a part of a quest, going back at least to the eighteenth century, for secular terms in which to analyze politics and social change. Rather than seeing the hand of God moving events, many antebellum Americans saw the hands of sinister individuals. That may not have been accurate, but it was about as good as any other explanation available before Marx and modern social science. While in the twentieth century conspiratorial explanations mostly served the cause of repression, in the nineteenth they also served reform.

That was true in part because the "paranoid style," besides being secular, was anti-elitist. It raised doubts about established authorities and leading citizens. Ministers, politicians, and "gentlemen of property and standing" were all fair game—it was they who plotted against the liberties of the people. In addition to venting class hostilities, such charges rested on long-standing beliefs in Anglo-American political thought, derived in part from classical republican writers: a conviction that power corrupts men, who then plot against liberty, and that loss of civic virtue leads to loss of freedom. For abolitionists, that view, combined with evangelical Protestantism, gave shape to their hatred of slavery and of the idleness, dissipation, and abuse of power it pro-duced. For other people it appeared in charges that selfish men (Ma-sons, rum merchants, Jesuits, congressmen, or whoever) secretly connived against the interests of decent folk. Fear of power can be crabbed and selfish—the ideology of a class that wants to be left alone to do as it pleases—but in antebellum America it also made men and women sensitive to many different issues, a few of which appear silly a century and a half later, but others of which, like slavery, were momentous.

Whether "paranoid" or healthy, moreover, mistrust of politicians can be a powerful force in bringing new leaders to the fore and raising the level of political participation. Reform movements, anti-Masonry, mobs, and nativism did precisely that. They drew into the public arena men and women who previously had not been involved in social ac-tion. Such people often gloried in not being members of the estab-lishment and indulged in a kind of politics of antipolitics. In some instances that took the form of a literal rejection of political means, as when abolitionists refused to vote or when mobs enforced their own "justice." At other times it was little more than open contempt for officeholders and the major political parties. Yet even the crusades that seem exceptions to the antipolitical rule fit it. The Anti-Masonic and

Know-Nothing movements, for example, produced parties, but these did best when they attacked professional politicians and at least appeared to be in the hands of fresh, inexperienced leaders. When political hacks and chronic office seekers climbed aboard the bandwagon, the movements lost credibility and support. Their temporary success and long-run failure are a sign that much of the electorate, not simply reformers, was uneasy with the party-oriented political system of Jacksonian America and responsive to people and organizations claiming moral detachment from it.

Anti-Masonry, proslavery, mobs, and nativism had still other characteristics of true reform movements, but each lacked a crucial element. Mobs, obviously, were not movements. They were spontaneous and sporadic, without institutions and often without clear long-range goals. Anti-Masons and nativists had reformers in their ranks and supported many reform objectives, but they were fuzzy about what sort of social order they wanted, once they purged America of sinister conspiracies. Proslavery writers often criticized Northern and Southern ways of life and presented alternative visions of society (and in that sense were reformers), but they did not have an organizational structure to spread their ideas and to channel the energies of the faithful. Instead of building a movement, they used publications and existing political bodies to carry the word.

The point of the comparison, however, has not been to argue that anti-Masonry, proslavery, mobs, and nativism were reform movements. It has been to demonstrate that reformers were more representative of their period than they seem to have been at first glance. They were Americans responding to change in a manner their society and culture allowed. Whether a person became a reformer, a nativist, politically active, a member of a mob, apathetic, or anything else was a matter of social position, upbringing, and events. The decisive factor in making, or not making, a reform commitment was how the transformation of America played upon the individual's life history and connected it, or failed to connect it, to some larger cause. For some the path led to reform; for others it led elsewhere.

•　　•　　•

How reform helped people respond to a changing world varied with the particular crusade. At one extreme were causes such as health reform and temperance, which assisted people, including reformers themselves, in achieving self-mastery and individual dignity. At the other extreme were antislavery and school reform, which acted as explanations of what had to be done to society and for others. Communitarianism played both roles by promising to transform both the believer and the world.

Important as the nature of a reform was, the position it held in a person's life depended greatly on whether one was a leader or a follower. Leaders found in reform a career that had not existed two or three generations earlier. Before 1800 very few people had been able to give themselves over entirely to moral or social causes. Full-time gadflies like Tom Paine were rare, and most of them in the eighteenth century were religious itinerants, like the great Quaker abolitionist John Woolman. Before the 1820s reform more commonly was a sideline for men, and some women, who had social position and a reasonable income. The archetype of such a reformer was Benjamin Franklin, who included good deeds among his other activities. Only with the technological and social changes of the nineteenth century did it become possible for large numbers of Americans to make a livelihood out of agitation. To be sure, some leaders of antebellum reform held other jobs, as clergymen and even in business, like Arthur and Lewis Tappan. But many either rejected conventional occupations (including a fair proportion of onetime or would-be ministers) or else kept half-heartedly at other work while devoting much income and emotional energy to a cause. A life such as William Lloyd Garrison's, which for thirty-five years consisted primarily of editing a reform newspaper, would have been unthinkable in Franklin's day.

Reform was a demanding profession, with poverty and violence among its risks; but it offered rewards. For women it was among the very few means of having public influence; for men it provided a kind of moral authority that law, politics, business, and (in some circles) the ministry no longer had. The greatest satisfactions, however, were personal, as reformers often acknowledged. Reform transformed them in much the same manner as a religious conversion. Lydia Maria Child described it well. In the 1830s and already a successful author, she met Garrison, who "got hold of the strings of my conscience and pulled me into reforms." The encounter changed "the whole pattern of my life-web." Child would have seasons of doubt and unhappiness afterward, but she found a meaning in antislavery she had not discovered in religion or writing fiction. For her and hundreds of her colleagues reform was more than just another job. It was an important part of oneself.

Most people involved in reform, however, were not leaders. They were obscure men with regular employment, single women, or women with family responsibilities. They drifted out of reform after a few years or, at most, stayed on the periphery of it throughout their adulthood. Although their participation, dues, and consumption of propaganda kept reforms alive, they made little mark in the historical record. There were hundreds of thousands of such people engaged in various causes, and the experiences of one of them, Henry Cummins, may have been more typical than were those of a celebrity like William Lloyd Garrison. A teenager in Eugene, Oregon, in the 1850s, Cummins described himself as "reformatory all round." His commitment to health reform gave him pride and self-discipline—as an eighteen-year-old he noted with satisfaction that "the cravings of my appetite, on account of my rigid abstemiousness, are fast subsiding." (It is not entirely clear which appetite he meant: the previous month he read Dr. Russell Trall's *Home Treatment for Sexual Abuses*.) Important though control of his bodily urges was, Cummins gained most from the social network his enthusiasms spun for him. From a small town, distant from the cultural centers of the land, he corresponded with friends throughout Oregon on reform matters and inquired about the possibilities of going East to study phrenology or the water cure. Cummins was dedicated to reforms for years, but many of his acquaintances passed through them as a brief stage in life. "Most of the young men who commence the study of Phrenology, in Oregon," a friend noted, "have finely [finally] turned out Preachers or Merchants or drunkards." (That correspondent gave himself two more years as a phrenological lecturer, after which he planned to "study medison," which he thought "will not take me long with my knowledge.")

Antebellum reform was not entirely a movement of lonely youth, but much of its significance among the rank and file appears to have come from the self-control, intellectual stimulation, and social contacts it provided young people like Cummins. The surviving minutes of some small-town temperance societies deal less with the evils of drink than with costumes, rituals, and members of the opposite sex. It does not demean reform to say that it did a great deal for reformers. It was no small blessing for individuals to have been able to put their lives in order, to have created emotional bonds with others, and to have done some good in the process. A reform commitment is meaningful only when there is a resonance between the reformer's life and a broader problem.

Antebellum reform had its place in history, just as it did in the lives of individuals. In some respects it looked backward to traditions long predating it. The obvious instances were its evangelical Protestant imagery and its use of several ideological strands from the American Revolution, including the language of "natural rights," a belief in conspiracies, and an insistence that freedom was the right of human beings to buy and sell in the marketplace with a minimum of interference. The latter view could be radical when directed against restrictive laws and entrenched privilege, as it was during the American Revolution. But by the end of the nineteenth century it became conservative dogma, ending up as little more than a rationale for allowing Americans to exploit their land and one another without having the government do anything about it. Yet such a definition of freedom still had much of its egalitarian thrust when it appeared in antebellum reform. A few people (communitarians, most notably) challenged it and attempted to substitute an ethic of cooperation and harmony. The idea of laissez-faire, nonetheless, gave a critical edge to many reformers' analyses of tyranny, particularly to the abolitionist argument that the slave rightfully owned his or her labor.

Despite the significance of what was old in antebellum reform, many

things were new about it. The prospect of making a career out of
reform was one of them. Another was the matter of how people believed problems ought to be solved. Eighteenth-century reformers
generally took human betterment—the limited amount of it they
thought possible—to be something for members of the elite to determine and implement. It was the responsibility of those with moral and
financial advantages to ameliorate suffering, without any expectation
that the millennium was at hand or that social relationships would be
fundamentally changed. Antebellum reformers saw things differently.
Some men and women, consistent with their evangelical Protestantism, insisted that change could be total, that perfection was possible
for people and for society, and that it began with the individual, no
matter how lowly. Making a sinner's heart yearn for good behavior,
not imposing morality by force or giving charity, was the task of reform.
Reformers, of course, were not of a single mind about that. Temperance advocates were especially committed to legislating morality, and
there were others who swam against the individualistic and voluntaristic currents of antebellum reform. The most important of them developed innovative forms of coercion—schools, asylums, and assorted
institutions to uplift or cure mankind. But antebellum Americans
broke with their eighteenth-century predecessors whichever course
they chose, whether they tried to improve humanity through conversion or through confinement, and when they imagined a radically better world dawning.

Another great transformation of American reform lay ahead after the
Civil War. Signs of change began to appear as early as the 1850s, when
many reformers lowered their goals and lost some of the evangelical
fervor of the 1830s. The trend continued, at an accelerated pace after
the Civil War, until by the 1870s a prominent faction of Northeastern
reform, consisting in part of ex-abolitionists and their children,
dropped its horizon to the point where it would have been satisfied
with little more than civil service laws, honest elections, and free trade.
That was less ambitious than wanting to save the world.

Some of the gloomier mood came from the bitter sectional conflict
of the late 1840s and 1850s and the Civil War. The majority of re-

formers lived north of the Mason-Dixon line and most were drawn to
the Northern cause, willing to subordinate their programs and swallow
their doubts in order to help it triumph. They had, moreover, to re-
consider their belief that the individual could be a force in history.
Despite acts of heroism, humans seemed irrelevant in modern war,
when large organizations deliver men and matériel to the front lines
and care for the sick and wounded. It was a massive army rather than
sanctified hearts that won the war.

It was not just the war that took the fire out of antebellum reformers.
Part of the change came about because of what had not been accomplished in decades of agitation. Sinners were harder to reach than anyone imagined; drunkards remained drunkards, the insane were not
made sane, and so it went. Reformers had been far too optimistic about
what propaganda and moral suasion could do. If nothing else, fatigue
and a lack of results began dampening enthusiasm for reform by 1860.

When success did come, it proved to have as much of a chastening
effect as failure. The destruction of slavery in 1865 deprived reformers
of their most emotionally compelling issue. Few white Americans
could bring to the cause of civil rights for blacks the same passion they
invested in antislavery. Some abolitionists kept faith in racial justice
down to the end of the nineteenth century, and most crusades persisted after 1860—temperance and woman's rights reached their peaks
much later. When people worked for causes after 1860, however, their
objectives usually were more modest than those of antebellum reformers, and their emotional pitch was lower. As hopes for humanity declined, so did the rationale for reform. Political corruption in the 1870s
provided more reasons for morally sensitive people to retreat in disgust
from social involvement: the most meaningful of wars ended with
elected officials wallowing in the public trough. Perhaps human nature
was fatally flawed and mankind was beyond redemption in this world.

By the 1890s other styles of reform began to emerge, types more familiar to us, although they may be passing as well. Their story is too
complicated to tell except in outline, as further reminder that modes
of changing the world also change like everything else. Since the late

nineteenth century, reform has been largely secular and often committed to science as a guide to managing human affairs. Only in rare
instances has a religious tone been as prominent as it was in the early
nineteenth century. Where God retreated, the state and expertise advanced. Beginning with the Populists of the 1880s, reformers called
upon the government to solve problems with a boldness that would
have appalled their early-nineteenth-century counterparts. There was
no precedent in antebellum reform for the zeal of Progressives and
New Dealers for constructing regulatory agencies to oversee social and
economic matters. This bureaucratic impulse was directed toward setting fair terms for competition in the marketplace and protecting
Americans from the worst hazards of the day. In desiring to do that,
rather than strive to create a perfect world, latter-day reformers expected less than their antebellum predecessors had. They were, nonetheless, more perceptive for recognizing that solutions to the evils of
modern life have more to do with industries and cities than with sinful
hearts.

Yet differences were not absolute between antebellum reformers
and their successors. Some individuals bridged the distance. Wendell
Phillips (to cite a notable case) began as an abolitionist and, after the
death of slavery, spent many years involved in less individualistic,
more secular crusades. In style as well as personnel the line between
older and newer modes of reform often becomes indistinct. The use
of law, institutions, and science to further social change, for example,
began in the pre–Civil War period, even though it would be central
to Progressivism. Millennialism and immediatism—characteristics of
antebellum reform—continued to crop up after 1860. They reappeared
in 1912 when Theodore Roosevelt's followers stood at Armageddon
and battled for the Lord (they lost) and again when "Freedom now"
became the rallying cry for the civil rights movement of the 1960s.

Still, much has changed since 1860 and many twentieth-century
Americans found it hard to be sympathetic to antebellum reformers
with the exception of the abolitionists. They seem quaint for their
follies, their naïveté about evil, and their hostility to sex, drink, and
rich food. We are battle-scarred by developments they could not even

imagine; we are less optimistic about progress; and many of us are more at peace with our bodies. But perhaps we can admire antebellum reformers for the nobility of their greatest vision, or at least feel a twinge of guilt for being cynical about it. In their best moments they believed in harmony and human unity. They thought the glorious and perfect time was near when sin would vanish and men and women would behave morally because they wanted to, not because they were forced to. Instead, as we know and antebellum reformers could not, industrialization, imperialism, and war were advancing upon the modern world.

# ONE

# The Missionary Impulse

The report on a Kentucky girl in 1801 was dire: "She was struck down fell stiff her hand and arm also became as cold as Death heer fingers cramp'd recov'd heer speech in 2 hours and was haled home on a sled continues in a state of despare which has lasted 3 weekes." The girl was not ill. She had a religious experience. Hers was more extreme than most, although not unusual for Kentucky in 1801.

Between the late 1790s and the Civil War, countless Americans like the Kentucky girl were caught up in outbursts of intense religious excitement. Few people outside the West had her kind of physical reaction, but men and women, girls and boys became convinced of their own sinfulness, went through intense emotional turmoil, and emerged with a belief that they had been saved. Whether it came in special camp meetings or from the pulpit of the local church, the evangelical message was proclaimed across the land and the public responded with explosions of spiritual zeal. These bore a special relationship to antebellum reform.

Revivals in the early nineteenth century were so frequent and widespread that historians sometimes apply the phrase "Second Great Awakening" to the entire period from 1795 to 1837. (The first Great Awakening crested in the 1740s.) Within that long span of years there were times and areas of greater and lesser enthusiasm. Between 1795 and 1810 much of the action was in Kentucky and Tennessee, in rowdy revivals presided over by Methodists, Presbyterians, and Baptists. More sedate awakenings occurred in New York and among New England Congregationalists, but the vigor was in the West. From 1810 to 1825 the focus of revivalism shifted to the East, where influential clergy—Lyman Beecher most prominent among them—began preaching the gospel in revivalistic fashion while making important, often unacknowledged, modifications in New England theology. After 1825 evangelism reached a peak in the work of Charles G. Finney. His impact on reformers and reform, like Beecher's, would be great.

In 1821 the twenty-nine-year-old Finney went through a typically agonizing conversion, after which he gave up a promising law practice in rural New York to study for the Presbyterian ministry. Although he distanced himself from "ignorant" Methodist and Baptist evangelists, he had less patience with formal theology than did Beecher and the New Englanders. His forte was using common sense, everyday language, and theatricality to drive his hearers to seek salvation. In drawing on such techniques, he was part of a much larger antebellum process of dissociating religion from doctrinal complexity and fusing it and popular culture in powerful ways. Soon after ordination Finney presided over remarkable revivals in western New York and was well on his way to becoming a major force in evangelical Protestantism. In 1832 he came to New York City to assume the pastorate of the Second Free Presbyterian Church, situated in a former theater. His arrival symbolized a closing of the gap between Western and Eastern, and rural and urban, revivalism.

That is not to say Finney's triumph, or revivalism's, was complete. He and other evangelicals faced many critics, both from non-evangelical sects like the Unitarians and from within their own denominations. Finney eventually left the Presbyterians and Beecher, at first a Congregationalist, joined their ranks only to be put on trial by the Cincinnati Synod for heresy. He survived the ordeal, but the Presbyterian Church—the largest sect in the nation—split into pro- and anti-revival groups two years later, in 1837.

Evangelicals also battled one another. In 1827 things reached such a bad pass between Western revivalists led by Finney, and Easterners clustered around Lyman Beecher, that they held a nine-day peace conference. It failed. With his customary vigor, Beecher warned Finney not to enter Massachusetts. He recalled saying, "As the Lord liveth, I'll meet you at the State line, and call out all the artillerymen, and fight every inch of the way to Boston, and then I'll fight you there."

Despite hostility and dissension in its own ranks, revivalism was the core of antebellum Protestantism. It was the faith of people as far apart socially and geographically as rude Kentucky backwoodsmen and wealthy New York merchants. It flowed across denominational lines and appeared in all the major Protestant sects, muddling distinctions between them. In times of awakenings, Baptists, freewill Methodists, and predestinarian Presbyterians muted their disagreements and became brothers and sisters in spirit. Laypersons and clergy changed from one denomination to another, with little effort. What counted more to believers than creeds and doctrines was whether a church was for or against revivals. In some guise or another, evangelical Protestantism was the religion of most Americans.

Connections between revivalism and reform were obvious at the time and have been much emphasized by historians ever since. Evangelical clergy and laity engaged in moral crusades of their own and led secular ones, for example, temperance and antislavery. Revivalistic institutions such as Lane Seminary and Oberlin College were breeding grounds for reformers, many of whom had been inspired by Beecher and Finney. In regions like the Western Reserve of Ohio and the Burned-Over District of New York, reform movements followed close on the heels of hellfire preaching. Even voting statistics bear out the correlation, with, for instance, the abolitionist Liberty Party doing best in areas where religious enthusiasm had run high.

Still, it is possible to make too strong a link between revivals and reform. Of the hundreds of thousands of Americans converted between 1800 and 1860, only a minority felt compelled to engage in social action, and others were on the anti-reform side of all questions. Not only that: many reforms had strong support from such non-evangelical sects as the Quakers and Unitarians. Some crusades, notably communitarianism and spiritualism, were especially attractive to freethinkers and atheists. Deism, with its mechanistic God and skepticism about doctrine and clergy, had a following in labor reform, where an eighteenth-century tradition of artisan radicalism and rationalism remained vital.

Even among evangelical reformers, Christianity was not the only source of intellectual and emotional stimulation. Many looked to science, natural law, and American political traditions, as well as the Bible, for inspiration. All reformers buttressed their arguments with enlightenment humanitarianism, the republican rhetoric of the American Revolution, and the sentimental conventions of the day. Yet it was evangelical Protestantism that provided much of the ideological and organizational foundation for antebellum reform.

Beginning in the early twentieth century, popular critics of revivalism such as H. L. Mencken made it seem the simple-minded epitome of anti-intellectualism. This gulf between intellectuals and radicals on one side and revivalism on the other, however, made it easy to forget the complex and sophisticated role evangelical Protestantism played in the history of ideas. It grew out of—and produced—impressive theological debates and permeated much eighteenth- and nineteenth-century social, moral, economic, political, and scientific thought. What mattered most for reform, nonetheless, was a handful of highly generalized beliefs, held in one form or another by all evangelicals. These were usually not formal doctrines (although they could be); more often, they were half-articulated assumptions about society, human beings, and the future.

The Second Great Awakening raised expectations that the Kingdom of God on earth was imminent. Similar notions appeared during the first Great Awakening and had surfaced throughout the centuries, but the quickening of religious fervor after 1800 seemed a sure sign to many Americans that the new day was dawning. One variety of these beliefs, called millenarianism (also known as premillennialism), held that there would be a literal return of Christ, and a Day of Judgment, prior to the thousand-year reign of God predicted in Revelation 20. In the antebellum period its most numerous exponents were followers of a New England Baptist preacher named William Miller, who set the year of Christ's arrival as 1843 (it was postponed to 1844, then indefinitely). Several prominent reformers became Millerites—one of their leaders was an ex-abolitionist—but millenarians generally had an anti-reform cast of mind. They usually maintained that times would inevitably become worse until the reappearance of Jesus and that godly people must withdraw from the sinful world and await the Judgment.

There was another way of thinking about the Kingdom of God, known variously as millennialism or, more clumsily and accurately, as postmillennialism. It was of much greater significance in antebellum reform than millenarianism. Postmillennialists disagreed over whether the reign of God was near or whether it would come gradually or swiftly, and whether it would begin with a cataclysm or quietly. But they agreed that it would be a real historical era occurring before the final Judgment—a thousand years of peace, prosperity, harmony, and Christian morality. That was a vision of the ideal society and an important one for reformers: the imperfections of their own day were stark by comparison with a time of God's justice. Postmillennialism assured them that a better world was possible (people have not always thought that to be the case) and gave them hope they might live to see it. Belief in the approaching Kingdom of God also had a darker side in its foreboding that the forces of light and dark would engage in a terrible final battle. But it broadcast the ultimate glad tidings: God would triumph. In these extremes of apprehensiveness and joy, post-millennialism gave reformers a language to express conflicting feelings about the direction in which the United States was heading. The troubled mood matched their fear of immorality, mobs, irreligion, political turmoil, sectional conflict, and similar signs of disorder and decay. The promise of a perfect future, on the other hand, embodied reformers' expectations that everything would turn out for the best.

Millennial optimism was particularly strong because it interacted with other common attitudes. It merged with a belief that the United

States was chosen by God to fulfill a great mission, an old notion given new life in the antebellum period by territorial expansion and religious revivals (sure marks of divine favor). This idea of national destiny was simultaneously accepted and used by reformers. They claimed that America's special place in God's design (a version of what scholars call American exceptionalism) meant that its sins were more heinous than those of other countries and that their reforms were urgently needed. The divine plan—the millennium—depended upon reform. Whatever the merits of the argument, it joined religious and patriotic fervor to make a case.

In much the same fashion, postmillennialism converged with prevalent attitudes toward economic development. It was easy for reformers (and many other Americans) to feel that a new era was beginning in the antebellum years. Evidence of God's favor was not just in revivals or addition of territory to the Union: it was also apparent in a rising standard of living and in scientific and technological advances. At some points millennialism became almost indistinguishable from the secular idea of progress, the bourgeois Victorian faith that Civilization was marching onward and upward.

In spite of its ability to adapt and survive, millennialism would not have been so influential in the antebellum period if clergymen had not told humankind it could help God usher in His Kingdom. Very much in tune with the activist spirit of their age, millennialists argued that people need not sit idle in anticipation of the glorious new day. Good deeds and improved public morality were omens of its approach and might well hasten it along.

When nineteenth-century preachers made this claim that human effort could bring about the millennium, they were abandoning a line of theology stretching from John Calvin through early American Congregationalism and Presbyterianism. Calvin and Calvinists maintained that human beings were innately sinful and could, of their own free will, do nothing pleasing to God. Salvation came only as an arbitrary, predestined judgment from an omnipotent deity. By the end of the eighteenth century, Methodists and a few other sects in America had repudiated those propositions, preferring to think that people might assist in their own salvation. As early as the seventeenth century, even Presbyterians and Congregationalists had been finding ways of mitigating the harshness of their theology without going over to the "free will" position later taken by Methodists. Beecher's generation softened Calvinism still further, and Finney, nominally a Presbyterian, overthrew it.

Among the means he used was the concept of "disinterested benevolence," which he saw as the sum of all "holiness or virtue." The phrase itself had an honorable history in American Protestantism, going back to Jonathan Edwards in the eighteenth century. Finney, however, took any trace of Calvinist hellfire out of it and turned it into an inspiration for reformers. Edwards had believed humans incapable of disinterested benevolence while in their natural, sinful state. Like any other good thing, it was one of God's gifts to regenerate individuals. Finney was more concerned with results than metaphysics. Where Edwards's universe revolved around God, Finney's centered on what the believer did; and he was certain people could act virtuously if they wished. In a practical manner he tried to persuade them of the "utility of benevolence." Often his reasoning was more reminiscent of Ben Franklin than of John Calvin (he declared that "if we desire the happiness of others, their happiness will increase our own"), but there was a moral earnestness to Finney. He insisted that men and women not only could but should "set out with a determination to aim at being useful in the highest degree." So much the better that being useful would make them happy and please God in the bargain—Finney's call for benevolent action was more effective for having a greater degree of self-interest than disinterest to it. His theology may have been muddled, but its message was firm. Of true Christians, Finney wrote: "To the universal reformation of the world they stand committed." It is little wonder that his preaching spawned converts to antislavery, temperance, and other crusades, as well as to the Gospel.

Finney (and most of his critics, for that matter) revised dramatically upward the old Calvinist estimate of human nature. The problem was deciding where to stop. Was it just that people could do good deeds of their own volition, even though remaining essentially sinful? Or might human beings become completely free from sin while on earth? The Bible, after all, commanded: "Be ye therefore perfect, even as your Father which is in heaven is perfect." In that passage lurked a doctrine: perfectionism, or the notion that individuals could become sanctified while on earth. Finney himself arrived at a version of perfectionism in the 1830s and helped spread it among his peers. He and the great majority of evangelicals, however, accepted a moderate form of the doctrine while staunchly rejecting a dangerous implication in it—the possibility that sanctified persons could do no wrong. That would have freed believers from all worldly laws, a horrifying prospect to Calvinists and anyone else who recognized the villainy that pious men and women can perpetrate. A few perfectionists believed that whatever they did was not a sin (we will meet some of them later), but the great majority, including Finney, avoided that radical conclusion.

The significance of perfectionism here is not the forms it took—which were many and strange—but rather that it existed in all branches of evangelical Protestantism. Although it could lead to self-aggrandizement and heresy, it was also an energizing principle, inspiring people who wanted to impose absolute moral integrity upon their own lives and upon a changing world. Perfectionism helped create an "ultraist" mentality, common among antebellum crusaders, that insisted anything short of millennial standards should not be tolerated. It was manifested in such things as utopian efforts to construct a new social order, calls for slavery to end immediately, a belief that any alcohol was evil, and an unwillingness to compromise. Unlike their eighteenth-century or twentieth-century counterparts, antebellum reformers seldom wanted merely to improve conditions. They wanted to make things right.

People felt and acted upon the crucial doctrines of evangelical Protestantism, including perfectionism, rather than analyze carefully. Evangelicalism was a religion of the heart, not the head. It asserted that salvation was an internal conviction, an experience, not something arrived at through study and contemplation. Theodore Dwight Weld, abolitionist and onetime student at Lane Theological Seminary, phrased it well when sympathizing with a friend who was puzzling his way through "mere intellectual theories of religion." Weld's advice was for the man to give up, turn "to direct communion with God," and bring his "spirit simply and utterly in contact with infinite purity and love." Weld was not repudiating intellectual activity, in the manner of some twentieth-century revivalists, but he was calling for a religion of emotion rather than dogma.

That evangelical faith in the heart was extremely significant. Like Finney's disinterested benevolence and perfectionism, it belonged to the nineteenth-century rejection of Calvinism. In practical matters, it was a proclamation that everyone, not just professors of divinity, could understand what was important to know, a doctrine as egalitarian as anything put forth by Jacksonian politicians. In common with much of evangelicalism, it joined easily with secular currents, including a democratic faith in the individual conscience and a romantic trust in feeling and intuition. Of singular importance for reform was the anti-hierarchical extreme to which this could be taken: all authorities, even the clergy, might be judged and found wanting by the true believer.

Christian benevolent activity was not new in the nineteenth century. Cotton Mather, in 1710, published *Bonifacius: An Essay upon the Good* . . . , reprinted off and on for decades. Mather influenced many people, including Benjamin Franklin, with his call for "REFORMING SOCIETIES," separate from, but allied with, the churches. These anticipated later voluntary organizations, but nothing in the eighteenth century came close to matching the size and range of benevolent groups that sprang up after 1800. It took westward expansion and loss of position in the Eastern states to push evangelicals into making their real contribution to the organizational, as well as intellectual, structure of antebellum reform.

Movement of population into upstate New York, Vermont, and the Ohio Valley meant that after the Revolution there were thousands of souls scattered along the frontier ripe for harvesting. The Methodists and Baptists, who had circuit-riding ministers and an evangelical tradition, were in a better position to provide religious services than were the older New England denominations, with their settled clergy. Aware of the deficiency, Presbyterians and Congregationalists developed techniques to proselytize Westerners. Among the devices they came up with was the Connecticut Missionary Society, which, by the 1790s, was busy spreading the gospel according to New England. The society was run by a committee, on which laymen had equal representation with clergy. With impressive efficiency, it raised money, supported agents in the field, and produced propaganda. Its methods could—and would—be adapted to serve any number of religious and secular causes.

Heathenism in the West was not the only enemy. New England and New York Protestants also faced challenges on the home front. By the end of the Revolution few states still had a legally privileged, established church. In parts of New England, Congregationalism retained a special status under law until after the War of 1812; but even there the handwriting was on the wall much earlier. Baptists, Methodists, and—more disturbing—Unitarians (who denied the Trinity) and Universalists (who believed all would be saved) were growing in influence. It was only a matter of time before they overthrew the "standing order" in religion. No longer able to count on the government to preserve their dominance, Congregationalists and their Presbyterian allies launched a counterattack. Evangelism was a part of it, but so was reliance on voluntary organizations like the Connecticut Missionary Society. Some of the latter were reform societies; others were not. All of them, nonetheless, provided models and personnel for every other antebellum crusade, including secular ones.

Most of the earliest nineteenth-century Protestant voluntary organizations clustered in New England and the mid-Atlantic states. A few aimed at specific sins. The name of the Anti-Duelling Society, for instance, revealed its purpose. (It was begun in 1809, and Lyman Beecher was a strong supporter.) But many of the first organizations were general in scope, much as Cotton Mather suggested a century before. Although important for its anti-liquor stand, the aptly titled Connecticut Society for the Reformation of Morals (1813) sought to suppress a multitude of evils, among which its founders included the

Democratic-Republican Party of Thomas Jefferson. The mandate of a similar organization—the Andover South Parish Society for the Reformation of Morals—was typically broad. Its members were "to discountenance immorality, particularly Sabbath-breaking, intemperance and profanity; and to promote industry, order, piety, and good morals." Such groups drew upon local clergy and pious laymen, and very likely served both useful religious and social functions. They released the Protestant energies of parishioners in a sustained fashion, in contrast to revivals, which were sudden and sporadic. Moreover, they acted as a kind of moral police, pointing out immorality and lawbreaking that elected officials might prefer to ignore.

Although such work was important to the people involved, the largest Protestant voluntary associations were dedicated to missionary activity rather than to harassing local wrongdoers. The first national one was the American Board of Commissioners for Foreign Missions, begun by Congregationalists in 1810, with Lyman Beecher among the founders. It owed something to the example of the British, who had long been spreading the Gospel to remote and uncivilized lands, including North America.

Inspiring though that task was, evangelicals quickly recognized that there were threats enough to deal with in the United States: most especially Unitarianism, Universalism, Catholicism, and irreligion and vice on the frontier. To fight them, evangelicals developed formidable instruments of propaganda and made use of all the latest advances in print technology. The American Bible Society came into existence in 1816, with the goal of putting the Scriptures into the hands of every family in the nation. The American Sunday School Union (1824) aimed its efforts at children and printed books, pamphlets, and periodicals for them. Probably the most significant of all was the American Tract Society, formed in 1825; it had up-to-date presses at its disposal and no shortage of manuscripts. By 1830 it was producing approximately six million tracts each year, at a time when the American Bible Society was publishing more than a million Bibles a year. The message these religious organizations proclaimed was firmly evangelical and, less firmly, reformist. Temperance and other moral causes were preached along with diatribes against heresy and lack of faith. The American Tract Society eventually went so far as to distribute anti-slavery material.

The missionary societies generally made a point of claiming to be national in scope. That was not entirely accurate: leadership and support concentrated in New York, Pennsylvania, and New England. Yet most of these organizations represented a consolidation of prior state and local efforts, sometimes after much resistance. (In Massachusetts and Pennsylvania, for instance, opponents tried to obstruct formation of the American Bible Society.) It was a considerable accomplishment to impose some central control over missionary enterprises (or over anything else in antebellum America). Being able to do so depended on several factors, the most obvious of which were improvements in transportation and in communication after 1815. Also playing a part was a rising sense of nationalism, fueled both by revivalism and by economic and political developments following the War of 1812. None of these large-scale missionary ventures would have been possible if evangelicals had not been able to look beyond the borders of their communities and regard a sin in one part of the Union as a matter of concern for all Americans.

In order to reach a far-flung audience, and to hold their organizations together, evangelicals developed institutions and tactics that were impressive by antebellum standards. Details varied, but the usual arrangement was for the national society to have local affiliates, sometimes a great many of them—the Tract Society claimed three thousand in 1837. These auxiliaries collected and spent funds, passed out propaganda, and engaged in work of their own. Connections between them and the parent society were often quite loose and disharmonious. ("Ideas of state-rights and state independence," an abolitionist noted, "determine the character of even our benevolent operations.") Annual conventions brought together members from throughout the Union, where they proposed resolutions, listened to inspiring oratory, elected officers, and quarreled. For the rest of the year most of the national society's affairs were left to a board of managers or an executive committee, which oversaw production and distribution of printed material, tried to meet expenses, and, in some instances, supervised paid agents who traveled about on the society's business. Almost all the devices necessary for any kind of agitation were refined by the Protestant ventures begun between 1810 and 1825 and were copied wholesale by later reform movements.

By 1830 Protestant voluntary associations constituted a loosely interconnected "benevolent empire." Although formally distinct from one another, evangelical organizations propagated the same worldview, tapped the same financial resources, and had many of the same men on their boards of directors. They often held their conventions at the same times, in the same cities. These linkages permitted a measure of coordinated action, as when, in 1829, the benevolent societies mounted an especially energetic campaign in the West. (Reports had been coming in of appalling moral and theological degeneracy there, and Eastern evangelicals feared for the safety of the nation.)

The agencies of the benevolent empire had other things in common besides ideology, members, and sources of revenue. Many of them were interdenominational in ways that went well beyond the usual cooperation between Presbyterians and Congregationalists, who engaged in joint ventures after agreeing to a Plan of Union in 1801. The managers of the Sunday School Union and the Bible Society, for example, included Presbyterians (the largest single group), Congregationalists, Methodists, Episcopalians, Baptists, Dutch Reformed, and even a stray Moravian and Quaker or two. (Unitarians were conspicuously absent.) The American Board of Commissioners for Foreign Missions was thoroughly Congregational, but its managers showed a sense of guilt about that—an 1860 publication they sponsored headed a section with the caption "The Board ceases to be Denominational." (It combined efforts with Presbyterians.) Cooperation across denominational lines sometimes broke down, but it was part of the evangelical spirit and it foreshadowed later secular reforms, such as antislavery and temperance, where there was a determined effort to keep the cause from becoming the property of any particular sect.

Another feature of the missionary organizations, likewise to reappear in antislavery and temperance, was the crucial role played by the laity.

Clergy, of course, were never absent, yet the driving forces of the benevolent empire were people like Arthur and Lewis Tappan, wealthy New York merchants who were at the center of nearly every one of the greatest religious and secular reforms of the day, and the men and women who carried the message at the local level.

Most of the benevolent empire's work met with a fair measure of public approval, at least until leaders like Arthur Tappan committed themselves to such controversial causes as antislavery. Still, the managers and agents of the various benevolent societies had enemies, including reprobates, skeptics, Unitarians, and anti-mission elements within the revivalistic denominations themselves. Politicians—Jacksonian Democrats especially—railed against the repressive goals of evangelicals and warned darkly about an alliance of church and state, simultaneously playing upon traditional American political values and appealing to the fears of Catholic voters.

The most recent critics of the benevolent empire are historians who charge evangelicals with serving their own narrow interests rather than truly aiding humankind. Their real ambition, supposedly, was "social control"; to say this accuses them of imposing their authority and their standards upon poorer folk at the expense of diversity and freedom. The Protestant voluntary associations, in the words of one scholar, were little more than "means to make people obey their [the evangelicals'] will."

To an extent, that argument rests on presuming to know the motives of the people who founded the associations—and it is difficult to find out what went on in the hearts and minds of long-dead human beings. The evidence does not entirely absolve evangelicals of selfserving and bigotry, but it indicates that there was more to the benevolent empire than social control. The first antebellum efforts—the Connecticut Society for the Reformation of Morals, for instance—came closest to supporting the accusation. It had a truculent dislike of deviance from the strict New England way and a determination to make unruly elements behave properly. Yet there were less repressive aspects to evangelical benevolence, especially after the mid-1820s, when millennialism became more pronounced and Finney and perfectionism entered the picture. Mixed with rhetoric about moral decline and heathenism was a genuine belief that things could improve, that people could and should be helped, and that a better world would result. There was, moreover, a capacity for growth in many of the supporters of missionary activity. Some of them shed sectarian prejudices after working with godly men and women in other denominations. They also saw that their own successes were not enough: getting the Bible and the Word to the public did not make America a Christian nation. That recognition led a number of people, including Arthur and Lewis Tappan, into antislavery and temperance and out of the more restricted religious concerns of the benevolent empire.

Evangelicals were uneasy about change and committed to a traditional morality, but they were not necessarily reactionaries. Rather than simply endorsing or opposing change, humans can want to guide it in what they believe to be a constructive manner, which is what the benevolent empire intended to do. In a very loose use of the term, "social control" may be what that was. But it was not sinister, even in cases where it was shortsighted and intolerant. There were worse ambitions than hoping that antebellum Americans might behave better toward one another and lead more moral lives.

Evangelical Protestantism released people from some of the old Calvinist suspicions about human nature and gave them an outlet for emotional and reformist enthusiasm. But like any liberating ideology, it could be taken to extremes that appalled its first supporters. As early as the 1830s even Finney, once attacked for unorthodoxy, was disturbed by what people were making of revivalistic techniques and impulses. His own theatrical style was imitated to absurdity by unscrupulous evangelists. Others fell into theological unorthodoxy too bizarre for Finney and most of the Christian world to stomach. A few preached and, worse, practiced scandalous sexual doctrines. In 1844 Theodore Dwight Weld reported that "within the last four years not less than thirty ministers of evangelical denominations have been guilty of the most flagrant licentiousness."

Reform urges also began to take on a life of their own, separate from evangelical Protestantism, and to grow in ways that caused problems for revivalists like Finney, who had done so much to stimulate social action. Finney endorsed temperance, health reform, abolition of slavery, and other worthy causes; but he insisted that revivalism came first. In common with most evangelists, he believed that excessive reform agitation alienated potential converts and diverted the enthusiasm of believers away from religion. He was not vocal about his own social views and he used his influence to discourage revivalistic publications and divinity students from taking controversial stands. That caution sometimes irritated influential laypersons who believed that reform was a sacred obligation (had not Finney said as much?) and that it should not be sacrificed to expediency.

As time went on, many reformers became disappointed, not just with Finney, but with revivalism generally. It appeared to have become mechanical, without real conviction behind it—Finney himself denied that revivals were miracles and gave instructions on how they might be produced (virtually a do-it-yourself manual for evangelists). There was mounting evidence that converts attracted by those methods did not engage in good works, as evangelical teachings said they would. Slaveholders saw the light, but kept their slaves; tipplers went through a change of heart, but continued to drink. To make the situation more puzzling, it was obvious that there were many decent, reform-minded people who were not evangelicals (some were Unitarians and Universalists). Perhaps the proper way for evangelicals to judge them was not by their theology but by their actions. On that scale they came out better than any number of revivalistic preachers.

Some evangelistic reformers kept their faith and preserved their sectarian prejudices. But even those men and women did not necessarily trust fellow evangelical Protestants to do the right thing. Arthur Tappan, for instance, virtually bribed Western churches into temperance by giving donations to non-drinking congregations. Many other reformers became less concerned about religious matters after years of crusading, and a few drifted into unorthodoxy. In some cases they did so in protest against the failure of churches to take stands on moral issues (generally slavery); in other cases they acted out of a feeling—itself a product of the revival—that a good heart and good deeds mattered more than religious formalities. For such people (and they included former clergymen) reform itself became a religion. Looking back on her career as an abolitionist, one woman wrote: "That is the only true church organization, where heads and hearts unite in working for the welfare of the human race." Her words echoed others spoken over the decades by men and women who transferred their zeal from religion to reform and from individual to social salvation. The irony is that when a cause such as antislavery or temperance became a church, it was many of the things evangelical Protestantism was at its best: passionate, interdenominational, and committed to improving the human situation.

All reformers, including non-evangelicals and ones who left their churches, owed much to revivalism. Their language was filled with its rhetoric of sin, damnation, and salvation. It gave them a way of viewing the world—even the most secular of reformers talked of "progress" and "civilization" in tones harking back to millennialism and perfectionism. Evangelical techniques and enterprises, finally, showed how crusaders could organize and propagandize on a national scale. Yet evangelical channels were too narrow to contain all reform energy. By the 1830s communitarianism, antislavery, temperance, and various social causes and pseudo-sciences were redirecting, as well as drawing upon, religious impulses.

# Heaven on Earth

"Since the war of 1812–1815," John Humphrey Noyes declared in 1870, "the line of socialistic excitements lies parallel with the line of religious Revivals." Even when Noyes wrote, his use of the word "socialistic" was beginning to sound antiquated. He did not mean Marxism or the kinds of socialism familiar in the twentieth century. He had in mind the bold experiments of small bands of antebellum men and women who gathered in their own ideal communities, as Noyes and his followers had done at Oneida, New York. These were little utopias carved out of the American countryside, dedicated to one or another social or religious theory, and designed to serve as models for the rest of the world to imitate. Noyes deeply regretted that the people who constructed these communities had not seen the "parallel" and joined forces with evangelical Protestants. Each sought what the other needed for success: revivalists "failed for want of regeneration of society" and utopians "failed for want of regeneration of the heart." The unwillingness of communitarians and evangelicals to unite "their two great ideas" was all the more tragic since the groups had much in common. They shared a faith in the perfectibility of humankind and a belief that the millennium was at hand. Both desired "to bring heaven on earth." Utopianism and revivalism, Noyes insisted, "are closely related in their essential nature and objects, and manifestly belong together in the scheme of Providence as they do in the history of this nation." Noyes was perceptive.

No one knows exactly how many communitarian societies were built in the nineteenth century, but more than a hundred were founded between the Revolution and the Civil War. The greatest wave of enthusiasm for utopian ventures came in the 1840s, in the aftermath of a deep economic crisis following the Panic of 1837. Most communities lasted no more than a few years, some only a matter of months. Yet there were long-lived ones as well: the Shakers began in the eighteenth century and lingered into the late twentieth. Two others, Oneida and Amana, transformed into ongoing business enterprises.

If one counts only active members, utopian societies were among the least popular expressions of antebellum reform and radical sentiment. At their height in the 1830s the Eastern Shaker communities had a little over 2,400 members, divided among several locations. All other communities were far smaller, and many consisted of no more than a few dozen people. Even so, there was no other period in American history, except possibly in the late 1960s, when such a large proportion of Americans joined communal societies.

The importance of these, however, goes far beyond the number of people involved in them. In some respects communalism was an exception in the midst of antebellum reform. It was genuinely radical: communitarians aimed at creating a totally new order rather than improving the old one, as reformers sought to do. Some communitarians, moreover, emphasized the influence of environment in shaping the character of human beings. In that, they disagreed with most antebellum reformers, who gave greater attention to the human heart than to the material world. Yet communitarianism also was the extreme that proved the rules of antebellum reform. As Noyes recognized, it was the ultimate expression of evangelical perfectionist and millennialist logic. In that, and in numerous other ways, communal ventures played out themes and tensions characteristic of reform and of American society generally.

It is difficult at first to see much coherence in anything so varied as antebellum communalism. The communities themselves ranged from highly structured to utterly unstructured, from theological to freethinking, from celibate to "free love." To make sense out of that diversity, historians and sociologists often divide utopian communities into those that were primarily organized around religious doctrines and those that were primarily secular. The distinction is helpful enough to be worth following, but requires a word of caution. Like many ways of classifying things, it is most interesting when it breaks down. As we shall see, and as Noyes grasped, one of the significant things about antebellum communalism was the manner in which it fused religious and secular impulses and sometimes combined religious, political, and scientific rhetoric.

Some of the largest and most stable utopian societies in antebellum America were neither antebellum nor American in origin. These ventures represent a particular kind of religious communalism, best labeled "pietistic." All such groups formed around a strong and magnetic leader whose unorthodox theological teachings gave the community its reason for being. The communities themselves were in the United States but not especially of it. Several traced their ancestry to German sects, the rest to other seventeenth- or eighteenth-century European religious splinter groups. The most notable of the German-speaking communities—Ephrata, Harmony, Zoar, and Amana—kept their Old World character.

Ephrata was not quite the first utopian society in North America, nor was it the largest; but by the antebellum period it was the oldest. Ephrata's founder, Johann Conrad Beissel, left the Palatinate in 1720, apparently with the idea of joining the Woman in the Wilderness, a mystical community of German pietists who gathered in the Pennsylvania forest to await the millennium. By the time Beissel arrived, most members of the Woman in the Wilderness had scattered or died. Beissel remained and spent much of the next twelve years in hermit-like spiritual contemplation. In 1724 he joined the Dunkers, a German sect, but in 1728 he published a work contradicting some of their doctrines. He attracted followers, and in 1732 they began Ephrata, located near Lancaster, Pennsylvania, as a communitarian society, or "cloister."

Those who lived within it were in no danger of being corrupted by luxury. Their days were filled with work and worship; their diet was sparse and vegetarian; their dress was homespun. Men lived in one large building, women in another. Little in those dwellings distracted them from spiritual thoughts. The passageways were exceedingly narrow; the rooms were small and spartan; and the residences were constructed and furnished without the use of metal, in imitation of Solomon's temple.

For all its plainness and religiosity, Ephrata did not have rigid rules on two matters crucial to later communitarians: sexual relationships and private property. Beissel did not insist upon chastity, although he encouraged it and most of his followers were celibate in the mideighteenth century, when their numbers may have reached three hundred. The community punished "the untimely intercourse of some of the brethren and sisters with each other," but over the years there was a decline in celibacy as well as in membership. By 1900 most of the seventeen remaining Ephratans were married. Beissel also did not demand that all property be held in common, although the community as a whole owned whatever was donated to it or produced by residents. Those who valued worldly goods (or sexual intercourse) simply left the cloister, took housing nearby, and became "outdoor" members, over whom Beissel and his successors exercised less rigorous discipline.

Nineteenth-century communitarians sometimes faulted Ephrata for its mystical theology, its isolation from the world, and its equivocation on marriage and property. That was to miss the point: spiritual contemplation was the essence of Ephrata and of the pietistic communities. Unlike later communitarians, Ephratans and most pietists never intended to provide the rest of humanity with models of such mundane things as relationships between the sexes and ownership of property.

By the early nineteenth century Ephrata was a relic. Beissel died in 1768. Peter Miller, his successor, survived him by twenty-eight years, leaving no one with his or Beissel's intellect and personal power to carry on. Ephrata inspired interest and at least one imitator in the nineteenth century, but by then it was not even the most vital of the German pietistic communities, an honor that belonged to George Rapp's Harmony Society or (after 1847) to Amana.

In 1791 Rapp, a thirty-three-year-old German farmer, told an official investigating his religious beliefs, "I am a prophet and called to be one." Prophet or not, Rapp had been in conflict with the established Lutheran Church of Württemberg at least since 1785. He remained in conflict until he left Germany in 1803 to find a New World home for his several hundred disciples. In December 1804 he purchased land in western Pennsylvania, and in February 1805 he and supporters formally incorporated the Harmony Society.

Although living conditions were primitive at first, the Harmonists were steady and industrious. In a decade they cleared and cultivated over two thousand acres of land. As early as 1807 they were selling goods to the outside world, including three thousand gallons of whiskey. They soon constructed several mills and a town. Dissatisfied with the climate, the soil, and the difficulty of bringing their products to market, the Harmonists sold their Pennsylvania property for $100,000 (less than its real value) and moved to Indiana in 1814. The Harmonists—of whom there were now about eight hundred—again prospered. In 1824 the society advertised its holdings as consisting of numerous buildings (among them a cotton and woolen mill, a distillery, and a tavern) and 20,000 acres of land on a navigable portion of the Wabash River. For reasons that are not altogether clear, the society again decided to move. By 1825 it had sold everything to Robert Owen, a wealthy British social theorist, and returned to Pennsylvania, to land north of Pittsburgh. This, the society's third home, was named Economy. The Harmonists did well, despite a slow decline in their population. By 1874 they had closed several factories on their own land for lack of a labor force, but they kept flourishing ones on the outside. In that year a visitor marveled over their cutlery shop at Beaver Falls, Pennsylvania, which he described as "one of the largest in the world, where of late they have begun to employ two hundred Chinese." By 1900 the society had fewer than ten members, as well as substantial investments in petroleum and railroads.

Harmony was a more worldly place than Ephrata, yet the two had similar characteristics. Each was the creation of a vigorous and compelling founder: Rapp's control over his followers, although occasionally challenged, remained firm until his death in 1847, at ninety. Each community was millennialistic. Rapp informed an inquirer in 1822 that Harmonists "believe without doubt that the kingdom of Jesus Christ [is] approaching near." If anything, the Harmonists were more consistent in banning private ownership of property than Ephratans had been. By the terms of the Articles of Agreement of 1805 members signed over to the society all their earthly possessions.

Like the Ephratans, Harmonists generally remained celibate. Rapp had advocated sexual abstinence as early as 1791, and had probably practiced it as early as 1785, but he did not initially insist upon it. His own son, John, married just before the society's ban on intercourse took place. Celibacy became policy in 1807 at the urging of members caught up in a new wave of religious enthusiasm sweeping the society. Apparently there was a brief relaxation of the rule around 1817, when several marriages were performed, but by the time Charles Nordhoff visited Economy in 1874 the residents practiced celibacy. Indeed, they attributed their long lives and good health to it. Be that as it may, celibacy and unwillingness to proselytize non-Germans had the same effect on the Harmony Society as on Ephrata: the membership grew old, died, and left none to keep the faith.

These were not the only German pietistic societies. Some others split off from the more famous ones—Harmony spawned settlements in Missouri and Oregon—and there were also several significant ventures that originated independently of Ephrata or Harmony. The latter included Zoar in Ohio (1817–98), Amana, Iowa (1843–1933), and Saint Naziancz (1854–96), a Catholic community in Wisconsin. The Germans, moreover, were not the only European people to form pietistic societies in America. A Swedish settlement at Bishop Hill, Illinois, may have had as many as 1,500 members in 1854. (It also had an extraordinarily turbulent history, punctuated by a cholera epidemic, extravagant speculation in land and businesses, and the murder of its founder in a courthouse shooting in 1850.) Colorful as Bishop Hill was, neither it nor Harmony was the largest and most influential pietistic community in the antebellum period. The Shakers were, probably because they were British in origin and thus more successful in recruiting English-speaking members.

The American career of the Shakers was rooted in the spiritual experiences of Ann Lee, the illiterate daughter of a blacksmith in Manchester, England. Her life, like her theology, was plain and demanding. Born in 1736, she performed factory and menial labor at an early age. While still a young woman she married Abraham Stanley (or Standerin), a blacksmith like her father. It was an unhappy match. Ann Lee apparently felt repugnance at sexual intercourse and, in any case, suffered through the birth and loss of four children, each of whom died without reaching maturity. Before marrying Stanley, she had joined the Shakers, a small sect tracing its lineage to seventeenth-century France and named for a convulsive dance that was part of its ritual. Fired with zeal, she preached, prayed, and went into trances. She was persecuted by mobs and by the authorities, who occasionally threw Ann Lee and fellow Shakers into prison. While in jail in 1770 she had a powerful revelation and upon her release attracted followers who accepted her as "Mother in Christ." In 1774 another revelation directed her to take passage to America, which she did, accompanied by eight others, her husband among them. He deserted her in New York.

Mother Ann lived apart from her tiny flock for nearly two years, but by 1776 she rejoined them at what is now Watervliet in upstate New York. They endured difficult times, because of the hardships of making a living and the hostility of neighbors, who disliked their practices and suspected them of pro-British sympathies in the Revolution. Although Mother Ann was central to Shaker theology, she died in 1784, three years before the sect formed its first true communal settlement in Mount Lebanon, New York, and well before its period of greatest expansion.

The Shakers began to grow after 1779, when a Baptist revival swept the country around Mount Lebanon. In what would prove to be a persistent pattern, they attracted men and women awakened but not satisfied by evangelical preaching. In 1805 the Shakers similarly took advantage of revivals in the West by sending out preachers of their own. The result was another rich harvest of converts and formation of a half-dozen new communities. Still later the Shakers received people jarred from their spiritual moorings by Finney's great revivals of the 1820s and 1830s.

The sect also owed some of its success after Mother Ann's death to the ability of her successors. In 1787 Joseph Meacham and Lucy Wright, both skillful organizers, became the first American-born leaders. Wright presided over the development of settlements throughout New York, New England, Ohio, Indiana, and Kentucky. In 1830, nine years after Wright's death, Frederick W. Evans joined the Shakers; in 1836 he became an elder, a position he held for fifty-seven years. While in his native England, Evans had been a freethinker and a believer in Robert Owen's schemes for social reorganization; upon his arrival in the United States he became involved in labor reform. He had come upon the Shakers, in fact, while searching for a place to locate an Owenite community in New York. He proved to be an effective administrator and propagandist for the Shakers, serving them well from their high tide in the 1830s and 1840s into their decline after mid-century.

For all the ability of Meacham, Wright, and Evans, much of the strength of the Shakers lay in their distinctive and compelling way of life. Mother Ann Lee had taught that God was both male and female in nature, with Jesus representing the masculine side. Since Mother Ann represented the feminine side, her coming, according to her followers, marked the completion of God's revelation and the beginning of the Kingdom of Heaven on earth. This was a variety of millennialism and an assertion of the spiritual equality of men and women. Both genders shared authority throughout the sect's hierarchy, from its "Head of Influence" at Mount Lebanon to the "families" (or smaller groups of men and women) that were the basic unit within each community. "Each brother," one visitor reported, "is assigned to a sister, who takes care of his clothing, mends when it is needed, looks after his washing, tells him when he requires a new garment, reproves him if he is not orderly." Wifely chores and other manifestations of gender inequality aside, there were few places in American society where women were so emancipated from their usual roles as wives and mothers and granted so much influence. It is no accident that women often were a majority among the Shakers.

Shaker men and women lived in chastity as well as relative equality. Mother Ann made "Virgin Purity" a pillar of her faith and insisted that followers be celibate, likely recalling her own sad marital career. Shakers believed that sexuality was an "animal passion" belonging to a lower, less spiritual order of existence. Even though many non-Shakers shared that view of sexual intercourse, few antebellum Americans tried to ban it altogether and many observers regarded the sect as cold and contrary to human nature.

Yet one of the secrets of Shakerism's appeal was the way it alternated self-denial with emotional release. Shakers spent much of the day in silence, hard work, and restraint. Rituals, however, provided moments of ecstasy. The most curious of these was the well-known "dance" that was part of Shaker services. The "dance" and its accompanying music changed over time; but it was always a performance in which both genders participated, parading in what visitors described as odd, regimented movements, sometimes dignified, sometimes spasmodic. The Shakers also went through periods of special enthusiasm, as in the late 1830s and early 1840s, when each of their communities was swept by spiritualism, mystical experiences, and speaking in tongues. Those outbursts and the dance help explain why Shakers gathered in men and women originally converted by revivals in the outside world: they gave regular expression to evangelical Protestant emotionality, and made it all the more intense by mixing it with Protestant asceticism.

Bizarre as their customs seemed to some commentators, the Shakers gained the admiration of such non-Shakers as John Humphrey Noyes and Robert Owen, each of whom considered them a precursor of more "modern" communitarianism. On the matter of private property the Shakers were indeed among the most radical of utopians. They did away with distinctions in "temporal blessings" about as completely as any American commune ever has. But theirs was "Christian Communism," not the later, secular variety. They shared their possessions because they did not value them much: their eyes were on heaven. That otherworldliness marks Shakerism as (in Noyes's phrase) one of the "antique religious Communities."

Most of the pietistic societies, including the Shakers, were European as well as "antique"—the significant exception was Jerusalem, established in New York in 1788 by followers of a Rhode Island woman, Jemima Wilkinson. What European pietists found in America was toleration for their practices, inexpensive land, and economic opportunity. Most also discovered that they could remain European if they wished—only the Shakers recruited Americans successfully.

Although pietistic societies were beginning to fade as early as the 1820s, Noyes and Owen were right to think that they had lessons to teach later communitarians. The pietistic communities had begun the process of breaking away from conventional notions of family relationships and private property, both of which generally proved destructive to utopian ventures. In that, and in their pacifism, millennialism, and ability to survive, they were a model and an inspiration to other antebellum utopians.

But they were a deceptive model. Antebellum communitarians saw the durability of Ephrata, Harmony, and the Shakers as evidence that communal living was possible. What they did not see was why it had been possible. Many of the German pietists were bound by Old World ties of kinship and friendship, or simply by the experience of speaking the same language in a foreign land. Also, they were peasants for whom farming, simplicity, and hard work were second nature. Virtually all pietists, moreover, subordinated themselves to authoritarian leaders like George Rapp or to an exacting regimen like those of Ephrata or the Shakers. In contrast, most native-born communitarians after 1825 were artisans, independent farmers, and petty entrepreneurs. They were individualistic, self-assured, and intellectually restless Americans—characteristics that made them chafe at the discipline of communal life. They were too impatient to await and contemplate the arrival of heaven on earth in the manner of the pietists. They could be ferociously dogmatic, but unlike the pietists, they did not completely accept the truth as given. They debated it among themselves and sought it in an even grander debate between ideology and experience.

American communitarians after 1825 generally operated within a Christian tradition, just as eighteenth-century pietists did; but each took different components from it, which, in turn, led to different modes of behavior. The pietists drew upon the communalism, monasticism, and mysticism of early Christianity. Later utopians lived out a social gospel, bringing Protestant principles to bear upon the wider world around them, as well as within the community itself. Nowhere was the divergence in styles of religious communalism more apparent than in the contrast between the old pietistic societies and Hopedale and Brook Farm, two of the most important New England communities of the 1840s.

Hopedale's founder, Adin Ballou, characterized it as a missionary, temperance, antislavery, peace, charitable, woman's rights, and educational society. True to his word, he and members of Hopedale regularly sallied forth from their Milford, Massachusetts, home to participate in those causes and others. While guiding Hopedale, Ballou lectured for temperance and for the American Anti-Slavery Society, and he served as president of the New England Non-Resistance Society, an offshoot of the peace movement and a forum for Christian anarchism. In spite of that, some disaffected residents charged Hopedale with being too isolated from the reforms of the day.

Ballou and his followers were religious enthusiasts and zealous reformers, but on a number of issues they were among the least daring communitarians and far more moderate than their doctrines suggested. Ballou was a Universalist minister who believed that all humans were destined for heaven (some, he felt, would need a period of probation and punishment). He also held to the nonresistant faith that human relationships should be free of coercion, including coercion by manmade governments. Yet he did not push those doctrines (as some did) to the point of denying human sinfulness or arguing that individuals should be free to do whatever they want. Hopedale elected "official servants" who used the power of persuasion rather than force to encourage proper behavior. Ballou even organized residents into an "Industrial Army" (the name was quickly changed to the less military-sounding "Industrial Union"). Ballou's "Army" was a far cry from the regimentation of the Shakers, whom he repudiated, but he likewise had no use for almost rule-less communities such as ones founded by his anarchistic contemporary, Josiah Warren.

Ballou was equally moderate on the matter of private property and downright conventional when it came to marriage. Hopedale organized along the lines of a joint-stock company with provisions for dividends and for repurchase of shares held by dissatisfied investors. It also permitted members to work at their own businesses and to maintain property separate from that of the community. The looseness of Hopedale's economic arrangements was a major, but understandable, weakness. Ballou was primarily a moralist, concerned above all with the relationship between an individual and God, not with relationships in the marketplace. He was appalled at "revolting extremes of wealth and poverty," but he saw avarice and exploitation as rooted in the human heart, not in the economic structure. Ballou was equally moralistic in his views on matrimony, which he regarded as "sacred," and on family life, which Hopedale encouraged. He was horrified when a case of marital infidelity occurred in the community, and he thought it appropriate that the offending couple departed for Modern Times, one of Warren's ventures. There, he noted disapprovingly, leaders tolerated "promiscuous cohabitation."

Despite his prudery, Ballou was gentle and charitable; Hopedale was pleasant and, for a time, reasonably prosperous. In the words of a man who disagreed with Ballou on many issues, Hopedale was "one of the most distinctively American communities, and one meriting more complete success than it attained." Yet it met an abrupt, unique, and largely undeserved demise. Around 1851 Hopedale enjoyed a brief period of affluence. Ballou resigned its presidency in 1853, convinced that the community, then numbering more than two hundred, was in good order. Its stock, meanwhile, had been passing into the hands of the Draper brothers, Ebenezer and George, who became majority shareholders. They threatened to withdraw their investment when Hopedale fell behind in meeting its obligations, thereby forcing the community to turn over its assets to them. In 1856 they incorporated its property into their other business enterprises, ending Ballou's dream.

Brook Farm, located in West Roxbury, Massachusetts, was, like Hopedale, a product of New England culture, but of a slightly different strand. Hopedale derived from Ballou's nonresistance, reformist impulses, and Universalism. It was firmly committed to a code of Christian ethics. Brook Farm was not as infused with reform zeal and was, if anything, more individualistic. But it, too, was religious in inspiration, although it appeared to be less so to contemporaries. Elizabeth Peabody spoke of an early plan for it as "Christ's Idea of Society," and it originated in conversations between two Unitarian ministers, William Ellery Channing and George Ripley, in 1840 and 1841. Issues raised by Channing spilled over into discussions of the "Transcendental Club" (loosely organized gatherings of Boston-area intellectuals). Fired with enthusiasm, Ripley and some colleagues purchased land and began the community in the summer of 1841.

Brook Farm is sometimes characterized as a "Transcendentalist Utopia," but what it owed to Transcendentalism is not completely clear. Transcendentalism itself was often as much a sensibility and a set of attitudes about humankind and nature as it was a set of coherent doctrines. From it, Ripley, the community's moving force, could have come to believe in the limitless potential of human beings, but other communitarians derived the same belief from evangelical Protestantism, through its perfectionist strain. Transcendentalism may actually have contributed a destructive element to Brook Farm: a feeling that individuals ought to free themselves from the restraint of institutions. That justified seceding from society in favor of utopian ventures; but it could also lead to the more radical conclusion that individuals ought to avoid all organizations, including communitarian ones. The great Transcendentalist Ralph Waldo Emerson agonized over whether to join Brook Farm and finally convinced himself (as he commonly did) that he was more valuable preserving his autonomy and remaining unaffiliated. He visited and observed Brook Farm with the same detachment his fellow Transcendentalist Margaret Fuller displayed when she spoke of going there to watch "the coral insects at work." When the influence of Transcendentalism was felt at Brook Farm, it was sometimes in the form of a thorny independence like Emerson's that weighed against the discipline essential to communal life.

That was, nonetheless, part of Brook Farm's charm. It had room for playfulness, fads, odd attire, unfashionably bearded and long-haired men, and sweet eccentrics like Burrill Curtis, who, according to one account, "had been a model for a portrait of Christ." The motive of the original Brook Farmers, according to Elizabeth Peabody, was to be "wholly true to their natures as men and women." Those natures were deliciously varied and more utopian than communitarian.

Although there was a frivolous side to Transcendental individualism, it also encouraged serious self-development. George Ripley had hoped "to insure a more natural union between intellectual and manual labor than now exists." The community, accordingly, organized so that all members not only worked with their hands but also had the means "for intellectual improvement and for social intercourse, calculated to refine and expand." Some were not enchanted by farm chores (Nathaniel Hawthorne's confrontation with a manure pile is one of the less elegant moments in New England literary history). But many were enthusiastic about Brook Farm's blend of physical activity with literature, poetry, and the other arts. "The weeds," George William Curtis recalled fondly, "were scratched out of the ground to the music of Tennyson and Browning." Whatever the effect upon weeds, Brook Farm's cultural ferment was unparalleled among American utopian societies and produced two impressive things: the *Harbinger* and the community's schools. In 1845 the Farm took over publication of the *Phalanx*, a New York Fourierist periodical, renamed it the *Harbinger*, and made it into an important weekly journal. After Brook Farm's failure in 1847, ex-members moved the *Harbinger* to New York and continued it for nearly two years. The schools were well staffed and remarkably flexible for the times. They had a broad liberal arts curriculum, broke with the practice of rote memorization, and attempted to combine learning with doing. They were also respectable enough to impress Harvard. Culture and students were Brook Farm's best crops.

They were not cash crops. From its beginning, Brook Farm was economically marginal. Organized more or less as a dividend-paying joint-stock venture, it was too Transcendental to be profit-making. The founders hoped to make "the acquisition of individual property subservient to upright and disinterested uses." They nonetheless sought to "reserve sufficient private property, or means of obtaining it, for all purposes of independence." The result was a tangle of community and private interests that would have been even more troublesome if Brook Farm had prospered. As it was, the real problem was making ends meet, not distributing profits.

In 1844 and 1845 Ripley and other leaders, newly converted to the socialism of Charles Fourier, reorganized the community into a "Phalanx" (Fourier's term). It gained some structure: workers were divided into three different categories—Farming, Mechanical, and Domestic—with each broken down into sub-groups, as Fourier taught. (Thus the Farming Series contained a Milking Group, a Haying Group, and so forth.) The system was cumbersome and the small community had about as many groups as members. No amount of reorganization, moreover, could solve the problem of finding a secure economic base for Brook Farm. Whatever chance it had disappeared in 1846, when a fire swept the expensive and uninsured new main building. The remaining property sold in 1849 for under $20,000, a paltry sum compared to the value of the Harmony Society's holdings, and even much less than Hopedale's.

Brook Farm enjoyed a fame out of proportion to its success or its size, which never exceeded one hundred members. Nostalgia for it lasted into the early twentieth century, when William Hinds reported that "so cherished are those memories that a few survivors of Brook Farm and a score of kindred souls gather annually in the summer months . . . to live again in the Brook Farm life." The community's reputation has a bittersweet air to it, a sense of a charming interlude too innocent to last. Much of this image stems from the fact that Brook Farm was put together by New Englanders who, unlike the German peasants at Harmony, wrote letters, articles, and books about their experiences.

And then there was Nathaniel Hawthorne. He turned a brief sojourn at Brook Farm into *The Blithedale Romance* (1852), a thinly fictionalized portrait of the community. It was this novel, more than anything else, that kept interest in Brook Farm alive outside New England literary circles. Hawthorne's perspective was complicated and ambiguous, but,

on balance, unflattering. At one point, the narrator of the novel reflected on the youthful naïveté that had taken him to the community.
"I rejoice," he declared, "that I could once think better of the world's
improvability than it deserves." Such disillusion was common enough:
when Ballou looked back on the failure of Hopedale he saw his "over-
sanguine" faith in human beings as "a weakness." But there was more
to *The Blithedale Romance*. Hawthorne showed an ugly side to the reform impulse. In the character of Hollingsworth, he portrayed "godlike
benevolence . . . debased into all-devouring egotism." That was a
powerful epitaph for the utopian spirit, no less influential on scholars
for being largely unwarranted.

·The problems with Brook Farm and Hopedale went deeper than
egotism and beyond the need to find an economic base. Adin Ballou
inadvertently put his finger on the difficulty when he tallied the virtues of a communitarian proposal he made in 1840. "It exhibits a
strong determination," he wrote, "to maintain unabridged individu-
ality of personal rights and responsibilities, the integrity of the
marriage and family relationship, and the great safeguards against communal tyranny and absorption . . . It contemplates no unnatural, exclusive monastic retreat from society at large." The list is remarkable
because it is generally accurate for Hopedale and Brook Farm and
because it contrasts with the characteristics of the longest-lived, most
successful pietistic communities. The latter subordinated individual
conscience, autonomy, and property rights to the community. They
altered family relationships. They drew sharp boundaries between the
community and the outside world. Hopedale, Brook Farm, and two
contemporary Massachusetts ventures, the Northampton Association
(1842–46) and Bronson Alcott's Fruitlands (1843), lacked the authoritarian structure and unorthodox living arrangements of the older communities. Although they appeared odd to outside observers, they failed
for being too moderate, too respectful of individual property and con-
sciences. They were too conventional to attract a zealously committed
membership, to isolate it from the world, and to hold it through hard
times.

●    ●    ●

Being too conventional was not a problem with Oneida. Like Hopedale and Brook Farm, it was an offspring of New England theology. Where Hopedale was shaped by Ballou's Universalism and nonresistance, and Brook Farm by Ripley's Unitarianism and Transcendentalism, Oneida was a product of evangelical Protestantism. Its founder was John Humphrey Noyes, a Vermonter by birth; a Dartmouth, Andover Theological Seminary, and Yale man by education; and a lawyer and clergyman by training. Probably possessing the most original mind of any American communitarian, he was, above all, a believer in perfectionism.

Noyes was literal, logical, and extreme. While at Yale Divinity School he came to feel that once a person was saved, he or she became absolutely perfect—incapable of sinning. He achieved that state on February 20, 1834. His theological notions cost him friendships, his license to preach, and his membership in the New Haven Free Church. By the end of 1834 he was a twenty-three-year-old perfectionist without a pulpit. For a time he wandered, trying to meet Charles G. Finney, the great revivalist. Noyes then worked among the poor in New York City where, according to rumor, he "lay dead *drunk* . . . by way of showing the perfection of his *flesh*." During his travels he met William Lloyd Garrison, the abolitionist, whom he strongly influenced; and he acquired a growing reputation as a propagandist.

In 1837 he gave the first sign of unorthodox sexual ideas that took final form at Oneida. Abigail Merwin, an early convert whom Noyes loved, spurned both him and his doctrines and married another man. Much grieved, Noyes wrote a follower that "when the will of God is done on earth as it is in heaven there will be no marriage." Noyes was not calling for Shaker-like celibacy. He meant that among those who had become perfect, all belonged to one another: there were no exclusive attachments. Merwin was his bride in spirit, even if she was another man's under law. "I call a certain woman my wife," he explained. "She is yours, she is Christ's, and in him she is the bride of all saints." The letter was published. It sounded too much like "free love" to sit well with the public, and Noyes lost a substantial portion of his small band of followers in the subsequent furor. Despite the letter's scandalous implications, Noyes was not ready to abandon monogamous marriage. In June 1838 he wed Harriet Holton, a good and loyal supporter and contributor since 1834. The couple settled in at Putney, Vermont, where Noyes's family lived. There his tiny congregation of disciples, most of them relatives, printed his works and developed the doctrines that would distinguish Oneida.

Noyes became a communitarian gradually. In 1841 the little group at Putney began to organize more formally and to pool resources. Noyes, his brother George, and two of his brothers-in-law created a financial partnership in 1844. Their assets were substantial, thanks to Harriet's generosity and to an estate left by Noyes's father. After a year they reorganized into a corporation open to any who invested money or labor. By Noyes's own account, he and his followers had been reading communitarian publications, especially the *Harbinger*. Although Noyes rejected Brook Farm's Fourierist principles, the community impressed him and, with more sentimentality than truth, he declared Oneida to be its direct successor. In any event, by 1846, the year of the Brook Farm fire, the Putney perfectionists were evolving the legal and economic structure of a communal society.

They were also beginning the marital experiments that would cause them to be driven from Putney. Despite the controversy surrounding his letter in 1837, Noyes continued to insist—privately—that what he called "communism in love" would eventually be part of the practice of perfection. He nonetheless reproved a few who were eager to start prematurely by sharing spouses. That changed in the spring of 1846. Noyes and a follower, Mary Cragin, were powerfully drawn to each other. They quickly discovered that Harriet and Mary's husband, George, were similarly attracted. Following a period of discussion and contemplation, the four began a system of "complex marriage," maintaining that it was not a sin for any sanctified man and any sanctified woman to have intercourse. Noyes's two sisters and their husbands joined the complex marriage, and by the end of 1846 the central members of the Putney group declared themselves a community of persons as well as of property. The word was soon out. Noyes's explanations and theological justifications did nothing to calm the enraged towns-

people of Putney. By the fall of 1847 he had fled to New York City
to avoid prosecution on charges of adultery. Shortly after, he and some
of the Putney group joined a communal settlement begun by fellow
perfectionists in Madison County, New York. Together they formed
the Oneida Association. Noyes led it for more than thirty years.

In addition to complex marriages, Noyes's sexual program at Oneida
involved birth control and, eventually, planned reproduction. Within
six years of their wedding, John and Harriet Noyes had five children,
four stillborn. To avoid the uncertainty and possible sorrow of another
pregnancy, Noyes experimented with contraception. Of the few methods available in the early 1840s, he chose "male continence," or intercourse without ejaculation. From 1846 onward Noyes insisted that
it be a part of complex marriage. He promoted male continence for
various reasons, including health: it freed women from pregnancy and
spared men the expenditure of seminal fluid, which Noyes, like many
nineteenth-century Americans, believed to be debilitating. The perfectionists also had in mind a commonsense consideration. Had they
not used birth control there would have been uncertainty about the
paternity of children. But Noyes added theological arguments to practical ones. Male continence, he maintained, was part of God's design.
It would "give new speed to the advance of civilization and refine-
ment." With fear of pregnancy banished, sexual intercourse "became
a joyful act of fellowship," even among near relatives. With male continence, intercourse became a religious ritual.

Religious or not, complex marriage and male continence were
shocking in the nineteenth century and critics viewed them as nothing
more than free love. Noyes, correctly and vainly, pointed out that any
libertine who came to the community expecting casual sex was bound
to be disappointed. Oneida accepted members only after close scrutiny
to make sure their characters were properly sanctified. Sexual encoun-
ters were subject to a variety of rules and regulations. By the 1860s all
requests for intercourse had to be made through a third party and duly
recorded in a ledger. Community leadership reproved individuals motivated by mere sensuality or couples having an "exclusive attach-
ment" for each other. As for male continence, Noyes was fond of

pointing out its demanding nature. He claimed that "licentious persons" treated it "with bitterness and scorn" because "the real self-denial which it requires cannot be adjusted to their schemes of pleasure-seeking." Its essence, he wrote with much truth, "is self-control, and that is a virtue of universal importance."

As Noyes indicated, the effect of his doctrines was not to unleash sexual impulses but to control them and make them simultaneously routine and cosmically significant. That was especially apparent in Oneida's ambitious experiment with planned reproduction, or "stirpiculture" (a word Noyes coined). The program began in 1869 and involved the formation of a committee at Oneida to approve, even suggest, "scientific combinations" of community members to become parents. Since Noyes believed moral characteristics were passed on to children, the men and women selected were supposed to be the most spiritually advanced in the community, although some attention was given to physical condition as well. During the next decade fifty-eight children were born at Oneida, thirteen conceived accidentally and forty-five as stirpiculture babies, nine of them fathered by Noyes, the most spiritually advanced member of all.

Noyes was not the only nineteenth-century figure to believe that extraordinary parents produced extraordinary offspring, although he was more literal-minded than most about encouraging "superior" people to reproduce. Noyes cited the biological works of Francis Galton and Charles Darwin to justify stirpiculture; yet despite his fancy references, his program was an intriguing blend of evangelical perfectionism with the newer language and authority of science. He felt that body and spirit were interconnected and that humankind could work toward perfection in both by following principles that were God-given and discoverable by rational analysis.

The community flourished in spite of the tensions its sexual practices aroused among its members and the hostility of the outside world. As Noyes grew older he became interested in learning about the economics of communal life and, in retrospect, attributed Oneida's endurance to what he saw as two of the essential features of stable utopian societies: community ownership of property and an emphasis on manufacturing and commerce rather than agriculture. Oneida had a difficult period after its founding in 1848, but large contributions from its first members carried it through. It had greater capital reserves than most communal societies, a fortunate thing, since the best estimate is that it invested more than $40,000 before its enterprises turned a profit. Oneida's initial success came from production of a superior animal trap, invented by a member; by 1875 that and other enterprises gave Oneida and a smaller satellite community at Wallingford, Connecticut, property amounting to $500,000. Prosperity showed in Oneida's buildings, which included a handsome Mansion House, a Turkish bath, and a theater to entertain its two hundred and fifty members. After the hardships of the first years, there was a pleasant style and pace of life at Oneida. Its demise as a community was not due to economic collapse.

In the 1870s Oneida's perfectionism became less theological and more secular. Younger members absorbed new ideas from the community's schools and through college education on the outside. Noyes himself showed an interest in social science and in secular socialism. The result was an undercurrent of questioning of the old ways and a decline in religious fervor. Noyes's failing leadership was a greater problem. He had exercised control firmly, but often indirectly, delegating responsibility to committees and depending on the community's "mutual criticism" sessions to reprove members who showed signs of falling by the wayside. Although Noyes was the driving force of Oneida, he was often absent. In 1851 he went to London, despite the community's financial difficulties, and he spent prolonged periods in Brooklyn or New York City watching over perfectionist publications. In 1875 he tried to impose his son Theodore, a Yale-trained physician, as head of the community. Theodore and Oneida balked. He finally succeeded in turning over much of his authority to Theodore and to a committee in 1877. That arrangement lasted until 1878, when Theodore, lacking sympathy with Oneida's religious principles and possibly ill, clashed with his father and left for New York City. Open rebellion against John Humphrey Noyes came the next year.

Appropriately enough, a sexual matter brought dissension into the open. It was the question of which male ought to act as "first husband" to virgin females in the community, a duty that Noyes had once taken upon himself but that he began to pass along to others. Neither the factions nor the issue was clearly defined, yet the dispute was bitter enough to send Noyes into Canadian exile in 1879, fearful that his enemies would prosecute him for statutory rape. Like many other communal ventures, Oneida depended on the personal power of its central figure. It could not survive the erosion of Noyes's authority and his permanent departure from the community. With him gone and leadership divided, and with a group of local clergy attacking the community, Oneida's governing council reluctantly decided that the system of complex marriage had to be abandoned. On January 1, 1881, Oneida ceased to be a community and became a joint-stock company. It would do well manufacturing silverware for generations of newlyweds.

Oneida, Brook Farm, and Hopedale represent a native American midpoint between two types of communitarianism originating in Europe: that of the German and Shaker pietists and the secular variety of Robert Owen and Charles Fourier, which entered the United States between the 1820s and the 1840s. Like the pietistic communities, Hopedale, Brook Farm, and Oneida were religiously inspired; like Owenite and Fourierist ventures, they were more engaged in transforming society than in fleeing from it. But Oneida had the greatest strengths of both communitarian traditions. It had the discipline of the pietists and their ability to give theological significance to all aspects of communal life. It also had an experimental zeal and an interest in "science" and economics, characteristics, as we shall see, of the Owenites and Fourierists.

# THREE

# Earth as Heaven

The purpose of secular communitarian societies was to restructure social and economic relationships: their focus was on this world, not on
the next. A few were quasi-religious, but many were freethinking or
let members believe whatever they wished. If they were not much
given to theology, each was, nonetheless, organized around an ideology, generally one taken from British or French utopianism. Some
were based on detailed and rigidly structured bodies of ideas, like
Charles Fourier's. In other ventures, central beliefs were loosely formulated or loosely enforced, as in Josiah Warren's communities, the
most notable of which was Modern Times, located on Long Island,
New York (1851–64). Warren wished to establish "equitable commerce"—a system giving people the full value of their labor—but he
otherwise sought absolute personal freedom, which meant, among
other things, freedom to quarrel. The diversity of secular communitarianism notwithstanding, it was dominated in turn by two men, Robert Owen and Charles Fourier. Between them they were responsible
for the greatest number of utopian societies begun in America after
1825.

Owen's was one of the success stories of the Industrial Revolution.
He was born in Wales in 1771 and left home at the age of ten to

become a draper's apprentice. Before he was thirty he was manager of the cotton mills at New Lanark, Scotland; under his charge they became the greatest in Britain. New Lanark was the primary source of the fortune Owen spent promoting his ideas, but it was also the inspiration for many of his theories. Sensitive to prevalent vice, ignorance, and misery among the workers, he found himself with a rare chance to shape their lives—in addition to managing the mills, he was a partner in the firm that owned the town. Seizing the opportunity his position gave him, Owen made numerous innovations at New Lanark and thus improved the financial security, living conditions, and educational opportunities of the townspeople. The experience in Scotland earned Owen a considerable reputation, left him with a sense of his own ability to alter social relationships, and confirmed his belief that the problems of his day required collective solutions. It did not, however, make him a communitarian. New Lanark was far from being a utopian society. It was simply a successful, profit-making venture.

After 1812 Owen turned his attention to broader industrial questions than those at issue in New Lanark. He presented proposals on national working conditions, unemployment, and poor relief to Parliament, which, by its failure to take them seriously, disillusioned him about the possibility of using governmental action to reform society. In the spring and summer of 1817 Owen took his case to the public in speeches, letters to London newspapers, and documents printed at his own expense. These put forth "the peculiar advantages to be derived from the Arrangement of the Unemployed Working Classes into 'Agricultural and Manufacturing Villages of Unity and Mutual Cooperation.'" The villages were to contain no fewer than 500 and no more than 1,500 people (later raised to over 2,000). They were to consist of healthy living quarters arranged in a parallelogram, with good schools for children and useful, mixed employment for adults. Even though Owen first represented his plan as an alternative to poor relief, he quickly came to see it as the prototype of a new social organization in which humans would cooperate with one another, lead decent and prosperous lives, and enjoy the benefits of the machine age without its vices. This was the beginning of his communitarianism, which was of a forward-looking sort, with only traces of the yearning for an agrarian past found in some other varieties of utopian thought.

Owen's beliefs after 1812 are neither extraordinarily complex nor easily summarized. He wrote copiously in the forty-five years between his *New View of Society* (1813) and his death in 1858. More a publicist than a philosopher, he neglected to analyze crucial concepts rigorously and sometimes skewed his logic, shifted his emphasis, and changed his mind. Owen's words and deeds, nonetheless, excited American communitarians. He fired their imaginations with visions of a perfect, practical future.

Owen's most distinctive proposition was the hardest for American reformers to accept wholeheartedly. In *A New View of Society*, he declared that "the character of man, is, without single exception, always formed for him" by his surroundings. This was a blunt statement of environmentalism, the doctrine that human beings are creatures of circumstances. Environmentalism was not entirely new to Americans —some of them had used it for decades to explain racial differences —but it was troublesome because it seemed to absolve individuals of responsibility for their sins. It rooted evil in a person's surroundings, not in his or her soul. Owen did not explore the logical implications of environmentalism and he occasionally fudged a bit, adding such factors as "constitution or organization at birth" as determinants of character. Yet environmentalism was central to his view of reform. It was the intellectual justification for his social engineering, particularly for its emphasis on creating a proper moral climate through education and an improved standard of living. Although most Americans persisted in believing that change had to begin with the human heart, not with external circumstances, Owen forced them to consider social conditions more than they might otherwise have done. He presented a challenging alternative to the old view that sinful humans were to blame for whatever evil befell them.

Owen's greatest contribution to American utopianism, in fact, was the way he departed from, rephrased, or modified Christian categories of thought. Where German and Shaker pietists, and even such utopians of the 1840s as Ballou, Ripley, and Noyes, imagined a sort of

Christian commonwealth, Owen rejected formal religion. He sought a new moral world based on "fundamental laws of nature" and the "science of man." After Owen, American utopian societies could rest on "reason" rather than on the Bible, or they could follow Noyes's intellectual path and join religious and secular languages in imagining a millennium that was simultaneously God's, nature's, and humankind's.

Owenism also provided antebellum communitarians with a new way to treat equality and property. Contemporaries often saw Owen as a radical egalitarian. Indeed, he assured members of New Harmony that "there will be no personal inequality, or gradation of rank or station; all will be equal in their condition." He wished laborers to receive the value of their work; he wanted the present "competitive system" to be replaced by cooperation—on those scores, he, the successful manufacturer, sounded a little like the artisan radicals we will meet in Chapter 8. He was even bold enough to examine gender inequalities and attack the family as an enemy of the communal spirit (accepting, in the process, such controversial practices as birth control, divorce, and employment for women outside the home). Owen, it should be said, was not always consistent: he preserved social distinctions in some of his plans; in none of his ventures did he abolish private property or effect revolutionary changes in family patterns. For women, the promise of a better life frequently dissolved into a weary round of service for the community as well as for family members, and diminution of one realm of power allotted them in antebellum culture, the individual household.

Ambiguities, failures of nerve, and unintended consequences aside, Owenism was the beginning of a secular critique of capitalist individualism. It promised American communitarians that by following a rational plan they could build a cooperative social order immediately, without revolution, without going through the conventional political process, and without God, although the latter was optional.

Some aspects of that imaginary new order were novel to Americans, but others were consistent with commonly held values. Owenism rephrased American clichés in its egalitarian rhetoric, devotion to ever-increasing prosperity, and advocacy of education. Even the size of

Owen's proposed villages played to American prejudices. With a population of one to three thousand, they were not large cities (those havens of vice), but they were big enough to support both agriculture and industry. They combined the moral advantages of rural small towns with the material advantages of a mixed economy. Despite these appealing aspects, however, Owenism grated on the American devotion to private property and conflicted, somewhat unnecessarily, with Protestantism, which helps explain why its life in the United States was brief and its communities ephemeral.

Word of Owen and his ideas reached America quickly. Owenism influenced a New York Society for Promoting Communities, founded in 1819, and a small circle of Philadelphia scientists and intellectuals. But the real outburst of enthusiasm came with Owen's visit to the United States in 1824. For a time he considered building a community in Scotland or elsewhere in Britain—he believed that once a model was constructed the rest of the world would rush to imitate it. His chance to find out came when the Harmony Society decided in 1824 to sell its Indiana property and return to Pennsylvania. Although the price amounted to more than half his fortune, Owen had an opportunity to purchase an already constructed community in a good location for a fraction of the cost of anything similar in Britain. Less than two months after being contacted by an agent of the Harmony Society, Owen sailed for the New World.

Landing in New York in November 1824, he circulated for nearly a month among a great variety of Americans—socialites, literary figures, businessmen, scientists, intellectuals, and a group of Shakers. It was not until mid-December that he arrived in Harmony to look it over and conclude arrangements for its purchase. Two and a half weeks later he was the owner of 20,000 acres of Indiana countryside and nearly two hundred assorted buildings, which he rechristened New Harmony. Journeying to the Eastern states for the winter and early spring of 1825, Owen continued to stir excitement. He addressed Congress twice, the second speech with outgoing President James Monroe and President-elect John Quincy Adams in the audience. Things were at such a fever pitch that Owen regarded America as his most promising field (he later decided differently). The Northern states, he predicted, would be converted to his theories by 1827.

He may have been too successful in kindling interest in New Harmony. When it opened for settlement under his auspices in May, it had more than eight hundred members. There was housing for seven hundred.

Crowding was only one of the problems to plague New Harmony in its short, troubled history. From the outset the community suffered confusion in purpose and leadership. Owen was not clear about property arrangements—his son William claimed he first thought about the matter a few days before purchasing Harmony. Owen likewise declined to state what form the community would take once it passed through a transitional stage as a "Preliminary Society." To compound his errors, Owen spent much of 1825 away from New Harmony, traveling along the Atlantic Seaboard and, for a few months, in Britain.

Owen's faulty leadership was matched by his lack of discrimination in admitting members. Confident that his system would work with anyone, he did not recruit dedicated Owenites. He took in people who came to him voluntarily, whatever their reasons or beliefs. The best of them were men and women like William Maclure, a prominent geologist and teacher, and his associate, Marie D. Fretageot, an educational reformer. They joined the community in 1826, along with some equally impressive Philadelphia scientists, and they were the heart of its fine educational apparatus. Such people gave New Harmony a substantial intellectual and artistic environment. Most of Owen's settlers were much less admirable. They lacked discipline, the willingness to compromise, and the skills of communal life. They were the majority.

In a four-month period in early 1826 New Harmony went through three reorganizations. Owen was pressed to govern more firmly, then to govern more democratically. He was pushed and pulled by his ideas, interests, and constituents. Some members demanded that he be true to his principles, relinquish ownership, and institute a genuine community of property. Others had different proposals. In May 1826 the community adopted Maclure's suggestions and divided New Harmony

into three semi-independent communities, defined by their functions
—education, agriculture, and manufacturing—and loosely coordinated
by a Board of Union. The chief benefit of the plan was to give New
Harmony a month of relative stability and Maclure and his colleagues
a freer hand to try their educational theories. The partition of New
Harmony proceeded without resolving problems. It may even have
had a negative effect by defining the warring factions more precisely
and giving them new ways to cripple each other (the agricultural and
manufacturing communities, for instance, withheld aid from the school
community). New Harmony's economic situation deteriorated.

The events of 1826 and 1827 did no credit to Owenism or to Owen.
The community was splintering out of existence while Owen generated confusion and distrust. He also managed to be taken in by a
crooked land speculator and to undermine Maclure's Education Society, one of the community's finer achievements. Maclure, a heavy in-
vestor in New Harmony, helped bring the sad situation to a close. He
made a large payment to creditors of Owen, who was financially em-
barrassed by that time, called in the loan, and forced the community
into dissolution.

Although it was a severe blow, the failure of New Harmony was not
the end of Owenite dreams. Other American communities were built
under his influence: they were smaller than New Harmony but equally
torn by conflict and equally doomed. More than twenty Owenite ventures sprang up, most in the United States, with others in Canada,
Wales, Ireland, Scotland, and England. Owenism also contributed personnel and ideas to other utopian societies. Frederick Evans, the
Shaker leader, had been a member of an Owenite settlement at Ken-
dal, Ohio, and Josiah Warren, the anarchistic communitarian, lived at
New Harmony as a young man. By the late 1820s, however, Owenism
had a fading hold on the utopian imagination. By 1840 there was a
new star on the horizon.

Owenism in America was bound up with the life of Owen; Fourierism
in America had little to do with Fourier. He died in 1837, before his
work reached its greatest influence in the United States. He was born

in 1772, a year after Owen. Unlike Owen, he was a poor and unhappy businessman, forced by his father to pursue the family trade of cloth merchant. His theories took shape amid the social and political turmoil of the French Revolution, not as a result of factory management, as Owen's did. Like Owen, he formulated his program in the provinces, away from his nation's metropolis; but, unlike Owen, he never moved in the highest social and intellectual circles: he was so obscure that it took one disciple two years to locate him. There was an attempt to form a Fourierist community in France in 1833, but in his native land Fourier was merely one of a number of interesting social theorists, and something of a crank at that. Only in America, and after his death, did Fourier triumph over French competitors such as Henri, Comte de Saint-Simon.

That was largely the doing of a wealthy young upstate New Yorker named Albert Brisbane. His conversion came in 1832, when he was in his early twenties and traveling in Europe. A friend gave him a book by Fourier, which, Brisbane said, carried him "away into a world of new conceptions." Brisbane repeated those conceptions energetically for decades as author of *Social Destiny of Man* (1840), as promoter of Fourierist communities, as a writer for various journals, and as a contributor to Horace Greeley's widely read newspaper, the *New York Tribune*. Fortunately, Brisbane did not advocate all his master's ideas (Fourier was capable of great absurdity), but he translated into American terms the French utopian's awkward vocabulary and intricate system of social relationships.

At the core of an ideal Fourierist "phalanx" was the "phalanstery," a huge structure to house the community's enterprises and the 1,620 people ("as varied as possible") Fourier saw as optimum. With great care, Fourier spelled out the kinds and quantity of rooms, where each should be located, and what should be reserved for whom. (Children had the mezzanine in order to keep them "separate from the adolescents, and . . . from all those who are capable of making love.") Fourier even calculated the minimum revenue a model phalanx would receive from charging admission to "curiosity-seekers." The jargon, fascination with numbers, and petty detail were characteristic of Fourier and made him easily ridiculed. They also made him appear to be of scientific bent.

In addition to designing the phalanstery, Fourier set up an elaborate method of defining and compensating labor, with highest wages going for the least pleasant tasks. His systematization sometimes ran amok and led to such documents as a report from a council of New York Fourierist societies in 1844. It broke Fourier's category of "Industry" into three "classes": Necessity (which included baking, washing, and ironing), Usefulness (which included raising silkworms and teaching), and Attractiveness (which included landscape painting and poultry keeping).

Fourier's instructions were obsessive and his speculations were daring, but the utopias his disciples built were more mundane. They were primarily agricultural, with some light industry, and they did not have a true community of property. Investors put capital into the phalanx and drew interest from its enterprises. That is not to say that it was the same as a conventional business corporation. Fourierists considered labor a form of capital and thought smaller investments of money should receive proportionally greater dividends than larger ones. Phalanxes, moreover, were communal living arrangements as well as economic ventures, even if they were staid in comparison with Oneida.

The economic theories and the occasional nonsense of Fourierism sometimes obscured its psychological and anthropological assumptions, which were among the most striking things it offered American communitarian thought. Fourier's enemy was "civilization." He believed it to be false to human nature; in its place he envisioned a social organization based on "association" and "harmony," key words in the Fourierist vocabulary. Although Fourier resembled Owen in basing his utopianism on a "science" of man, the two were at loggerheads about what science revealed. Owen believed that human beings were shaped by circumstances, while Fourier proposed to make circumstances fit an unchanging human nature. Mankind, Fourier calculated, consisted of twelve passions. Each person had all of them, in varying intensity. It was the particular mix of passions that made one's personality. Here Fourierists introduced the notion of "attraction," or "attractive industry" in the case of work. Different personalities, they felt, were "attracted" to different sorts of labor. Under the "civilized" way of doing things, people were either misemployed or unemployed and their passions were therefore thwarted. In the phalanx, men and women would gravitate to occupations suited for them. Work would be the pleasure it was meant to be. Like virtually all American communitarians, but more explicitly than most, Fourierists believed the present world had falsely separated humankind's physical and moral selves and that people had to be reconciled with their own true being.

In adapting Fourier's ideas for American audiences, Brisbane and his colleagues both held out the utopian promise of a perfect new world and fashioned a critique of individualism and conventional social and economic structures. This was all the more powerful because it challenged the notion that the United States was "exceptional"—that is, exempt from the inequalities and barbarisms of the rest of the world. "We have the same repugnant, degrading and ill-requited system of Industry as Europe," Brisbane and his collaborator, Osborne Macdaniel, declared, "the same system of Free Competition . . . the same menial system of Hired Labor . . . the same wasteful, intricate and grasping system of Trade; the same exclusive ownership of machinery by capital . . . and the same system of isolated or separate Households." With words like these, Fourierists cut through self-congratulatory American rhetoric and found darkness at the heart of Western civilization.

No brief summary can do justice to the density and obscurity of Fourierism, but its promises were clear and ironic. It offered a rigid, almost regimented plan designed to free people to be what nature meant them to be. Thus a European ideology offered the United States a chance to avoid a European fate many Americans thought they had already escaped.

Brisbane and his colleagues were tireless propagandists, and effective ones, too, particularly after the literati of Brook Farm joined the cause. American Fourierists wrote, lectured, held conventions, and formed clubs. More impressive, they actually constructed communities, at least twenty-eight of them between 1841 and 1858, with settlements as far afield as Michigan, Wisconsin, Iowa, and (possibly) Texas. These phalanxes, however, were much smaller than Fourier's ideal of 1,620 residents and the scaled-down American minimum estimate of approximately 400: the Alphadelphia Phalanx in Michigan claimed "upwards" of thirteen hundred members in 1844, but that figure was given before the community even began construction of its central building. The longest-lived phalanx, the North American in Red Bank, New Jersey, had a little over a hundred residents in its best years.

Brisbane, Greeley, and others hoped that these small beginnings would lead to a world transformed. The difficulties, nonetheless, were considerable when real people confronted real crops and animals. "Association" and "harmony" were elusive ideals for Americans—indeed, it was their absence in the United States that helped make Fourier's system attractive to utopians. Phalanx members refused to be passionately attracted to all the things they needed to do to run a community; and the old civilization's corruptions, including greed and religious disputes, refused to vanish.

Yet there were bright spots for the Fourierists. The conversion of Brook Farm was one, but the North American Phalanx was probably the brightest. Begun in 1843, it had the leading Fourierists, Brisbane and Greeley, involved in its affairs. It also was close enough to New York City to be a showcase of Fourierism. Blessed with capable managers, the North American was reasonably sound financially and paid some dividends to investors. Its nearly seven hundred acres of land produced a variety of crops, many sold outside the community (one source credits the phalanx with being "the first to grow okra or gumbo for the New York market"). In the early 1850s it was looking toward increasing and diversifying its manufactures.

Life at the North American was pleasant. The community had its Fourier-inspired buildings: a common dining room and great houses to accommodate families, individuals, and guests. It had its own school, more modest than New Harmony's, but well taught. There was the usual carping about wages, and more serious bickering over how democratically the association should be governed. But members worshipped as they pleased, without the religious strife that agitated some Fourierist ventures. Visitors remarked on the apparent joy of residents as they engaged in dancing and other amusements. If it lacked the idyllic reputation of Brook Farm, the North American Phalanx was nonetheless a more genial enterprise than any Shaker community and a more stable one than New Harmony.

It was sold in 1856. The precipitant was a fire, as it had been with Brook Farm. It set in motion a downward financial spiral even though the mill that burned was not vital to the community's livelihood and Greeley offered to lend money to build a new one. By the mid-1850s Fourierism had almost run its course. It worked for a time in New Jersey, but it failed in too many other places. Fourierists (and Owenites, for that matter) did not have a powerfully unifying creed or a charismatic leader to hold them together through rough periods. In that respect, they were weaker than the German and Shaker pietistic communities and Oneida.

There is another point of comparison, likewise relating to the staying power of the pietists and Oneida, on the one hand, and the lack of endurance among Owenites and Fourierists, on the other. It has to do with how drastically communal societies altered social relationships. Fourier's assault on "civilization" was sweeping; and Owen, although more restrained, was equally committed to abolishing outmoded thought and former ways of doing things. Their communities, however, were not nearly so radical as the pietistic societies, many of which did away with private property and conventional marriage and one of which, the Shakers, gave much authority to women. The more a community deviated from American norms, and the more authoritarian it was, the better its chance of survival.

Still, the radicalism of the pietists was a dead end. Their equality was that of the saints in Christ: they shared property and did away with families because they felt the things of the world were meaningless. Owenism and Fourierism asserted the right of people, here and now, to live happily, cooperatively, and productively. Secular communitarianism was not thoroughly anticapitalistic or truly communistic, and, at heart, it was based more on moral impulses than on economic analysis. But, above all, it demanded a just measure of the good things of the earth for every human being. That cast of mind, in its infinite variations, outlasted Owenite and Fourierist utopias and was more dynamic in the industrial age than pietism could ever be.

Useful as the distinction between religious and secular utopian societies is, the behavior of communitarians ought to be a warning against drawing it too rigidly. There were numerous examples of people who moved back and forth between religious and secular ventures with no trouble—a surprised visitor to the North American Phalanx in 1851 immediately met an ex-Shaker and an ex-resident of Hopedale. One whole community, Brook Farm, went easily from "Christ's Idea of Society" to Fourier's in less than three years.

Although not many recognized what it was, a real bond existed between almost all communities. It was millennialism and perfectionism. Those doctrines were obvious in religious utopias, but they were central to Owenism and Fourierism as well. Robert Owen, irreligious though he was, informed his feuding supporters at New Harmony that his system might "be termed the beginning of the millennium." Nearly twenty years later he was still hoping: in 1855 he issued his *Tracts on the Coming Millennium*. Elizabeth Peabody, promoting Brook Farm, interpreted Fourier as believing "the earth would be cultivated and restored to the state of Paradise." Religious and secular communitarians alike had a faith that humankind could arrive at a state of perfection, and that it could be achieved only collectively and by setting an example for the world to follow, not by politics or revolution.

Converts came to the task with hope and zeal, yet in the secular societies, at least, they wandered off in a matter of months, or a few years at most. Some of that was due to blundering, mismanagement, and personality conflicts, but it also reflected the difficulty of getting Americans to suppress their desires for autonomy, even when they voluntarily became part of a collectivity. Utopianism itself was a reaction against what many perceived as selfish individualism, particularly in political and economic affairs. Communal life was supposed to—and obviously did not—replace the go-getting, self-aggrandizing spirit of the age and create harmonious human relationships.

Paradoxical as it may sound, those were goals of even anarchistic utopians (who were no more successful at reaching them than were Owenites or Fourierists). Josiah Warren, for instance, was so complete an individualist that he once declared that "everybody has a perfect right to do everything." He inspired four communities (including an ill-fated settlement named Utopia) to free humans to do what they felt like doing. The most notorious venture to follow his theories was Modern Times, in Suffolk County, Long Island, which had more than a hundred members by 1860 and which horrified decent folk by its disdain for marriage and economic orthodoxy. Tolerant as Warren was of deviance, he was also committed to social harmony. He insisted that people would live in peace only if they obeyed their conscience rather than any external authority. He and his colleague Stephen Pearl Andrews advocated a "sovereignty of the individual" that, like its apparent opposite, the rigid moral and institutional structures of most communitarians, was an effort to make the lives of men and women consistent with a larger purpose.

Although utopian societies deprived men and women of the family life and autonomy Americans valued, they offered much in return. For disillusioned labor reformers in the 1840s and for others, they were a refuge from the failures of politics and radical agitation. For some people they were an escape from self-doubt, from anxieties about sex and marriage, or from the burdens of having to make choices. Communities promised a stable, morally perfect environment in which a person could find meaning and, at the same time, serve the cause of human uplift. Things did not always work that way, but the prospect was appealing in a time of uncertainty and change.

Communitarians, like antebellum reformers generally, were at too early a stage in the Industrial Revolution to grasp fully how it was transforming the world or to be certain whether its effects were good or evil. A number of communal ventures rejected urban and capitalistic society (in that, they resembled the communes of the 1960s). A few even challenged racism: the Northampton Association, for example, provided a home for Sojourner Truth and for at least one escaped slave, Stephen C. Rush. A Nashoba, Tennessee, community begun in 1826 was even bolder. The handiwork of a Scottish colleague of Robert Owen, Frances Wright, it was a short-lived interracial venture that aimed at the education and emancipation of African Americans.

Many communitarian societies, however, were more compatible with American economic and social mores. Several engaged in business enterprises and some were successful. Very few utopians chose to get away from it all by settling on the frontier, and even the most agricultural-minded ventures usually sold crops rather than practice subsistence farming. In that case a society became part of the larger market economy, not a rural paradise, unpolluted by commerce. Many communitarians, moreover, admired the science, technology, and rising standard of living produced by industrialization, despite being appalled at the misery "progress" brought with it. They did not so much oppose economic development as feel that humankind had to assert rational control over it, whether through religious principles such as Noyes's or the "social science" of Owen or Fourier. Such communitarians were too much products of their times to give up the nineteenth-century middle-class god, Progress, even though other utopians were practicing Christian asceticism or trying to learn how to farm.

It would be simpler if antebellum communitarianism had been one thing or another. It was not, but in it we see American reform and radicalism at an exciting and unique moment: moving from religious to secular modes of social thought, trying to harness American individualism in the name of responsibility to mankind, and confronting —often half-consciously and indirectly—the modern industrial world.

# FOUR

# Antislavery

In membership, communitarianism and the antislavery movement had little in common. A few abolitionists became involved in Hopedale and similar ventures, yet these were exceptions. As abolitionists saw their duty, it was not to retreat from society, even though they withdrew from such corrupt institutions as proslavery churches and political parties. They were determined, in the words of a New Hampshire editor, "to stay amid the great community [of the world], destitute of *communion*, as it is, and go for *community-zing* the whole" by breaking down slavery and other barriers separating individuals from one another and from their own potential. That was an impulse almost as utopian as any to be found among communitarians—a rarefied vision of human unity and a challenge to a system of racial injustice deeply embedded in American life.

On January 1, 1831, William Lloyd Garrison, a young native of Newburyport, Massachusetts, published the first issue of *The Liberator*. During its thirty-five-year run, the Boston newspaper would be abrasive, vituperative, and consistent in its loathing of slavery. It would never have a large circulation, nor would Garrison ever represent the whole of abolitionism—the movement was diverse, decentralized, and divided along lines of region, ideology, personality, gender, and race. Still, the founding of *The Liberator* marked the beginning of an antislavery movement that was new in tone, social composition, and doctrine.

Two gestures by African Americans framed the newspaper's appearance and gave it special significance. In 1829 a free black man who lived in Boston, David Walker, published his *Appeal to the Coloured Citizens of the World*, an incendiary pamphlet aimed at "all coloured men, women, and children," including the slaves of the South. It was a militant declaration that white slaveholders are "our enemies by nature." Walker's *Appeal* provoked defenses of slavery and greater repression against slaves, suspected abolitionists, and free blacks, including African American seamen, who were suspected of bringing insurrectionary doctrines from the outside world to their enslaved Southern brethren. By the summer of 1830 Walker was dead, his body found under mysterious circumstances near his used-clothing shop. A little over a year later another African American insurrectionary, Nat Turner, led the largest slave revolt in North America. Coming shortly before and after *The Liberator*'s first edition, these events posed the alternatives: abolition or insurrection. For the majority of white Southerners, however, abolition, not slavery, was the cause of insurrection. Their answer—an unsuccessful one, as it turned out—was to try to suppress the debate over slavery.

Before 1831 opposition to slavery had taken several forms. From the outset blacks made their feelings clear by flight from bondage, by day-to-day resistance, and by occasional insurrections. In the eighteenth century—and especially by the time of the Revolution—increasing numbers of whites were preaching abolition, inspired by religion, Enlightenment humanitarianism, and their own republican and egalitarian rhetoric. Most Northern states ended slavery before 1800, while simultaneously limiting the rights of free blacks. Abolition sentiment was on the wane by then and the institution of slavery was, if anything, becoming more strongly entrenched in the lower South, as the newly invented cotton gin and population growth pushed cotton production farther west.

Organized antislavery persisted in the early nineteenth century and differed strikingly from the caustic brand Garrison and his colleagues promoted after 1830. It was concentrated in the upper South, was conciliatory to the master, and had little sympathy for blacks. Above all, there was no particular urgency to it. Prior to 1831 most white critics of slavery assumed that manumission would be gradual and ought not to cause social or economic dislocation. No organization better typified such an approach than the American Colonization Society, founded in 1816. Its mission was to send ex-bondsmen out of the country, preferably to its African outpost, Liberia. The society's supporters included slaveholders, prominent politicians, and distinguished men of the sort who later shunned abolitionism. Their motives were varied and conflicted. Some genuinely hated slavery but believed the races could never coexist without it. Their solution was to expel black people. Other colonizationists were proslavery and merely wanted to dispose of the small free black population of the South and to eliminate bondsmen who might become a burden on their owners or society. Without much consistency, idealism, or practicality to recommend it, the Colonization Society nevertheless profited from this ability to satisfy contradictory viewpoints. It sent few black people to Africa, but it discharged some white anxieties about slavery and race, and otherwise did well in the 1820s.

Most post-1830 abolitionists regarded colonization as their great enemy. Their hostility was a combination of ideology, disillusion—many of them had once believed in it—and tactical necessity. From personal experience they knew how powerful its appeal was and how difficult it would be to persuade whites to accept a truer, more demanding antislavery position. Yet even allowing for understandable exaggeration, later abolitionists were right to contrast their crusade with colonization. The platform Garrison proclaimed on New Year's Day 1831 was different. It found no favor in the South. It made few concessions to the sensibilities of slaveholders (they were "oppressors," "man-stealers," "despots," and "tyrants"). Although tainted with streaks of racism, post-1830 white abolitionists like Garrison dismissed any thoughts of exiling blacks, accepted the idea of civil equality for them, and greeted the slave as "A Man and a Brother" or "A Woman and a

Sister," phrases borrowed from British abolitionism. Most important, antislavery after 1831 repudiated what Garrison called the "pernicious doctrine of gradual abolition." "Immediate emancipation" was the new battle cry.

The phrase was ambiguous. Even Garrison seldom insisted that it meant slavery should cease right away. It was, instead, a demand immediately to renounce slaveholding. Abolitionists admitted that emancipation might take time. Immediatism, however, tolerated no delay in beginning the process, as earlier, gradualistic approaches had. It was a call to break off an evil practice without hesitation or equivocation, just as sinners, when saved, utterly repudiated sin. The revivalism of the 1820s encouraged abolitionists and most other antebellum crusaders to see reform as something akin to an act of repentance. That approach to problems slighted social, political, and economic factors in favor of moral imperatives, and it could be narrow and self-righteous; but it had a passion and clarity badly needed when men and women espoused unpopular issues in a society where compromise was second nature. Instead of describing a well-worked-out plan, "immediate emancipation" jolted the complacent and infused abolitionism with a fervor it seldom had before 1831.

Immediatism quickly made converts in New England, New York City and upstate New York, Pennsylvania, and Ohio. The first organization based upon the doctrine was the New-England Anti-Slavery Society (1832). Nearly two years later, in December 1833, delegates from several states gathered in Philadelphia and created the American Anti-Slavery Society. For the next half decade it played a crucial role in spreading abolitionism throughout the North.

Garrison was instrumental in founding the American Anti-Slavery Society, but control of it passed to able and dedicated men at its New York headquarters. Chief among them was Lewis Tappan, blessed with ample financial resources and fine managerial experience gained as a leader of the "benevolent empire" of Protestant charities. He and several energetic co-workers marshaled support for the cause and guided an outpouring of antislavery activity up to 1837, when internal disputes and hard times slowed the crusade. Affluent members like

Tappan subsidized the printing and distribution of a wide range of American Anti-Slavery Society publications (at least three-quarters of a million pieces of propaganda by 1838). In 1835 the organization flooded the mails with this literature in an attempt to reach clergy, editors, and other influential people in every state, particularly in the South. Two years later the society began to encourage and coordinate circulation of antislavery petitions directed at Congress. Abolitionists —especially women—were so diligent in collecting signatures that they gathered more than 400,000 by 1838.

Among the national organization's most significant enterprises during Tappan's stewardship was the recruitment of agents. These were zealous young men charged with carrying abolitionism across the American countryside. Like Theodore Dwight Weld, their greatest orator, many were would-be or former ministers; several had been brought into the abolitionist fold during highly emotional debates over slavery at Lane Theological Seminary in Ohio in 1834. Whatever their background, the agents sparked controversy and inspired rapid formation of town, county, and state antislavery groups. By 1838 the American Anti-Slavery Society claimed a membership of a quarter of a million and more than 1,300 local branches. Once begun, these local organizations worked in cooperation with the parent society, published newspapers of their own, and waged campaigns of special importance to their areas (including challenges to segregation and racist legislation in the North). Before the 1830s were over, immediatism passed into the hinterland and the agency system had served its purpose.

Neither the blistering rhetoric of Garrison nor the bureaucratic expertise of Tappan fully explains what drew men and women to antislavery. The motives of African Americans in the movement were more straightforward than those of their white colleagues. Some, like Frederick Douglass, Harriet Tubman, Sojourner Truth, and many others, had been slaves and knew the institution from the inside. Their hatred of it was rooted in personal experience as well as moral conviction, which made them especially effective in helping others flee bondage and in writing and speaking against slavery. Their lives were witnesses to its evils, and their testimony moved audiences in Europe as well as in America.

But the crusade against slavery also owed much to free black communities in such Northern cities as Boston, New York, and Philadelphia, ones whose men and women were educated and had financial resources. For them, discrimination was a daily reality and slavery only the most extreme part of a general denial of citizenship, opportunity, and dignity to African Americans. In common with their brethren and white allies elsewhere, they sheltered fugitive slaves or helped them along the "underground railroad" to Canada. They also did a great deal more, sometimes in cooperation with white abolitionists, sometimes independently. Free blacks provided generous financial support for antislavery efforts, including a disproportionate share of the subscriptions to *The Liberator*, and devoted their organizational, tactical, and rhetorical skills to every branch of the movement. Even before 1831, nonetheless, their communities had institutions capable of carrying distinctly African American forms of abolitionism and other reforms. Among these were black churches, voluntary associations, and the beginnings of a National Negro Convention movement. Such organizations, and later ones, proved durable and effective, especially by the 1840s, when many black abolitionists felt confined by their white colleagues' lingering racism and refusal to share power equitably. Increasingly, as the Civil War approached, they came to articulate a distinctly broader, more militant agenda. Even Frederick Douglass, who acknowledged a considerable debt to Garrison for bringing him into the movement, made a painful break with his mentor in 1847, largely because of the latter's efforts to control his beliefs and actions.

More puzzling than Douglass's opposition to slavery is the matter of why thousands of whites dedicated themselves to immediate emancipation. Most came from highly moralistic families, influenced by evangelical Protestantism, Quakerism, or Unitarianism. In their own accounts, they made much of discrepancies between the way the United States was and the religious and political ideals they held. That, however, described rather than accounted for their objections to slavery. Thousands of equally moral and sensitive Americans felt no urge to attack the institution, even though they came from the same areas and similar families as those who did. It is difficult to say what caused some people to ignore slavery while others, very much like them, condemned it.

For those who became abolitionists, exposure to antislavery often came at a crucial moment in their lives and helped them find direction, meaning, and companionship. To be an abolitionist was to declare allegiance to the principles of brotherhood and equality of opportunity, to suffer for those ideals, and to band together with like-minded individuals. It was to find a moral community in an immoral society.

Antislavery also attracted support because it spoke to a complex set of hopes and fears about the future. These were social in origin and were expressed in a kind of moral drama present in much abolitionist propaganda. The chief protagonists in it were the master and the slave. The former was lustful and tyrannical; dominion over others, not greed, was what abolitionists usually regarded as his primary motive. The slave, on the other hand, was the epitome of powerlessness: his or her degradation came not primarily from cruelty but from the loss of the right to exercise choice. Real freedom, abolitionists maintained, meant the absence, as much as possible, of external restraints on one's behavior. Only then could people be morally responsible for their actions and justly rewarded for their labor.

Most of those assumptions were familiar to Americans and permeated other reforms of the day. There was nothing novel about the abolitionist notion that restraint was the mark of a virtuous person, nor were a fear of power and a desire for individual autonomy unique to antislavery. Those attitudes had been current at least since the late eighteenth century and had a complex history in Anglo-American religious and political thought. Conditions in the 1820s and 1830s, however, gave them a special urgency and made it easier for abolitionists to draw upon them to interpret slavery and other evils. By the antebellum period, Americans had become mobile, energetic, and heterogeneous; they capitalized on the opportunities available to them and paid scant attention to anything except personal advantage. Religious and political leaders, according to abolitionists, did little to make the situation better; they were either ineffective or corrupt, or both. Reformers thought it necessary to find some means to make certain that virtue was not trampled in the rush to get ahead. One half of the abolitionist answer looked backward to classical republican thought; it was not to trust anyone with too much power, lest he turn it to his advantage at the expense of everyone else. The other half involved a mixture of evangelical Protestantism, individualism, utilitarianism, and an emerging middle-class morality; it was for people to be sufficiently self-disciplined to do what was right and resist what was wrong without help from ministers or politicians.

Abolitionists aimed that message at all Americans. In their bleak images of the slaveholder, the slave, and the South, they constructed a model of what happened when people failed to conquer their worst cravings. The slave states, according to antislavery rhetoric, were characterized by laziness, contempt for honest work, insolvency, violence, licentiousness, irreligion, and a lack of respect for the family. Tyranny and disorder prevailed. Moral desolation turned the South into a cursed land, upon which God showered few blessings. It lacked such signs of progress as railroads, factories, public schools, and other benefits of Yankee culture. Abolitionists, however, refused to let Northerners take too much comfort in the contrast between their "civilization" and the "barbarism" of the South. The cardinal sin of Southerners—loss of moral control—appeared in the North in the guise of social turmoil and rampant selfishness; surely the free states would be punished for their transgressions just as severely as the slave ones were, unless repentance came in time. Unconsciously, abolitionists saw in the South a mirror of their concerns about their own region and about people like themselves.

Although many values behind that view were old, abolitionists applied them in a manner unthinkable in the eighteenth century, before economic growth sharpened differences between the sections. Only after slavery vanished in the North, and factories and cities blossomed there, was it possible to believe that the free states represented a higher level of development than the South. Even then it was a debatable point, given the strength of the Southern economy and poverty and exploitation of Northern workers. Antislavery men and women did not entirely endorse the emerging urban and industrial order of their region—its excesses were what they had in mind when arguing that Northerners were in danger of losing self-control and becoming like Southerners. Yet abolitionists shared many of the assumptions of Northern capitalism, particularly when they insisted that liberty meant the ability to buy and sell property and labor (although not humans) without hindrance. They used that definition to indict slavery and, to their credit, they worried about the consequences of economic individualism even while they accepted it. They always insisted that entrepreneurship had to conform to Christian morality and declared that the free market had to be opened to blacks on an equal footing with whites.

Far from being uncritical apologists for their section, abolitionists demanded that the North live up to its best standards and fulfill its greatest promises. Only a few explored the radical outer edges of antislavery logic. Some, like the woman's rights activists and Christian anarchists we will meet in the next chapter, followed their commitment into a sweeping critique of gender inequality and state power. Others, many of them African Americans, insisted on a thoroughgoing expansion of the rights of citizenship and the granting of those rights, including the vote, to all men (and, in the case of feminists, to all women). Only a small number of abolitionists advocated the genuinely radical course of granting land to former slaves in order to ensure their economic autonomy. On that issue, former slaves were often ahead of former abolitionists, including some African American ones.

Racial prejudice prevented the majority of Northern whites from acknowledging how thoroughly antislavery expressed many of their own economic and religious beliefs. But there must have been some recognition of the fact: much of the strength of abolitionism was in cities, towns, and rural areas transformed by commerce and evangelical Protestantism.

The spread of immediatism in the mid-1830s came in the face of suppression. Defenders of slavery saw antislavery as a dangerous assault on the status quo and believed it had to be stopped by all possible means. Their response, in retrospect, seems out of proportion to the actual threat—at the time abolitionists were a tiny minority in the North. There were, nonetheless, reasons to be outraged and fearful. Some abolitionists, especially African American ones, did indeed proclaim radical social doctrines, including the heretical notion that blacks ought to be equal, under the law, with whites. If that idea ever became current, the system of race relations in the South (and in the North, for that matter) would come tumbling down. Moreover, many white Southerners were wrongly convinced that slave revolts such as Nat Turner's were related to "agitation" from the North. Abolitionists denied the charge and countered by saying that the only way to ensure the safety of Southern whites was to free blacks, words that did nothing to calm the defenders of slavery.

White Southerners and their Northern allies used force and the political system to thwart abolitionists in the 1830s. The American Anti-Slavery Society's propaganda campaign of 1835 (a year of much anti-abolition violence) prompted a mob in Charleston, South Carolina, to break into the post office to steal and burn antislavery publications mailed in from the North. Instead of deploring this illegal act, public officials in the South, and some in the North, applauded. President Andrew Jackson put his seal of approval on the Charleston riot when he suggested that the real problem was with antislavery propaganda and the solution was banning it from the mails. No such bill ever passed, but proslavery forces were successful in stopping Congress from considering antislavery petitions. In 1836 the House of Representatives resolved that all of them should "be laid upon the table, and that no further action whatever shall be had thereon." Some form of this "gag resolution" remained in effect until December 1844.

Repression was not confined to Congress and the South. Connecticut in the mid-1830s passed legislation to outlaw racially mixed schools and to silence antislavery lecturers. Although politicians in other Northern states were similarly inclined to give the South a helping hand, there was very little they actually could do. Mobs proved to be much more of a danger to abolitionists—from 1834 through 1838 they were victims of several major riots. One occurred in Boston in 1835, where a crowd led Garrison through the streets by a rope. On the same day a similar fracas took place in Utica, New York. In yet another and far more violent episode two years later, Elijah Lovejoy, an antislavery editor, lost his life while defending his press in Alton, Illinois. As abolitionists were fond of noting, substantial citizens— "gentlemen of property and standing"—were prominent in creating most of these disturbances. Such people cared less about the South's "peculiar institution" than about the federal Union and the nation's racial and social hierarchy, both of which they thought the abolitionists were out to destroy. South of the Mason-Dixon line, mobs left an even bloodier legacy of harassment and murder of blacks and whites suspected of threatening the racial order.

Efforts to stop antislavery agitation were probably more effective in making converts than in slowing the crusade. Among those joining the movement in the 1830s were people who dated their commitment from revulsion at anti-abolition mayhem. Abolitionists appreciated that and made much out of incidents such as the slaying of Lovejoy and the passage of the gag resolution. (The American Anti-Slavery Society's great petition campaign, in fact, got under way after the first gag resolution passed.) Besides providing opportunities for publicity, repression strengthened the resolve of abolitionists and confirmed two cardinal tenets of their propaganda. The first was a belief that American institutions were dominated by the "slave power" (an alleged conspiracy of slaveholders and their Northern lackeys). The second was an insistence that proslavery men had no respect for the civil liberty of whites. Congress, President Jackson, and mobs confirmed that every time they denied white abolitionists their right to free speech and to petition the government.

Abolitionists may have been helped by their enemies, but the results were less beneficial when they battled one another, as they did with increasing frequency after 1836. The issues were seldom as clearly defined as the warring factions thought they were, and both geographical distance and irascible personalities played a part in dividing abolitionists. These disagreements, nonetheless, were severe enough to fragment the movement in 1840, a feat no amount of proslavery violence had accomplished.

William Lloyd Garrison was the center around which most internal conflict revolved. He was deeply disturbed by mobs, by the mindlessness of partisan politics, and by the reluctance of many ministers to endorse antislavery. There was nothing unusual about Garrison's perception of things: most abolitionists shared his disgust with the level of public morality in the country and with weak-willed politicians and clergymen. But where other abolitionists tried to purge the churches and the government of corruption, the Boston editor sought alternatives. Disillusion and his own spiritual restlessness made him susceptible to notions that upset his straitlaced contemporaries.

Within a short span of time in the mid-1830s Garrison adopted an impressive number of unconventional positions. He questioned whether Sunday ought to be celebrated as the Sabbath (all days should be holy, he maintained). He denounced both the Protestant denominations and the majority of clergy for "sectarianism"—the sin of putting selfish interests ahead of morality. In addition, Garrison came to believe in a form of Christian anarchism known as nonresistance. It involved repudiating all varieties of force, among which Garrison included laws and governments. As we shall see in the next chapter, nonresistance was subtle beyond simple summary and rooted in evangelical Protestantism. Yet neither its complexity nor its origins made it acceptable to most Americans or to many within the antislavery movement. Along with the rest of Garrison's crusades, it struck the public as silly at best, horrifying at worst.

But there was more. At the very moment Garrison's multiple heresies offended many former supporters, he added woman's rights to the controversial causes he favored. Garrison himself had no particular responsibility for raising the issue, which largely grew out of the activities of female abolitionists. By the mid-1830s women were deeply involved in antislavery agitation, working within separate organizations affiliated with those run by men. That kind of arrangement was common in the antebellum period and suited contemporary notions of propriety. What some antislavery women did, nevertheless, was less consistent with a Victorian sense of decorum. For instance, they welcomed blacks as equals (stirring white fears of miscegenation), and they left the family circle (supposedly their "sphere") for such unladylike ventures as lecturing and petitioning the government to end slavery. Women chafed at opposition from the public and at the condescending attitudes of male comrades. Yet it took an unforeseen event to elevate the "woman question" into a matter of open contention among abolitionists and to alienate Garrison further from some of his colleagues.

The catalyst was a lecture tour of New England, undertaken in 1837 by two valuable additions to the antislavery crusade, Angelina and Sarah Grimké. Unlike most abolitionists, the sisters were Southerners, members of a prominent South Carolina slaveholding family. Their public appearances drew curiosity seekers. Originally, the Grimkés were to talk only to female audiences—it was generally thought improper for women to address "promiscuous assemblies" (those with both sexes in attendance). Men frustrated the sisters' intentions by sneaking into antislavery gatherings to hear what they had to say. This outrage to public decency attracted the attention of New England clergy, ever vigilant to spot sin and preserve the social order. A grandiose *Pastoral Letter*, circulated to the Congregationalist churches, chastised the sisters. It declared that women should not speak in public and should obey men, rather than lecture to them.

Some abolitionists shared the clergy's consternation over the Grimkés' tour, while others, perhaps a majority, had trouble arriving at a consistent view of the matter. They could not entirely repudiate the sisters, nor could they endorse the *Pastoral Letter*, which made extreme claims for ministerial authority; yet they were unwilling to fly in the face of public opinion on issues other than slavery. Garrison was not the least uncertain. He argued that there was nothing immoral about the sisters, or any woman, participating in public life or addressing men. Like many other abolitionists, he was in the process of shaking loose from his old assumptions about feminine roles and beginning to comprehend the implications of women's activism of the sort we will see in the next chapter.

Taken along with his other enthusiasms, Garrison's support of the

Grimkés convinced many abolitionists that he was either abandoning antislavery or leading it to ruin by associating it with strange crusades that assaulted the sensibilities of decent folk. Garrison responded that expediency should never prevent a person from speaking out against evil and, moreover, that his views on questions other than slavery were his own, not an essential part of abolitionism. He advocated an "open platform" where all who believed in immediate emancipation were welcome, no matter what their differences on other social or theological questions. That point was lost on anti-abolitionists, who saw Garrison as representative of the cause and cited him to show that the movement consisted of dangerous crackpots. Some of his colleagues felt they had to distance themselves from him to refute such charges and gain credibility. Garrison, meanwhile, subtly closed the "open platform" and frittered away support by using harsh language to describe allies who disagreed with him. By 1838 he had repelled many admirers while retaining an intensely loyal cluster of followers, concentrated in New England and labeled Garrisonians. They were diverse in religion, had a high proportion of women and blacks, were flamboyant in their tactics, and were extreme on social issues.

Abolitionist opponents of Garrison were not of one mind and did not form a single, coherent group. They included evangelical Protestants put off by Garrison's heterodoxy and convinced that, if approached tactfully, the clergy and other influential men would support the movement (a notion many of them lost with time). Some, such as Lewis Tappan, were quite traditional regarding the role of women, while others, such as Theodore Dwight Weld—who married Angelina Grimké—took a woman's rights position but felt it should not be proclaimed openly, lest it detract from abolitionism.

Divisive as Garrison and the "woman question" were, the most serious dispute among abolitionists came over politics. From the beginning, antislavery had been nonpartisan as well as nonsectarian. Abolitionists, however, expected to have political influence by acting as a pressure group, by changing public opinion, and by forcing major-party candidates to declare their positions on slavery. In the late 1830s a number of abolitionists in New York and Ohio, led by such men as

James G. Birney, Myron Holley, and Henry B. Stanton, became dissatisfied with those tactics. They recognized that abolitionists were being taken in by politicians who made promises more easily than they kept them. Politicking, moreover, seemed a good way to focus abolitionist energies and to give publicity to the cause. Since many abolitionists regarded the Whigs and Democrats as corrupt and chained to Southern votes, the logical conclusion was to form a separate antislavery political organization, with its own candidates. After months of talk, the Liberty Party emerged in time to run Birney for the Presidency in 1840.

Garrisonians opposed the move on practical and philosophical grounds. Politics, they felt, demanded unacceptable moral compromises as the price of success. They further argued that an antislavery party would do poorly in elections (they were right) and would actually diminish the influence of abolitionist votes, since the major parties would no longer bother to compete for them in close elections. Even if they had swallowed those objections, many Garrisonians could not have joined the Liberty Party. As Christian anarchists, they believed the proper course of action was not to vote or to have anything else to do with human governments, which they regarded as inherently sinful. Yet Garrison and his followers did not entirely reject political means—for others.

Garrison frequently said that he expected antislavery to be manifested at the ballot box. He added that it would get there only if abolitionists kept their moral purity (which meant staying clear of party politics) and if they persuaded public opinion of the evils of slavery. What Garrison failed to see was that the Liberty Party did not necessarily have to make moral compromises or win elections in order to have a purpose: in a highly political nation, electioneering can serve as a valuable form of propaganda.

Well before the Liberty Party, cracks in antislavery unity occurred. The worst of the early ones appeared in Garrison's home territory. In 1838 his critics created an alternative organization to the Massachusetts Anti-Slavery Society, which he dominated. In the meantime, politically minded abolitionists such as Henry B. Stanton and James G. Birney pressed for resolutions defining the voting obligations of antislavery men. Although Garrisonians suggested compromise declarations, Birney and his allies stuck to a formula calculated to purge the movement of nonresistants and of abolitionists who wanted to stay within the Whig or the Democratic Party. The "woman question" also remained a source of irritation. It nearly broke up the American Anti-Slavery Society in 1839, when female delegates were admitted for the first time on equal terms with men.

The following year the American Anti-Slavery Society split under the accumulated weight of internal disputes. With the election of a woman, Abby Kelley, to serve on a previously all-male committee, a substantial minority of delegates walked out of the annual meeting. Some left to work primarily within the Liberty Party; others joined Lewis Tappan in a new, largely ineffective venture, the American and Foreign Anti-Slavery Society.

The schism might have been averted. Positions taken by Garrison and his critics appeared in various state and local organizations without causing comparable disruption. Abolitionists in places remote from the battles in Boston and New York commonly regarded the feuding as silly and refused to take sides. The antagonists, and historians, nevertheless persisted in blaming the division of 1840 on drastic and irreconcilable differences between the factions. Supposedly, it was Garrison, the radical, against moderates who accepted Protestant orthodoxy and the legitimacy of American institutions. That interpretation, however, fails to acknowledge that Garrison's "radicalism" grew out of the values of the day (it stemmed from Protestant perfectionism and millennialism) and that he was capable of altering it with circumstances. In spite of his pacifism and anarchism, for example, he accepted the Civil War and the Republican Party as means of achieving reform goals. His abolitionist opponents, furthermore, were not always so "moderate" as they seemed to Garrison. They, too, made drastic criticisms of the political system and of American religion (James G. Birney called it the "bulwark" of slavery). Non-Garrisonians also had visions of a future America morally transformed and they endorsed causes in addition to antislavery, although usually in more temperate fashion than did the Boston editor. All factions recognized that the basic principles of abolitionism—control of oneself and one's labor, personal moral responsibility, human brotherhood, and so on—applied to a great many situations beyond the institution of slavery. Still, whatever underlying agreement there was among abolitionists, personality conflicts and disagreements over tactics made a parting of the ways difficult to prevent by 1840.

Garrison blamed the schism on "traitors" and insisted that it was a blow to antislavery. The results were less dramatic. Neither the American Anti-Slavery Society nor the American and Foreign Anti-Slavery Society was especially effective in coordinating abolitionist efforts after 1840; yet the movement may have no longer needed firm central direction. The American Anti-Slavery Society seems to have been past its prime before the division occurred. The Panic of 1837 dried up funds for major undertakings of the sort it mounted earlier. More important, the functions of the national society were already passing down to the auxiliaries—probably a healthy thing, since local control permitted maximum participation in decision-making and allowed abolitionists to modify tactics to suit circumstances in their areas.

For better or worse, the fate of the American Anti-Slavery Society paralleled that of other religious and reform organizations in the antebellum decades. National voluntary societies were a new development, a product of early-nineteenth-century improvements in communication and transportation. Virtually every antebellum movement generated its own central organization, although some, such as phrenology, did so belatedly. Virtually every such organization fell apart within a short span of years. Central reform institutions—national institutions of any sort—were hard to maintain in a diverse country with a tradition of localism. Indeed, much the same thing was happening outside the realm of antebellum reform. A schism occurred between Presbyterians in 1837, marking what one historian characterized as "the first major North–South cleavage in American institutions . . ." Methodists and Baptists likewise divided in the mid-1840s. A reform issue—slavery—was central to these schisms, but if the major denominations could not sustain central organizations, other groups were even less likely to do so. More remarkable than the failure of organizations like the American Anti-Slavery Society is the fact that antebellum Americans built them in the first place.

After 1840 Garrisonians continued to rely on "moral suasion," believing that slavery would end when Americans were convinced of its sinfulness. But they shifted tactics, most notably when they endorsed "disunionism," the idea that the free states ought to secede from the Southern ones. First promoted by Garrison in 1842 and officially proclaimed by the American Anti-Slavery Society in 1844, disunionism shocked public opinion, garnered publicity, and provoked defenders of slavery into behaving foolishly. It also fit well with the "ultraist" desire, prevalent among antebellum reformers, to separate from anything impure.

Disunionism, finally, expressed a principle abolitionists had long held: that slavery was the responsibility of all Americans, not just Southerners. To a degree, abolitionists had to make that argument or find some other line of work, since they had no audience among whites in the South. But they sincerely believed that slavery depended upon Northern military might, available to put down slave insurrections, and upon Northern economic assistance. Remove these, Garrisonians argued, and the institution must fall. In its own fashion, disunionism was both a politically sophisticated tactic and an affirmation of American nationhood—a curious thing coming from the branch of abolitionism that seemed most nonpolitical and most sectional. The irony was that the South, not the North, made disunionism a reality in 1860, and in the name of preserving slavery.

After 1840 non-Garrisonians worked to free slaves in their own fashion, with little sympathy for disunionism. Lewis Tappan corresponded with foreign abolitionists, financed propaganda, and mounted religious and legal campaigns to help blacks. Liberty men continued electioneering, with minimal success, until 1848, when political antislavery was drastically redirected.

Even earlier, there were stresses and strains apparent within the Liberty Party. The lines of conflict crisscrossed in complicated ways and, as usual, personality differences played a part. Some members were dissatisfied with Birney, the presidential candidate in 1840 and 1844. He spent much of his first campaign in London and cast aspersions upon the morality of the electorate, neither of which did much to stir enthusiasm among voters. Matters of more substance also divided Liberty men. There were debates over whether to stay with the one issue of slavery or to add others in an effort to apply abolitionist ideals to all social problems and thus to become a party with a broad platform. There was disagreement over the constitutionality of slavery and over Congress's power to touch the institution. Some wanted to keep to the purest possible antislavery position and others were willing to make concessions in order to attract moderate, even racist, voters.

Quarrels continued among abolitionists into the 1850s, but by the late 1840s events upset the calculations of Liberty men and Garrisonians alike. At first the trouble had to do with Texas. In the 1830s American settlers there declared independence from Mexico, sparking controversy over whether their Texas republic ought to join the Union. To bring it into the United States meant adding slave-state representation in Congress and shifting the delicate balance there. Not to bring in Texas implied a censure of slavery and denied political and economic advantages to the South. Texas eventually became a state in 1845, through a devious procedure that reinforced abolitionist suspicions that Southerners controlled the federal government. The worst was yet to come. Shortly after annexation of Texas, the United States and Mexico went to war over a disputed boundary. The United States won. The total amount of real estate acquired from Mexico (counting Texas) came to more than a million square miles, including what is now the state of California.

The war disturbed many white Northerners who cared nothing for black people and who were not especially hostile to the South. So long as slavery stayed where it was, they could tolerate it and comfort themselves by believing it would die a natural death. They were not prepared to see it expand and they were uneasy about the acquisition of fresh soil for the South's "peculiar institution." In 1846 David Wilmot, a Pennsylvania congressman, spoke for them. A piece of legislation he sponsored—the Wilmot Proviso—demanded prohibition of slavery in territories taken from Mexico as a result of the war. The upshot was sharp sectional conflict in Congress, where the South defeated the Proviso in the Senate, and the emergence of a new force in American politics. In 1848 an odd coalition—disaffected Democrats, Liberty men, and a few stray politicians looking for a home—formed the Free-Soil Party. Its candidate was ex-President Martin Van Buren, once obnoxious to abolitionists. Its platform advocated the non-extension of slavery, the position of the Wilmot Proviso.

The Free-Soil Party posed an intellectual problem for all abolitionists and a tactical one for Liberty men. It was not truly antislavery: it did not demand immediate emancipation, nor did it propose to touch slavery where the institution already existed. It depended, as the Colonization Society did, on an alliance of ardent racists and genuine racial egalitarians. To the former, it promised that Northern whites could preserve western land for themselves and keep out blacks. To the latter, it offered the possibility of a broadly based coalition to check the power of slaveholders. Perhaps because of its ideological adaptability, the Free-Soil Party met with far greater success than did the Liberty Party. It drew 10 percent of the presidential vote in 1848, a respectable showing for a hastily assembled organization, and it elected candidates to state and national offices.

Quick to point out the party's moral lapses and personally unable to endorse it, Garrisonians cheered nonetheless. They interpreted Free-Soil gains as signs that the Northern public was moving toward abolitionism and that the South would soon be at bay. Many Liberty men agreed, and a few prominent ones such as Salmon P. Chase of Ohio were among the Free-Soil Party's founders. James G. Birney and other key Liberty men, however, saw the party as a betrayal and had nothing to do with it. They persisted in waging hopeless, but morally pure, campaigns of their own in the 1850s, running as self-styled "radical political abolitionists." Free-Soil further fragmented the abolitionists at the very time public controversy over slavery was intensifying.

The question of the territories remained unresolved throughout 1849, only to be "settled" in the Compromise of 1850, which created new tensions while trying to soothe old ones. The terms of the Compromise cost the South political leverage. Until then the number of states—hence the number of U.S. senators—had been evenly balanced between slave and free. Admission of California in 1850 as a free state changed that. In return for accepting minority status in the Senate, the South received concessions. The most significant was a Fugitive Slave Act to assist masters in retrieving their runaway human "property," some of whom provided Northern audiences with scathing eyewitness testimony about the South. The Act was not the first of its kind, but it was offensive because, contrary to the principles of Anglo-American justice, it stacked the deck against escaped slaves and because it gave Northerners direct responsibility for helping to retake them. As almost no other piece of legislation could have done, the Act gave credence to the abolitionist argument that slavery rested on disrespect for civil liberties and that it could not survive without the support of Northerners, now called upon to do the slaveholder's dirty work.

The Act created hardships in Northern black communities—thousands fled to Canada to avoid being taken into slavery—and increased the despair that African American abolitionists had begun to express in the 1840s of ever receiving justice within the United States by peaceful means. It also led to well-reported episodes of civil disobedience in which blacks and whites fought slave catchers, shielded fugitives, and attempted to rescue them from courts and jails. In one such episode, a party led by a Maryland slaveholder, Edward Gorsuch, entered Pennsylvania to recapture runaways. At Christiana his group ran into determined resistance from a group led by a free black man, William Parker, long involved in helping African Americans escape slavery, by violent means if necessary. At the end of the fray, Gorsuch lay dead and his son wounded, some of the principals took flight, and various trials, including ones for treason, dragged the affair out long after the confrontation itself.

Abolitionists made the most of such incidents and wrote movingly of runaways and their quest for freedom. Antislavery politicians added their voices to the chorus. Ohio congressman Joshua R. Giddings declared that Parker and the fugitives "stood up manfully in defense of their God-given rights . . ." The Fugitive Slave Act also inspired the single most effective piece of antislavery propaganda, *Uncle Tom's Cabin*, published in 1852 by Harriet Beecher Stowe. With a vivid cast of characters, the novel was wildly popular in the North and was quickly transformed into countless stage productions, leading one abolitionist to note wryly that the theater became antislavery before many churches did.

It is in the nature of compromise to outrage people at the extremes, to please no one fully, and yet to work, at least for a while. Despite the furor over the Fugitive Slave Act, the Compromise of 1850 undercut abolitionism by settling the fate of slavery in the territories, seemingly in favor of freedom. The Free-Soil Party did poorly in the election of 1852.

The relative calm was easily shattered. In 1854 a Democratic senator from Illinois, Stephen A. Douglas, introduced legislation to organize territory west of Iowa and Missouri. In order to secure Southern support for the Kansas-Nebraska Act (as it was known), he wrote in the principle that settlers ought to be able to decide for themselves whether the newly formed territories would be slave or free. He graced this notion with a glittering phrase, "popular sovereignty." The problem, so far as Northerners were concerned, was that this changed the rules of the game. According to the Missouri Compromise of 1819–20, slavery had been prohibited from much of the area. Now, with passage of the Act, slavery might retain a foothold there.

Dismay over this brought together ex-Free-Soilers, a few old Liberty men, a smattering of disaffected Democrats, and many onetime antislavery Whigs, who created the Republican Party. Like its predecessor, the Free-Soil Party, it stood against the extension of slavery while professing not to want to harm the institution in the Southern states. Even so, the party's rhetoric made white Southerners edgy. In addition to criticizing slavery, Republicans (again like Free-Soilers) envisioned a nation consisting of independent, prosperous white property-holders. That image implied a criticism of the Southern way of life and was powerfully appealing to Northern voters. In a short time the Republicans made remarkable gains and threatened to win the Presidency and control Congress without any support in the South.

These events of the mid- and late-1850s partially vindicated abolitionists, and then passed by them. As Garrison and others predicted, the major parties could not ignore slavery: it broke up the Whigs, divided the Democrats, and produced the Republicans. Southern aggressiveness and political maneuvering also made it appear that abolitionists had been right in their charge that there was a sinister conspiracy in the government hell-bent on promoting the interests of slavery. The actions of Southerners and their Northern supporters, furthermore, lent weight to the abolitionist argument that the institution was a national evil. The Fugitive Slave Act, of course, did that, as did an 1857 Supreme Court decision in the important case of Dred Scott, a slave suing for his freedom, which appeared to write slavery and racial discrimination into the Constitution. Yet while Northerners edged closer to abolitionist views, older members of the antislavery vanguard had little to do with guiding public affairs. Initiative and leadership came from such people as Charles Sumner and Henry Wilson (senators from Massachusetts) and Salmon P. Chase. Many of these men were ex-Whigs, some former Free-Soilers; all were antislavery politicians and Republican stalwarts. Few came out of the original abolitionist organizations.

That was not especially disturbing to the older abolitionists. Most had always assumed that their greatest effect would come from persuading others. Many, including Garrison, were pleasantly surprised to find a politician as righteous as Sumner winning office and they had cordial feelings for such leaders, while remaining critical of their public stands and suspicious of their involvement in partisan activities. For abolitionists, the unsettling thing about Republican victories was their partial nature. Northern voters were indeed beginning to elect moderate abolitionists. They were also beginning to see slavery as a threat to the Republic and to the civil liberties of whites. They were not, however, convinced of the sinfulness of slavery, ready to demand its immediate extinction, and prepared to accept black people as fellow citizens. Clearly, there was a great deal left to do before the abolitionist message reached the white public in its entirety.

Yet the time for propaganda seemed to be passing and violence, not moral susasion, was the order of the day by the late 1850s. For some black abolitionists, that day had dawned much earlier. At an 1843 National Negro Convention in Buffalo, New York, Henry Highland Garnet exhorted slaves: "Brethren, arise, arise! Strike for your lives and liberties." "Let your motto be resistance! Resistance! RESISTANCE!" he declared. Frederick Douglass, then still an ally of Garrison, used his influence to help narrowly defeat endorsement of Garnet's position. By 1849 Douglass, although clearly ambivalent about the issue, said he would welcome news of a slave insurrection "spreading death and destruction" in the South. In 1857 he defended a slave's right to revolt, characterizing it as a "duty" under "favourable circumstances." By then he was warily involved in the scheming of a strange, charismatic old white man, John Brown.

Although the Fugitive Slave Act began the slide toward advocacy —or at least acceptance—of violence for some abolitionists, events in the middle years of the 1850s accelerated it. Vicious guerrilla warfare raged in Kansas between free- and slave-state settlers, each exercising "popular sovereignty" with firearms rather than honest ballots. Violence even invaded the chambers of the United States Senate. A speech made by Sumner in 1856 maligned slavery, administration policy toward Kansas, and a fellow senator from South Carolina. The senator's kinsman Preston Brooks (himself a representative from South Carolina) approached Sumner, then seated at his desk, and beat him savagely with a cane, presumably vindicating the honor of Brooks's relative and his region. Feelings about slavery were running so high that each man became a hero. In the North, Sumner was a martyr to Southern brutality; Brooks, whose cane broke over Sumner's skull, received replacements from Southern well-wishers.

The bloodiest and most ominous episode of the late 1850s was the work of John Brown, a veteran of antislavery battles in Kansas. In October 1859 he and a small band of both black and white followers attacked the federal arsenal at Harpers Ferry, Virginia. Most were killed or captured. Brown survived, to be tried and executed soon after. In the minds of white Southerners the raid raised the nightmarish prospect of future slave revolts, as David Walker had thirty years

earlier. This time Northerners, abolitionists among them, had a harder
time dealing with Brown's actions. Insurrection was abhorrent to them,
yet the old man had taken up weapons to strike down evil—a noble
gesture, many thought. A failure in most things in his life, Brown
helped his reputation in the North by dying well: he accepted his fate
with eloquence and dignity. He was an avenging angel, at peace with
God. Even pacifists like Garrison and the Transcendentalist Henry
David Thoreau stood in awe.

From the beginning abolitionists advocated peaceful means to end
slavery; but they also predicted it would die violently if emancipation
did not come quickly. Kansas, the beating of Sumner, and Brown's
raid justified their darkest fears. Some wondered, in the bleak days of
the 1850s, whether America's sins might not have to be washed away
in blood.

They were. On December 20, 1860, South Carolina responded to
the election of Abraham Lincoln, the Republican Presidential candidate, by declaring that the Union between it and the other states was
"dissolved." Four months later the Civil War began. As usual, abolitionists divided. Consistent with pacifism and Garrisonian nonresistance, many believed the Southern states should be allowed to secede.
Others endorsed the use of force to prevent them from leaving. Abolitionists were far more agreed upon the moral inadequacy of Lincoln's position that the North was fighting to preserve the Union,
rather than to meddle with Southern institutions. Opposition to the
war, however, faded as the Emancipation Proclamation (to take effect
in 1863) and the course of events made it impossible to deny that the
conflict was over slavery. In 1864 Garrison, for thirty years a non-voter
and a nonresistant, cast a ballot for Lincoln.

The war ended slavery. Many abolitionists, pleased with the North's
victory, were aging and ready for retirement. A weary Garrison published the last issue of *The Liberator* and left the American Anti-Slavery
Society in 1865. The organization continued another five years, until
the Fifteenth Amendment to the Constitution promised to guarantee
civil liberties for blacks. Yet even in 1870 there was much left undone:
racism lived on, although slavery did not.

A few white abolitionists recognized that only the first battle had been won and continued to press for equal justice. They were not, however, prepared to agitate for the freedman with the same passion and thoroughness they brought to the cause of the slave. In common with most antebellum reformers, abolitionists tended to believe that both evil and success were problems of the human spirit, not matters of economics and social structure. With freedom, ex-slaves could fend for themselves. Those who were virtuous would succeed; those who were not would fail. Although some former abolitionists—especially African American ones—recognized the weaknesses in that line of reasoning, it was commonplace, even if it tragically underestimated the economic, psychological, and social damage slavery inflicted on both sections and both races.

It is difficult to gauge precisely the importance of the antislavery crusade. Unlike temperance and school reformers, abolitionists were not directly responsible for any great amount of legislation. Other than some successful local challenges to discriminatory practices, the original band of abolitionists did not wield much influence in government, although such antislavery politicians as Charles Sumner eventually did. Propaganda campaigns, nevertheless, had an effect. Reformers remained unpopular, but voters and leaders came, in time, to accept much of what they had to say. Certainly antislavery images and language passed into common usage and into the rhetoric of elected officials. When that happened, it was because abolitionists phrased things in a manner making sense out of events and speaking to general concerns of the day in words and symbols intelligible and compelling to many Americans. Antislavery talk about a conspiracy of slaveholders, for example, both played to long-standing American fears of arbitrary power and seemed to many Northerners to describe the behavior of slaveholding Southerners. The importance of antislavery (or any antebellum reform) came through a similar ability to help the public perceive situations, or institutions like slavery, in a new, emotionally charged way, often by reworking commonly shared values, beliefs, and language. The pity is that abolitionists could not communicate their entire vision: their higher goals of racial harmony and of a society ruled by God's law remained elusive, even, in many cases, to themselves.

# Women and a
# World without War

Virtually all the major figures in antebellum reform participated in several causes that commonly fell into predictable patterns. Secular communitarians, for instance, often were interested in health, labor, or educational reform; prison reformers tended to be concerned with such related issues as construction of almshouses, insane asylums, and schools. Among abolitionists the secondary reforms frequently had to do with health and morality—temperance and anti-licentiousness campaigns, for example. But the causes most closely linked to antislavery were the woman's rights and peace movements. The connection was not entirely a matter of numbers: probably more abolitionists were active in temperance than in either of the other crusades, both of which were relatively small. The common bonds were a set of assumptions about human beings and human society and the dynamic of an antislavery commitment, which pushed many men and women far beyond where their reform careers had begun.

"The investigation of the rights of the slave," wrote the South Carolina–born abolitionist Angelina Grimké, "has led me to a better understanding of my own." What she had come to realize was that power and domination were sexual as well as racial. In the antebellum period Grimké and thousands of other reformers created the first "feminist" movement in the United States—to use a twentieth-century term to describe what she and her contemporaries saw as a crusade for "woman's rights." In hindsight, their demands for increased educational and economic opportunities, the vote, and legal protection seem a reasonable, modest reaction against discrimination. Only the most hardened latter-day male chauvinist would not accept much of what they sought. Yet the fact that there were legitimate grievances does not entirely explain why protest began in the 1830s and 1840s. Many injustices these reformers attacked were centuries old and had never been met with more than isolated assaults, such as Mary Wollstonecraft's *Vindication of the Rights of Women*, published in England in 1792. The real roots of nineteenth-century feminism lie not simply in inequities between the sexes but also in social and cultural changes and in the consciousness-raising potential of abolitionism.

Divisions of labor along gender lines were not especially invidious so long as every member of the household clearly contributed to the well-being of all, as was the case in a world of family farms, small shops, and cottage industries, where young and old, male and female, each had an important, socially valued role. Economic development after 1800 changed that by widening the range of careers available for men (and closed to women) and by altering the chances for individuals to rise or sink on the social scale. The best of the new opportunities required spending long hours away from the rest of the family. The home increasingly became a female domain, cut off from business and public affairs. Running it might fully occupy a woman's day and require considerable management skills; but if she was middle-class, she no longer worked in ways that society recognized as work. Low-paid servants, schools, and fewer children reduced some traditional duties of homemaking; store-bought bread, clothing, and candles took away others. At the same time, family success required self-restraint. The costs of child-raising and of maintaining a suitable home—itself an emblem of middle-class respectability—favored couples who waited until they could afford marriage and delayed having children. Such calculations show up explicitly in literature advising men and women on marriage and sexuality and implicitly in demography: the birth and fertility rates declined steadily from 1800 through the antebellum period and beyond.

Antebellum images of masculinity and femininity both reflected these social changes and shaped them. According to most writers on the subject of gender, men were naturally strong in body and mind, aggressive, and sexual. Women were innately weak, passive, emotional, religious, and chaste. These were complementary qualities—men supported women; women provided the sensitivity men lacked. Such stereotypes reassured middle-class readers that each gender played its proper role. Woman was too fair a flower to survive in business or politics, where man's cunning and intellect were virtues; in the home she was protected, her goodness blossomed, she refined man's coarseness and shaped future generations.

From a twentieth-century view, those notions bespeak a belief in female inferiority. But that was not how most antebellum commentators presented it. Their respect for emotion and intuition—part of nineteenth-century romanticism—led them to cast these views of women in highly positive terms. Some suggested that feminine traits were morally superior to masculine ones and that women had a great social role to play, despite being excluded from politics and the professions: through their influence over men and children they controlled the destiny of humankind. Although a woman "may never herself step beyond the threshold," a clergyman gushed, "she may yet send forth from her humble dwelling, a power that will be felt round the globe. She may at least save some souls that are dear to her from disgrace and punishment, present some precious jewels to shine brightly in the Saviour's crown."

That sort of rhetoric—called the "cult of domesticity" by twentieth-century scholars—may have described some lives, but it was sheer nonsense for others. To poor women who often worked outside the home it represented, at best, a standard to which they might aspire; at worst, it was a measure of their inferior status. Middle-class women also had problems matching the ideal to their reality, particularly when faced with heavy demands on their time, financial insecurity, or troublesome children. Men, furthermore, often failed to live up to their part of the bargain. They drank, frittered away money, philandered, or generally behaved like scoundrels—with perfect impunity because their wives had neither the legal right nor the economic independence to defend themselves from their protectors.

Some women, however, discovered that common assumptions about them justified public roles, albeit in ways that did not necessarily challenge gender stereotypes or the male monopoly of the political process. If woman's influence was so beneficial, why should it be kept at home? Why not bring feminine virtues to the outside world to counteract masculine vices? Answers to those questions came almost before they could be asked.

Implicitly rejecting the notion that the household was their only sphere of influence, American women from the 1810s onward participated in public life through voluntary associations of their own and by providing organizational and financial support for other, male-dominated ones. These associations took several forms and eventually engaged women, a majority of them married, across a wide spectrum of the middle and upper classes. Some organizations were benevolent in purpose and closely tied to religious denominations; others were nonsectarian and related to larger reform movements such as antislavery or temperance. Before the antebellum period ended, still others focused on the rights of women. These female voluntary associations were most common in the North, in part because women's activism came to be tied to antislavery in the public mind and in part because the South had fewer cities and towns of the sort where such organizations flourished. But, like temperance, women's activism did not stop at the Mason-Dixon line. Petersburg, Virginia, for instance, had a Female Orphan Asylum in 1813, thanks to the bequest of one woman and the actions of others.

By the 1830s American women were involved in a growing number of secular as well as religious and charitable causes: health reform, temperance, antislavery, and campaigns to redeem prostitutes and curb licentiousness. A radical few were interested in communitarian ventures and had started talking about rearranging relations between the sexes. In the late 1820s the daring Scotswoman Frances Wright lec-

tured audiences of men and women—bad enough in itself—on her
heretical ideas about education, religion, economics, and marriage. (So
scandalous was her thought and behavior that "Fanny Wrightism" became a pejorative term, liberally applied to the Grimké sisters, Angelina and Sarah, and later woman's rights advocates.) Most of the first
generation of female reformers, however, posed no direct challenge to
the status quo. If anything, they reinforced feminine stereotypes by
displaying the moral impulses everyone expected of them, by doing
little that was unladylike, and by deferring to masculine leadership,
particularly of the clergy.

Antislavery changed that. At the outset it generated intense hostility, largely because of anxieties about race relations and social stability.
Quite probably the Grimké sisters—in the episode we saw in the previous chapter—would have been treated gently by clergy in 1837 had
they been lecturing to "promiscuous assemblies" on the conversion of
heathen in foreign lands or on a similarly safe subject. Instead, they
were talking about slavery and, to make it worse, about licentiousness
in the South. Consequently, the assault on them was harsh, as it occasionally had been on other antislavery women (literally so in the case
of the Boston Female Anti-Slavery Society, a target of mob violence
in 1835). Resistance forced the Grimkés and their supporters to examine their own beliefs and to confront the social restrictions placed
upon women.

Critics, in fact, provoked the sisters into writing classics of American
feminism. Sarah responded at first with a direct rebuke to her clerical
opponents and then, in 1838, with a less defensive and more sweeping
work, *Letters on the Condition of Women and the Equality of the Sexes*.
Angelina's main contribution came in a series of *Letters to Catharine E.
Beecher*, also published in 1838. The sisters defended woman's "moral
and intellectual capacities" and attacked "subordination to man." In
forceful language, the pamphlets insisted that both sexes had the
"same rights" and "same duties."

This egalitarianism was anathema to conservatives, but it similarly
disturbed people like Catharine Beecher, whose position was more
complex. Herself a pioneer in female education, Beecher—in common

with many feminists—accepted the idea that there were inherent moral differences between the sexes and that woman was the better of the two. Her view, however, was that feminine power should be exercised in the family. (Angelina suggested that "the Presidential chair of the United States" might be a more appropriate aspiration.) The Grimkés likewise assumed that woman's character was different from man's. Yet in the exciting days of the late 1830s each sister grappled with the question of how to believe in difference without also believing in inferiority and superiority. They issued ringing declarations of gender equality and rejections of domesticity.

Abolitionists could have repudiated the Grimkés, and some did; but many joined with assertions of female rights. An influential minority in the antislavery crusade were Quakers (the Grimkés among them), whose religious practices predisposed them to accept women speaking in public. For many, however, the crucial element was a powerful identification between the condition of free white women and the plight of enslaved African Americans. "The comparison between women and the colored race is striking," declared Lydia Maria Child. "Both are characterized by affection more than intellect; both have a strong development of the religious sentiment; both are excessively adhesive in their attachments; both . . . have a tendency to submission; and hence, both have been kept in subjection by physical force, and considered rather in the light of property, than as individuals."

Seldom have so many racial and sexual stereotypes been compressed in so small a space, or used for such a radical purpose. Child's message was not that women belonged in the home and blacks on the plantation, the conclusion of anti-feminists and racists. Instead, she argued that women and blacks (including black men) were morally sensitive, innately good human beings degraded by the authority white males exerted over them. Both were victims of the white man's lust; both lacked economic independence; neither had a role in public affairs. The solution was to end male tyranny and to allow weaker, but morally pure, people to act as responsible citizens. Certainly, abolitionists such as Child accepted notions about gender and race most latter-day Americans found offensive, yet the effect was for middle-class women to be able to see slavery as a metaphor for their own lives. (Whether or not it also led them to misperceive African Americans is another matter.)

Although abolitionists divided in 1840 partly over the "woman question" (both sexes were on both sides), hundreds took the step from antislavery to feminism. The leading lights of the post–Civil War woman's suffrage movement—Elizabeth Cady Stanton, Lucy Stone, and Susan B. Anthony—began their careers in the antebellum period and had abolitionist backgrounds. Early feminist gatherings were comprised of antislavery crusaders, usually Garrisonians and often including such prominent black abolitionists as Frederick Douglass and Sojourner Truth. Even the anti-Garrisonian Liberty Party admitted women to some of its meetings in the West.

It would be 1869 before there was a separate national organization to coordinate feminist activities—at which point there were two of them, thanks to a division in the ranks. As early as 1840, however, there was talk of creating an institutional structure to advance the cause. In that year Elizabeth Cady Stanton was in London with her abolitionist husband, Henry, a delegate to a World's Anti-Slavery Convention. Female representatives from America were excluded after an acrimonious debate. Stanton's indignation at the insult coincided with her discovery of those whom she later called (probably incorrectly) "the first women I had ever met who believed in the equality of the sexes." Among them was an American Quaker and abolitionist, Lucretia Coffin Mott. The two became friends and, according to Stanton, "resolved to hold a convention as soon as we returned home, and form a society to advocate the rights of women."

For eight years nothing came of their idea. Stanton traveled in Europe briefly, then settled in for a period of motherhood and intellectual stimulation in Boston. By 1848 her circumstances changed. The family moved to upstate New York, where life was hard and drab for her. She realized, as she had not before, "the impossibility of woman's best development" under the usual order of things. A visit with Mott, then passing through the area, led to a call in a local paper for a meeting at Seneca Falls on July 19 and 20. That left five days to prepare for the first woman's rights convention.

Working in haste, Stanton, Mott, and three friends presented the antebellum feminist case effectively and comprehensively. For the opening, they wrote a Declaration of Sentiments modeled upon the Declaration of Independence. It began with the premise that "all men and women are created equal" and substituted "man" for King George III as the tyrant. This was clever and revealing in its appeal to the natural-rights rhetoric of the American Revolution. Religious language, prominent in most antebellum crusades and very much a part of the lives of the women who gathered at Seneca Falls, was problematic in justifying gender equality. Male clergy responded with biblical quotations, especially Paul's calls for female subordination. Avoiding that, Stanton and Mott submitted "to a candid world" a bill of indictment against male domination, just as their forebears had done against the British seventy-two years earlier. The chief points and suggested remedies would be repeated for decades.

Stanton and her collaborators accused man of endeavoring, "in every way that he could, to destroy her [woman's] confidence in her own powers, to lessen her self-respect, and to make her willing to lead a dependent and abject life." They specifically objected to the lack of educational and professional opportunities for women, as well as to laws depriving wives of control over property and awarding custody of children to fathers in divorce. The convention considered eleven resolutions asserting gender equality, advocating a single moral standard for males and females, and urging woman to "move in the enlarged sphere which her great Creator has assigned her." They did not mean the home. In the final hours, Lucretia Mott offered an additional resolution calling for "the overthrow of the monopoly of the pulpit, and for the securing to woman of an equal participation with men in the various trades, professions, and commerce." The most controversial proposal approved at Seneca Falls—and the only one not to pass unanimously—was Stanton's. It insisted that women fight to gain "their sacred right to the elective franchise."

The vote may have been too much to ask for in 1848, but within three years a Massachusetts feminist convention labeled it "the cornerstone of this enterprise," as it would continue to be from the Civil War until woman suffrage became a reality in 1920. Emphasis on the franchise posed a problem for the Garrisonian abolitionists in the woman's rights movement, many of whom did not believe anyone should vote. Even they, nonetheless, could uphold the proposition that the chance to do so should not be confined to one gender. Rightly or wrongly, feminists became convinced as early as the 1850s that obtaining the ballot was the crucial objective and that, once achieved, it would permit women to protect their own interests. In the minds of some critics, the quest for the vote stressed a limited goal, and one not especially relevant to the lives of poor and minority women, at the expense of agitating against basic social and economic injustices. However that may be, the campaign for women's suffrage was not the sum total of women's activism after 1848, but it gave force and coherence to the crusade for gender equality.

Seneca Falls inspired the formation of local woman's rights groups, and numerous other meetings followed. Among the more noteworthy were two in 1850: a gathering at Salem, Ohio, unique for prohibiting men from speaking or voting, and the first "national" convention, held at Worcester, Massachusetts, under Garrisonian auspices. Such events kept the movement alive in the 1850s, as did feminist publications (including journals like the *Una*, run by Paulina Wright Davis in Rhode Island in the mid-1850s). Yet woman's rights remained closely tied to antislavery and were often promoted by abolitionist lecturers and newspapers.

The union between antislavery and woman's rights had both negative and positive effects. On the debit side, it closed Southern ears to feminism (anything connected to antislavery was suspect), and it continued to complicate matters after the Civil War. The Fourteenth and Fifteenth Amendments (1868, 1870) were particularly divisive. These granted voting rights to African Americans, something abolitionist women could not oppose, but the Fourteenth used the word "male" in defining suffrage and citizenship. The net effect of the two amendments was to make it unconstitutional to ban men from voting, but not to ban women. Thereafter, to secure the franchise for all American women would require following one of two difficult courses, either another constitutional amendment or positive action by every state.

For many abolitionists the painful choice was between supporting one important goal at the cost of making another harder to achieve. The result was a deep rift in the woman's movement in the late 1860s, as some leaders backed the amendments and others did not. The old bond between abolitionism and woman's rights, nonetheless, had been valuable. It provided feminism with articulate supporters and with an established forum in such antislavery journals as *The Liberator*. Most important, it gave both crusades the kind of emotional power that comes only when personal grievances resonate with a larger social situation.

Antebellum feminism, however, was not just an adjunct to abolitionism. Like their antislavery sisters—although more slowly and more cautiously—women in most crusades grew in perception of their own grievances as they helped others and battled predominately male sins. Female reformers of all sorts often began by staying within the bounds society and culture set for them, only to challenge or subvert these restrictions as time went on. From being meek, discreet, and deferential, they reached the point by the end of the antebellum period where they took charge of their own organizations, lectured to mixed audiences just as Frances Wright and the Grimkés had done, waged political campaigns, and left their domestic "sphere" in favor of public life. By the end of the century, women's activism expanded further to include a wide range of causes, crusades, and professional organizations in such fields as social work and nursing. What women found in reform throughout the nineteenth century was one of the small number of careers open to them. Although it frequently played to, rather than challenged, conventional ideas of femininity, it gave ever-expanding opportunities for talented women.

It would, moreover, be a mistake to imagine that the only activity of significance for antebellum women came from reformers in the conventional sense of the term. Margaret Fuller, a Transcendentalist whose commitment was more to art than to social causes, produced an influential feminist statement, *Woman in the Nineteenth Century*, published in 1845. For that matter, there were many middle-class nonfeminists doing things of long-range significance for women. Catharine Beecher and other female educators, for instance, had little sympathy for woman's rights, yet they founded antebellum schools that gave girls confidence in their mental abilities and presented them with intellectual skills that were difficult to confine to the home. In still other fields changes were taking place more or less independently of feminist pressure. Legislation increasing the property rights of wives owed something to female lobbying, but it had been proposed, before the Seneca Falls convention, by male lawmakers concerned about daughters' inheritances. (Elizabeth Cady Stanton listed public discussions of these bills as an "immediate cause" of female awareness of political inequality.) Contraception—aimed at reducing the burdens of childbearing—was practiced by people whose motives were not especially ideological. Some woman's rights advocates, for that matter, opposed it as an encouragement to male lust: their preferred form of birth control was abstinence.

While these developments were taking place primarily among the middle classes, working women, largely ignored by feminists or regarded as objects of charity, made demands of their own and conducted their lives in ways that often bore little resemblance to the "cult of domesticity." As early as 1824 female factory hands participated in a strike in Rhode Island. Larger protests came in Lowell, Massachusetts. The town itself was a marvel of the American Industrial Revolution. It had not existed in 1820; by 1840 it had thirty-two mills and a labor force of eight thousand, the great majority of it female. These were mostly women in their twenties, native-born farm girls, away from family life for a few years of hard work and marginal economic independence before marriage. In 1834 they struck to block a cut in wages. They struck again in 1836. To justify this unfeminine conduct the mill women, like woman's rights advocates, drew upon a language of natural rights and republican rhetoric similar to the one we will hear their male counterparts using in Chapter 8. Calling themselves "daughters of freemen," they declared their resistance to the factory owners to be in the "spirit of our Patriotic Ancestors, who preferred privation to bondage." They lost both times.

Failure in 1834 and 1836 did not stop collective action at Lowell or elsewhere. There were more strikes and organization-building among New England women operatives. In 1833, for example, wage cuts in shoe factories prompted formation of a "Female Society of Lynn and Vicinity for the protection and promotion of Female Industry." It called a meeting for December 30, 1833, held at a Friends' Meeting-house because of the Quaker tradition of women speaking in public. (This was four years before the controversy over the Grimkés' lectures.) The gathering drew approximately a thousand women, who, like their male artisan colleagues, believed that their labor created their employers' wealth, that they were not fairly compensated, and that low wages jeopardized the republic by threatening their independence and respectability. Mingling radicalism and the rhetoric of domesticity, they declared: "Equal rights should be extended to all—to the weaker sex as well as the stronger." Such moments were not unique in the antebellum period and we will meet similar-sounding male artisan radicalism in Chapter 8, but working women's and artisans' radicalism generally lay beyond the pale of the woman's rights movement, although sharing some of its language and goals.

In the 1840s important, if short-lived, Female Labor Reform Associations appeared, the result, in good measure, of the organizing skill of Sarah Bagley, a former factory hand at Lowell. These groups channeled most energy away from strikes and into petition campaigns, often in cooperation with men and designed to bring about the ten-hour workday. To some extent, such activities were peculiar to New England, where industrialization and feminine self-confidence were most advanced, and they were related to a general labor reform movement. Yet the efforts of mill operatives marked a growing assertiveness among women who were neither part of the "cult of domesticity" nor within the mainstream of antebellum reform.

Quite obviously, developments affecting women were so diverse that no antebellum organization could have comprehended or guided them all. It is no wonder that woman's rights had the least developed institutional structure of the important pre–Civil War crusades—by 1860 it was still more a movement in potential than in form. Yet there was a good, if limited, beginning. In books, pamphlets, and resolutions at Seneca Falls and elsewhere, feminists had begun to define problems and to articulate widely held grievances. They were clear and to the point in advocating such things as educational and economic opportunities, political power, legal protection, control over childbearing and intercourse, and greater autonomy. Moreover, by trying to change the world, middle-class reformers (like their poorer cousins at Lowell, Lynn, and elsewhere) were demanding a place in it for women, edging themselves and men away from the idea that feminine influence should hold sway only in the home.

Although critical of man's behavior, woman's rights activists were not arguing for a female universe. They wanted a society in which each gender had both independence and interdependence. Supposedly male and female characteristics—intellect and emotion, ambition and sympathy, and aggression and passivity—would balance each other harmoniously. Thus, feminists simultaneously accepted many of the stereotypes of the "cult of domesticity" and fashioned them into an image of human unity transcending gender, just as abolitionists and pacifists hoped to transcend race and national boundaries.

One of the most beloved antebellum paintings commemorates William Penn's eighteenth-century treaty with the Indians. It illustrates its theme of peace by showing animals, both gentle and savage, coexisting harmoniously with small children in the American wilderness. The artist, Edward Hicks, did approximately a hundred variations on this theme, entitled *The Peaceable Kingdom*. As an image of America, it is deeply moving, the more so for being out of touch with reality. Hicks turned out *Peaceable Kingdoms* in the 1830s, a period of mob violence and of extreme cruelty to Indians. He continued through the late 1840s, during the war with Mexico. The strength in Hicks's art was the ideal behind it. His sect, the Quakers, had been pacifistic since its seventeenth-century beginnings. In the eighteenth century non-Quakers, touched by religion or Enlightenment humanitarianism, also repudiated war as inconsistent with Christianity or reason, or both. This view was so widely shared that a major figure of the Revolutionary era even suggested that the new nation ought to have a Peace Office to counterbalance, and eventually replace, its military departments.

The suggestion was ignored and the peace movement in America did not begin until a generation later, in 1815. That year, not coincidentally, marked the end of the War of 1812, an ignominious conflict staunchly opposed in New England. It had done a great deal to make pacifism attractive. Well before then, however, war had been a burden on the mind of a devout New York Presbyterian layman, David Low Dodge. A well-to-do merchant, Dodge first committed his ideas to print in 1808, marshaling biblical quotations to demonstrate the evils of violence. In 1815 he published a penetrating essay, *War Inconsistent with the Religion of Jesus Christ*, and helped found the nonsectarian New York Peace Society, the first of its kind in the world. Almost simultaneously, Noah Worcester, a Unitarian minister and a veteran of the Revolutionary army, was preaching on peace (as were many New England clergy) and offering to the public his *Solemn Review of the Custom of War* (1814). On December 28, 1815, he and several friends created the Massachusetts Peace Society.

At the outset there were disagreements. Dodge rejected all violent means and declared governments to be under "Satan's dominion" for using them (he came close to the nonresistant position that William Lloyd Garrison adopted two decades later). Recognizing that Dodge's ideas were too elevated to suit the majority of pacifists, the New York Peace Society restricted leadership to people who shared his beliefs, but opened membership to those who considered force permissible under some circumstances. The latter held what Dodge called "lax doctrines"—the sort preached by the Massachusetts Peace Society.

Its leader, Noah Worcester, believed pacifism would gain followers gradually, and he was willing to take half measures in order to encourage its growth. He did not insist upon Dodge's absolutist proposition that war was inherently evil, nor did he demand that everyone follow the Quakers and refuse military service, although he admired those who did. For him, armed conflict between nations was the primary evil, to be eliminated through arbitration and reason. In private,

Worcester may have been more radical, but his public expressions of moderation and his "expediency" annoyed Dodge. The two men— and all antebellum pacifists—used a variety of arguments to show that war was un-Christian, contrary to republican principles, and economically wasteful. Beyond that, serious disputes brewed over tactics, the moral duty of individuals, whether or not defensive wars were justifiable, and how far to go in doing away with coercion in society, including use of police powers and capital punishment.

By the early 1820s there were more than a dozen local peace societies. Concentrated in the Northeast, they attracted respectable men —politicians, merchants, judges, professors, and preachers. The greatest support came from Presbyterians, Congregationalists, and Unitarians (the denominations most committed to reform), with surprisingly little participation by Quakers. These early organizations quickly established close contact with their overseas counterparts—a London Peace Society began in 1815, independently of the American pacifists, who were organized the same year. All antebellum reformers had international contacts, but such contacts were especially highly developed among pacifists.

For the first decade the American side lacked dynamic leadership. Worcester and Dodge, both capable men, made their major contributions through publications. Neither was able to fashion a unified movement. That was the task of William Ladd, a prosperous Maine farmer and former sea captain. Already middle-aged when he became a pacifist in the early 1820s, Ladd dedicated the remainder of his life to the cause. Not particularly theoretical, he nonetheless wrote perhaps the most significant pamphlet of the antebellum peace movement, his *Essay on a Congress of Nations* (1840). As the title indicates, Ladd suggested formation of world organizations to resolve conflicts through moral means, very much like a plan that emerged sixty years later from the Hague Conference of 1899.

Ladd's significance in the 1820s, however, came from his ability to bind peace groups together. His energy, persistence, and personality prepared the way for creation of a national organization in 1828, the American Peace Society. It was tiny—about three hundred members at the start—and never expanded much beyond New England; but it was useful in coordinating pacifist activities and it provided a' pulpit for Ladd, who was its secretary and the editor of its journal, the *Harbinger of Peace*.

Privately, Ladd grew closer to Dodge's absolute pacifism as time went on, yet he resembled Noah Worcester in his conciliatory public posture. In the *Harbinger of Peace* he remained neutral on the controversial question of whether defensive wars might be justified, and his platform was so broad that the American Peace Society had military men on its rolls. Ladd's tolerant policy worked for nearly a decade. Under his direction, the number of peace societies increased to around fifty and notable converts joined the fold; one of them, Thomas Grimké, a distinguished South Carolina lawyer, was the brother of Angelina and Sarah.

For all his good humor and hard work, Ladd could not smooth over conflicts between pacifists. In 1838 the American Peace Society split, just as the American Anti-Slavery Society would two years later (with some of the same people involved). The problems in both instances were sociological, temperamental, and intellectual. As the peace movement grew, it attracted middle-class reformers who were less distinguished and more impassioned than the founders of the New York and Massachusetts Peace Societies. Such people were impatient with moderation and unequivocally against whatever evil they were fighting, whether it was slavery, ill health, sexuality, ignorance, alcohol, or war. Some held to an extreme variety of pacifism—nonresistance, or Christian anarchism—and in their eyes Dodge had not gone far enough in opposing force. Their ranks included the abolitionists William Lloyd Garrison and Henry C. Wright, who argued the position vigorously and, in the case of the latter, promoted its growth within the APS in 1836 while serving as field secretary. Like the woman's rights movement, the antislavery cause led men and women to explore the outer edges of their own reform principles.

At its most elementary, nonresistance rested on a syllogism: force is sinful; governments use force; therefore, governments are sinful. However straightforward the reasoning might seem, critics were appalled.

Humankind, they insisted, would always do evil deeds and thus need laws, courts, police, prisons, and other restraints. In responding, non-resistants argued that governments, by relying on coercion to achieve their goals, set the lowest possible moral standard and gave legitimacy to force as a means of settling disputes. Nonresistants believed the best defense was no defense and the most orderly society one in which there was no effort to compel people to be orderly. That logic was yet another reflection of evangelical Protestant millennialism and perfectionism. Nonresistants literally believed that men and women could cease sinning and become sanctified while on earth. When they did, the Kingdom of God would supplant present-day political institutions. Rather than encouraging chaos, as critics charged them with doing, nonresistants had as their goal the ultimate in harmonious social relationships: all human beings knit together in love and sympathy, behaving decently because the most exacting law of all—God's—lived in their hearts.

Millennialism, perfectionism, and yearning for the Kingdom of God were not the exclusive beliefs of nonresistants. Such ideas ran throughout antebellum reform, and older pacifists like Dodge had preached doctrines similar to Garrison's since 1815. These religiously inspired beliefs, moreover, combined with political values derived from republicanism and individualism, notably the old American fear of power, especially of its corrupting influences, and the Jeffersonian bias against strong political authority. What made younger nonresistants like Garrison seem so radical in the 1830s was not their hostility to the state but their strident tone and extreme position. Dodge himself had refused to vote or hold office, but he believed some government to be necessary. The nonresistants were more consistent: they totally rejected human governments.

In practice, things were not so clear-cut. There were obligations to the state even the most dedicated anarchist could not avoid. (Ideology has never been an adequate excuse for not paying taxes.) Nonresistant doctrine, moreover, meant different things to different people. For some, including Garrison, it was as much a metaphor as a program. The nonresistant Kingdom of God served as an ideal against which to measure the imperfections of the status quo; it was a model of what the world should be and a counterimage of what it actually was. It was also an effective way of focusing attention on a wide range of coercive relationships in American society, including those between men and women and between master and slave. Others regarded Christian anarchism literally as a plan of action. Their beliefs impelled them to separate from morally corrupt and coercive things such as religious denominations, society as a whole, and marriage. In many of these instances, nonresistance was virtually indistinguishable from "come-outerism," or withdrawal from supposedly impure churches (an impulse not confined to anarchists in the antebellum period); but it also inspired more thoroughgoing responses, such as the construction of utopian communities based on pacifist principles—Adin Ballou's Hopedale being the most conventional and successful.

Wherever it may have taken individuals, Christian anarchism led the peace movement into a schism. After months of criticizing the American Peace Society for accepting men who were not complete pacifists, Garrison and his followers called a convention in Boston in September 1838. Ladd and other moderates from the national organization were present, although many quickly fled, realizing they were a minority and dismayed at the participation of women in the gathering (yet another bit of Garrisonian unorthodoxy). Ladd—much respected by Garrison—stayed, but his influence was negligible. Nonresistants were in charge and they soon adopted a Declaration of Sentiments, largely written by Garrison. Those who accepted it pledged themselves to deny the validity of social distinctions based on race, nationality, or gender. They refused allegiance to human governments and recognized Jesus as "our only ruler and lawgiver." They were against any kind of violence or retaliation, whether it took the form of war, self-defense, or prisons. To promote their views, they created the New England Non-Resistance Society. Believers in human unity and individual autonomy, they divided the peace movement and created yet another organization, albeit an anarchist one.

For several years after the schism all branches of the peace movement, in common with other antebellum crusades, suffered the financial effects of the Panic of 1837. In the 1840s, however, there was a strong upsurge of pacifist sentiment brought about by the annexation of Texas and the subsequent war with Mexico. The bullying behavior of the United States, as well as the complex issues involved, suddenly made peace respectable. Pacifists of all sorts mobilized to stir public outrage and, without success, to prevent armed conflict.

Rather than present a united front, peace advocates quarreled once more. The center of controversy this time was the Reverend George C. Beckwith, successor to Ladd (who died in 1841) as secretary of the American Peace Society. Beckwith opposed international wars but believed the society should not oppose other kinds of conflict. He and his followers wished to dilute a controversial article in the organization's constitution, which condemned all wars as un-Christian. Although he controlled the society, his machinations alienated the large number of absolute pacifists. At first they tried to displace him. When they failed, they seceded in 1847. There were then three major groups of peace advocates, not counting religious sects like the Quakers: Beckwith's faction of the American Peace Society, which believed some kinds of conflicts might be moral; the Garrisonians of the New England Non-Resistance Society; and, somewhere in between, people who wished to do away with war but who granted governments the right to use force, including capital punishment, to maintain internal order.

If the last group had a leader, it was Elihu Burritt, the heart and soul of American pacifism from the mid-1840s until his death in 1879. While in England in 1846 Burritt founded the League of Universal Brotherhood, which soon absorbed the energies of many who abandoned the American Peace Society over Beckwith's policies. By 1850 more than fifty thousand people in Britain and America signed its pledge not to participate in anything related to war. Throughout the 1840s and 1850s Burritt also engineered propaganda campaigns and mass meetings to ease international tensions. In addition, he traveled ceaselessly and put together societies to accomplish various goals, ranging from aiding immigrants to codifying international law. All those things he did in the United States and in Europe, in more or less equal measure.

Burritt was as impressive as his accomplishments. His nickname—

the "Learned Blacksmith"—marked him as the exotic he was. Except for people prominent in working people's organizations, he was, among leading reformers, almost alone in having been an artisan. Most of the others came from the middle classes. Burritt's erudition, the second remarkable thing about him, was largely self-acquired and principally represented an interest in languages (he knew several dozen). In common with many pacifists, he believed that improved transportation and communication among the world's peoples fostered human unity. His linguistic studies and travels were a personal witness to that faith, as was his crusade to have the transatlantic postal rate dropped from twenty-five cents to a penny.

Burritt's internationalism and his background as a workingman gave a different flavor to his propaganda. He recited the familiar litany about the un-Christian nature of man-killing and about the economic destructiveness of international conflicts. But, more than his peers, he spoke of the burden that war laid upon the laboring classes. Perhaps because of that, his League of Universal Brotherhood drew support from poorer folk than those usually reached by other pacifist organizations. By 1850 Burritt was urging workingmen to take collective action for peace and in 1867 he wished for the day when they "will form one vast Trades Union, and make a universal and simultaneous strike against the whole war system."

The rhetoric was radical, and Burritt had the firsthand knowledge of European socialist thinkers to have made it even more so. He did not. His perspective remained that of a devout Christian and a skilled craftsman—a petty entrepreneur as much as a worker. He neither thoroughly understood the factory system nor fundamentally questioned capitalism (in that respect he resembled the nonresistants, whose anarchism rarely challenged private ownership of property). Burritt's economic analysis of war had more passion than depth and he remained respectful of governments and of the men who ran them. During his last decade he devoted much of his failing strength to international arbitration, a distinguished cause by that time, and to religion. Statesmen listened to him courteously and prestigious institutions such as Yale honored him. War-making continued.

Despite Burritt's hard work, pacifism waned in the 1850s. It had never made headway in the South, in part because it, like the woman's rights movement, was closely tied to abolitionism. Whatever else peace advocates disagreed on, they almost uniformly considered slavery an unjust use of force, in the same category as war. Southern actions after 1848 made it difficult for them to believe slaveholders would accept peaceful overtures. Many pacifists also began to wonder if it was right to ask slaves to turn the other cheek after all the wrongs inflicted upon them. Even Christian anarchists reconsidered their objections to coercion. Garrison and Henry C. Wright, leaders of the nonresistants, came to emphasize the difference between their ideal world, in which force had no place, and the corrupt reality of American society, where it was a fact of life. That distinction allowed Garrison and Wright to condemn coercion in the abstract and still—judging by the standards of a violent society—to root for the best side to win, no matter what weapons it used. If given the choice, many pacifists cared more for the abolition of slavery than for accomplishing it without bloodshed.

By 1860 few were as firm in their principles as they had been in the 1830s. A year or two later, after the Civil War had begun, it was a rare peace man or woman who was not cheering for the Union Army. The American Peace Society did its part by declaring in 1861 that the war was not a war but rather an internal rebellion that required police powers to suppress it; by this reasoning, the Lincoln administration was correct in trying to crush the Confederacy. Slightly earlier, Garrison admitted to a friend that his "sympathies and wishes are with the government, because it is entirely in the right, and acting strictly in self-defense and for self-preservation." He added, not completely convincingly, "This I can say, without any compromise of my peace-principles." He regarded the war as God's just judgment upon a nation that had lived by the sword, and could not conceal his pleasure that slavery was dying, although by the wrong means.

A minority of pacifists kept the faith. In the late 1850s Burritt hoped to avert war by convincing the North and the South to accept a plan under which masters would be paid as their slaves were freed. Bitter at the unwillingness of all sides to consider his scheme, he remained certain to the end that the Civil War was both wrong and unnecessary. Only Adin Ballou and a handful of other colleagues agreed.

Burritt's isolation was not completely surprising. In some respects he was an unusual figure among antebellum reformers. His dream of brotherhood and his desires for a society based on choice, not coercion, were commonplace and fundamental to the antislavery movement. But he was atypical because of his artisan origins and, especially, for the tenacity with which he clung to his ideal. Despite their absolutist and uncompromising rhetoric in the 1830s and 1840s, many of his fellow reformers showed a great capacity for choosing lesser evils in the 1850s and 1860s.

There was a common conviction shared by antislavery men and women, woman's rights advocates, and pacifists (especially nonresistants) as their causes evolved in the antebellum period, propelled in part by events and in part by the logic of abolitionism itself. They all expressed a belief that the world should be ruled by God's law, not force, and that people could act morally and of their own free will. This was both a millennial dream and a response to a basic question in Jacksonian America. How could men and women be made to behave properly in a mobile, heterogeneous society where traditional governing institutions such as church and state had little hold on the country's citizens? The answer, for abolitionists, pacifists, woman's rights advocates, and some other reformers, was to do away with external restraints and to trust moral people with freedom.

Different answers were possible, however, and there was always a tension, sometimes within individual reformers, sometimes between them. On the one side were voluntarism and anarchistic impulses of the sort appearing in nonresistance and, less consistently, in mainstream pacifism, antislavery, and woman's rights. On the other side, reformers wanted to be certain that people would not sin, even if it took coercion to deliver the nation from evil.

# Strong Drink

With some exceptions, historians treat abolitionists with a respect they seldom received in their own times. In contrast, the temperance* movement had dropped into scholarly disrepute by the mid-twentieth century, when a leading historian of the day, Richard Hofstadter, characterized it as "a pseudo-reform, a pinched parochial substitute for reform . . ." A revival of scholarly interest beginning in the late 1970s, and greater awareness of the costs of addiction, led to a partial rehabilitation of its importance in academic circles by the late twentieth century. Nonetheless, in the popular imagination it continued to suffer from its supposedly crabby, joy-denying demands and from its greatest disaster, the failure of Prohibition in the 1920s. The most famous temperance photograph tells the tale: it is of Carry Nation, steely-eyed, grimly holding the hatchet with which she smashed turn-of-the-century saloons.

However much bad press it may have received, the nineteenth-

---

* I am using "temperance" in the conventional but misleading way. It is a catchall term—the lowest common denominator for the crusade against alcohol. Some reformers believed in temperate use of alcohol, others were for total abstinence, and some were for prohibiting its manufacture and sale. For the sake of convenience, I—and most historians—lump them all together under the label "temperance."

century crusade against alcohol was extremely significant for its practical consequences and its effect on reform tactics. In the 1850s, when slavery overshadowed every other issue, the temperance crusade became a major force in state and local politics and achieved remarkable, if temporary, legislative triumphs. In terms of longevity and membership alone, the crusade against alcohol far surpassed abolitionism. It has continued to the present day and, in the antebellum years at least, attracted the largest, most diverse collection of supporters of any reform. They ranged from pious churchwomen to militant feminists, from freethinkers to fundamentalists, from the high and mighty to the lowly and degraded. It was one of the few things upon which William Lloyd Garrison, abolitionist, and Robert Barnwell Rhett, Southern defender of slavery, agreed.

William Cobbett, an Englishman who closely observed drinking habits in the United States and Britain, lamented in 1819 that "Americans preserve their gravity and quietness and good-humour even in their drink." He believed it "far better for them to be as noisy and quarrelsome as the English drunkards; for then the odiousness of the vice would be more visible, and the vice itself might become less frequent." He was on to something. Drunkenness is partly what people make it. Even in such closely related societies as America and England, there are great differences in how individuals act when they drink, in what groups commonly drink, and in where, when, and why they do it. Equally important, cultures, classes, and generations vary in how they define "excessive" drinking and in the moral judgments they pass upon it. Although many late-twentieth-century Americans regard alcoholism as a disease rather than as the moral failing their ancestors believed it to be, drinking nonetheless has a history and takes place in social and cultural settings. And so do efforts to reform the drinker and eliminate the source of his trouble.

At the time Cobbett wrote, alcohol was an acceptable part of life in the United States. "You cannot go into hardly any man's house," he lamented, "without being asked to drink wine, or spirits, even in the morning." Men put down beer or harder beverages to fortify themselves for work, to be sociable, or out of habit. Rum was a staple of New England trade, and farmers in the West converted their grain to whiskey, a less bulky commodity to transport to market and a convenient medium of barter in a currency-poor region. There are stories of frontier clergymen paid with jugs of the local product; even New England ministers, the most priggish in the land, were not opposed to taking a drop or two. Alcohol was everywhere, whether used for commerce or for conviviality, and few people were much disturbed by it. That, however, was beginning to change not long before Cobbett put his critical words to paper.

There had been scattered protests against alcohol in the late eighteenth century, primarily from religious groups such as the Quakers and, especially, the Methodists, who after 1780 were among the more strident opponents of hard liquor. But the most distinguished and persistent early temperance advocate was neither a clergyman nor a Methodist. He was a physician, Dr. Benjamin Rush, signer of the Declaration of Independence and a major figure in the histories of medicine and reform alike. In 1784 he published *An Inquiry into the Effects of Spirituous Liquors on the Human Body and Mind*. Rush accepted the notion that beer, cider, and wine were good for health and well-being, but he put his prestige behind the argument that distilled beverages led to physical, mental, and moral destruction. Rush's *Inquiry* continued to be quoted, reprinted, and plagiarized into the middle of the nineteenth century. He generated sentiment against liquor, both by his writings and through personal appeals to influential people; but anti-alcohol organizations were slow in coming.

The first seems to have formed in Saratoga County, New York, in 1808, when a doctor and a clergyman persuaded more than forty of their neighbors to create the Temperance Society of Moreau and Northumberland. Members forswore use of wine and distilled spirits, "except by advice of a physician, or in case of actual disease." That loophole may have been an act of deference toward the doctor, but it was consistent with Rush's teachings and with temperance activity for the next generation. Up to the late 1820s most reformers opposed hard liquor while believing that beer and, usually, wine had medicinal value. Some merely criticized intoxication, not temperate drinking. The leading lights of one local society reportedly met in a tavern and drank a toast to their own moderation.

The Moreau and Northumberland society quickly inspired an imitator in nearby Greenfield, New York, but for half a decade little organizational work was done. The cause was carried largely by church groups and individuals, some destined to become important later. A young clergyman, Lyman Beecher, began to speak out against liquor, and by 1812 the General Assembly of the Presbyterian Church went on record against drunkenness, appointing a committee to see what could be done about it. There were similar rumblings from Congregationalists.

Finally, in 1813, the year of Rush's death and three decades after his *Inquiry*, two promising organizations formed with the idea of stamping out intoxication. They were the Massachusetts Society for the Suppression of Intemperance (MSSI) and the Connecticut Society for the Reformation of Morals. Their founders included clergy, laymen, and some non-church members, most of them Federalists. Neither organization bound its members to do much more than agree to lead godly, temperate lives, and both engaged in respectable and dignified activities. Cautious though their approach was, it led to the creation of auxiliaries in Massachusetts and Connecticut and encouraged people elsewhere to form similar groups.

Although more focused on drinking than the Connecticut Society, the MSSI was far from the sum total of anti-alcohol sentiment in America. There were, for example, scattered and quite distinct pockets of activity in the West, such as in Livingston County, Kentucky, where in 1817 a self-described group of humble folk pledged "to abstain entirely from the free use of ardent spirits, and use their personal influence to deter others from indulging in so pernicious a practice." The organizational expertise for a national movement, however, lay in the East. For one to materialize, the association with New England Federalism, already a political dinosaur, would have to loosen; temperance would need to shed some of its elitism and become more passionate in seeking a constituency.

Those conditions began to be met in the mid-1820s. Federalism did its part by dying. Lyman Beecher helped supply the other ingredients, even though he shared many of the narrow prejudices of the other early leaders of temperance. (He hated Unitarianism and described Jefferson's followers as "Sabbath-breakers, rum-sellers, tippling folk, infidels, and ruff-scruff generally.") Whatever support his views cost the movement among political and theological liberals he made up for with his ability to stir evangelical Protestants. In the fall of 1825 Beecher preached six thunderous sermons on temperance; published the next year, these had a tremendous influence, both at the time and over the decades.

What Beecher said was not entirely novel, but he said it well and gave a badly needed sharpness to the debate. Moderate drinking, approved by some temperance writers, was anathema to Beecher. According to him, to take any amount was to be intemperate, whether or not it resulted in drunkenness. Having cut away any happy middle ground, Beecher envisioned "banishment of ardent spirits from the list of lawful articles of commerce"—an omen of the political turn temperance would take in the next generation. His goal in 1825, however, was more immediate. He demanded a new, vigorous attack on alcohol carried across the land by voluntary associations.

There were, as Beecher knew, many temperance societies at the time he gave his sermons. What he had in mind was increasing the number of them and fashioning a national organization to provide central direction, sponsor publications and speakers, and supervise creation of auxiliaries. An answer to Beecher's call came in February 1826 in the form of the American Society for the Promotion of Temperance (or the American Temperance Society). Members repudiated moderation in favor of abstinence from hard liquor—Beecher's position.

Beecher himself was not present to sign the constitution of the American Temperance Society, but of the sixteen who did, several were his confederates in various Protestant religious and charitable enterprises. This close connection with the evangelical "benevolent empire" helped the society greatly. Its first secretary, the Reverend Justin Edwards, adopted techniques made familiar by the American

Bible Society and drew upon the churches and laymen who backed other Protestant crusades. The benefits of annexing temperance to the benevolent empire were apparent in the statistics. By 1834 there were estimates that five thousand state and local societies promoted the cause, that millions of pieces of propaganda were in circulation, and that a million members had pledged to avoid alcohol.

Even allowing for exaggeration, the figures are impressive. They are also deceptive. Many local groups originated independently of the national society, and a majority of them remained unaffiliated with it. The American Temperance Society acted as a valuable clearinghouse for information, but it could not provide firm direction for the movement. Supporters of the cause in different places continued to interpret their obligations differently and to keep their vows with greater or lesser faithfulness.

In part to bring about a degree of consistency, the society's executive committee called for a convention to meet in Philadelphia in 1833. The gathering was attended by delegates from throughout the country and they put together a more genuinely national organization, the United States Temperance Union (American Temperance Union after 1836). Its first president was a wealthy New Yorker, Stephen Van Rensselaer, whose popularity at the meeting was undoubtedly increased by his willingness to pay for the publication of 100,000 copies of the proceedings. Like Van Rensselaer, the officers of the union and of its state auxiliaries were men with money and prestige, many of them successful in business and a few in politics.

By the mid-1830s prospects looked bright. There was still opposition, even within the churches, but much of the weaponry of evangelical Protestantism was in the service of the cause. Temperance had many of the high and mighty behind it and the message seemed to be filtering down to workingmen, groups of whom began taking the pledge. In common with conservative temperance reformers, they, too, had come to see drinking as a cause of poverty. There was a national organization, many newspapers in support, no shortage of pamphlets, and grass-roots enthusiasm.

Arguments in favor of temperance had also come to maturity. Several lines of attack developed by the 1830s and persisted throughout the century with slight shifts and alterations. One appeal was personal and threatening. "The Holy Spirit," according to a circular, "will not visit, much less dwell with him who is under the polluting, debasing effects of intoxicating drink." Intemperance, in short, led to hell. In a more secular vein, temperance propagandists pictured alcohol as a form of tyranny, resembling slavery in depriving people of the ability to act as autonomous, morally responsible creatures.

If damnation and loss of self-control were not threatening enough, there were other temperance themes. Facts and figures demonstrated that alcohol produced insanity, poverty, and crime. By devastating families, it robbed society of a crucial institution and sent innocent women and children out into the cruel world, their lives destroyed by the husbands and fathers who were supposed to be their protectors. Everyone would gain by banishing alcohol, from the ex-drunkard to the hardworking taxpayer bearing the financial costs of crime and indigence. Temperance propagandists also played upon a powerful blend of patriotism and middle-class dismay at Jacksonian politics. They conjured visions of rum-soaked debtors using their votes to take charge of the country (a credible notion, given the realities of antebellum electioneering). The Reverend Heman Humphrey warned in 1828 that "if the emblems of liberty are ever to be torn from our banner—if her statues are to be hurled from their pedestals—if the car of a despot is to be driven over our suppliant bodies, it will be by aid of strong drink." Temperance advocates (including Abraham Lincoln in the 1840s) sometimes claimed that drunkenness was a worse national evil than slavery and that doing away with alcohol would uplift America, Americans, and the world.

Although they were often among the more conservative antebellum reformers on social matters, anti-alcohol crusaders were not blue-nosed reactionaries, as latter-day critics made them seem. They had a sense of progress and of the nation's potential. As they saw it, prosperity, godliness, and political freedom were the fruits of sobriety. Poverty, damnation, and tyranny were the consequences of intemperance.

Between 1835 and 1840 the temperance movement became a victim of its logic, which led to ever more extreme assaults on alcohol.

Beecher and the American Temperance Society worked to destroy the notion that moderate drinking was tolerable. They were not entirely successful, although the pledge after 1825 usually required abstaining from "ardent spirits," which could be interpreted to exempt fermented ones such as wine and beer. Yet the sin was supposed to be in the alcohol, not in distilling, and one could get as drunk on beer as on an "ardent spirit" such as whiskey. By 1836 a large faction, which included Beecher and Justin Edwards, pressed the American Temperance Union to adopt a "teetotal" pledge, binding signers to abstain from any alcohol. That view prevailed, but it cost the union some auxiliaries and continued to meet resistance from people who believed that wine and beer were healthful as well as useful in weaning tipplers from harder drink. The teetotal position had in its favor the moral purity, or "ultraism," many antebellum reformers insisted upon; yet it raised further problems. What about communion wine? Was it sinful? Some people thought so. Others, equally pious, read the Bible differently.

Not that teetotalism exhausted opportunities for temperance reformers to quarrel. Like abolitionists, they disagreed among themselves on the role of women in the movement. Unlike abolitionists, they often did not press the issue: some societies separated the sexes into different organizations, others included both. More divisive was the question of whether temperance meant going beyond trying to convert individuals. In his sermons of 1825 Beecher had raised the possibility of legislation to stop the making and selling of liquor. The matter was openly debated in the Philadelphia convention of 1833 and it continued to be for years afterward.

Battles over such questions split organizations. The most socially prominent leaders had begun to drift away in reaction against teetotalism, and there was a general decline in membership by 1836. The movement was in the doldrums by the time the financial panic of 1837 cut further into its resources, as it did for reform in general. Within three years, however, temperance revived, although changed. The new inspiration did not come from New England or evangelical reform.

•  •  •

The setting was Chase's Tavern in Baltimore and the unlikely heroes of the piece were six friends, later to describe themselves as ex-drunkards. Their story was the stuff of which legends are made. They met on the night of April 2, 1840, with anything but sobriety on their minds. Tavern humor being what it was, they delegated a "committee" to attend a nearby temperance lecture, presumably to know their enemy. The committee report, duly delivered, was unexpectedly persuasive. The six swore off intoxicants and formed an organization, called the Washington Temperance Society in honor of the first President (a drinker but a virtuous man nonetheless). By Christmas there were a thousand Washingtonians in Baltimore, and before a year passed, the society established a beachhead in New York City. At the end of three years supporters claimed—with more enthusiasm than accuracy—pledges from 600,000 intemperate men, 100,000 of them formerly habitual drunkards.

Existing temperance organizations first greeted the Washingtonians as allies, but tensions soon appeared and were based on more than competition for members. Several things separated the new phase of the movement from the old. The first anti-alcohol societies had been dominated by clergy and wealthy evangelical laymen. The Washingtonians had help from ministers and many of their methods derived from revivalism, but their leaders were neither clergy nor men of social prominence. Of their two greatest lecturers, one had been a hatter and the other a bookbinder and minstrel. Such men were uninterested in theological niceties; occasionally they were hostile to the formal trappings of religion, much to the disgust of American Temperance Union officials.

An equally crucial difference between Washingtonians and their predecessors had to do with the people they tried to reach. Older temperance societies had not been eager to deal with drunkards. The Massachusetts Society for the Suppression of Intemperance was candid about its position. "The design of this institution," it admitted in 1814, "is . . . not so much to wrest the fatal cup from those who are already brutalized and ruined, as to keep sober those who are sober." In contrast, the Washington Society's chief goal was getting tipplers to pledge total abstinence. Not every member was an ex-alcoholic, but many were, and almost all were workingmen or from the lower ranks of society.

Temperance would never be the same after the Washingtonians. Before 1840 anti-alcohol crusaders had used a fair number of devices, ranging from sermons and pamphlets to temperance hotels for the sober-minded traveler. Leaders of such organizations as the American Temperance Union, nevertheless, primarily worked through religious groups, engaged in fairly logical discourse, corresponded with like-minded people elsewhere in the United States and Britain, and held meetings which, despite sharp debates, were reasonably staid. The Washingtonians adopted many of the same instruments of reform—they also gave lectures, published newspapers, and had conventions. There the resemblance ended. Like their clientele, the Washingtonians' behavior and tactics were not genteel.

Using wit, pathos, and the language of common folk, their orators moved audiences to tears, laughter, and signing the pledge. More unusual, they gave accounts of their own careers as drunkards and demanded similar confessions from the audience, a practice older temperance reformers found vulgar. The Washingtonians also sponsored picnics, parades, and fairs, techniques they learned from political parties and, probably, from abolitionists. They used the streets and public space more effectively than earlier temperance reformers, as when they staged spectacles like a giant day-long parade in Boston in 1844, addressed by the governor of the state, a temperance man. It was an easy step to move from that sort of festivity to popular entertainment, a transformation represented in the work of Timothy Shay Arthur. Already a believer in temperance by 1840, Arthur was inspired by the Washingtonians to write fiction for the cause. He was not the first or the last to do so, but his output was formidable and easily translated into stage productions. His enduring reputation rests upon the anti-alcohol equivalent of *Uncle Tom's Cabin*, entitled *Ten Nights in a Bar-Room* (1854), a novel, a widely produced melodrama, and, for a time in the mid-twentieth century, a staple of dinner-theaters playing it as parody. In the 1840s, however, Arthur's work was emblematic of the inventiveness of antebellum reformers in taking advantage of new opportunities in communications and popular culture. A considerable distance separated Benjamin Rush's scientific critique of alcohol from temperance as theater.

The Washingtonian movement, however, was past its prime when Joe Morgan, the fictional hero of *Ten Nights*, first took the pledge. The Washingtonians could not control their auxiliaries—the typical fate of national organizations in the antebellum period. Growth was as haphazard as it was swift and there was not enough central direction to sustain local societies. Despite their flair for parades and picnics, the Washingtonians had trouble figuring out what to do once the pledge was taken, the confession made, and the first enthusiasm gone. People lost interest or joined newer organizations. The Washingtonians also suffered from putting too much faith in men who were better at swearing off alcohol than staying off it. One lecturer disappeared for nearly a week in New York City, only to be found sobering up in a bawdy house. Such episodes, combined with institutional weakness, personality conflicts, and disagreements over issues, led to the quick decline of the Washingtonians. Within a few years most auxiliaries vanished.

Their influence lingered. The American Temperance Union and other, older organizations took on some of the Washingtonians' fervor, although they found the public confession and the use of popular entertainment hard to swallow. Thanks to the Washingtonians, the drunkard received more attention than he had in the past and efforts were made to broaden the movement still further, even to extend it to anti-liquor Catholics, with whom there had been no real chance for cooperation so long as evangelicals dominated temperance. The Washingtonians, on the other hand, were not especially concerned about religion and in their public festivities they embraced organizations like the St. Mary's Mutual Benevolent Total Abstinence Society, a Catholic participant in the Boston parade of 1844. The most ardent recruiting of Catholics would come later, in a lecture tour by Father Theobald Mathew, an Irish priest, in 1849; but the Washingtonians had helped prepare the way by separating temperance from Protestant sectarianism.

The Washingtonians were valuable to the cause in their failure as well as for their innovations. Several societies begun after 1840 remedied weaknesses in the Washingtonian movement. The majority of these new organizations were similarly nonsectarian, committed to total abstinence, and aimed at common people, but they had the sturdy institutional structure the Washingtonians lacked. The Sons of Temperance, begun in 1843, was among the most important, although there were others of consequence, including the Independent Order of Good Templars (1852), which admitted women as full members (a few lodges also admitted African Americans). With an elaborate hierarchy and centralized control, the Sons recruited a quarter of a million dues-paying brethren by 1850. (There was an independent women's organization, the Daughters of Temperance.) They exercised discipline over those who took their pledge, adopted the air of the secret fraternal orders then popular in America, and offered important forms of mutual assistance—all things that secured the loyalty of members to a degree unapproached by the Washingtonians.

The magnetism of secular groups like the Washingtonians and the Sons does not mean that religious campaigns against alcohol ended in the 1840s. The evangelical tradition persisted in the American Temperance Union, in churches, and in later organizations like the Woman's Christian Temperance Union (1874). They, too, learned from the Washingtonians, particularly from their tactics, some of which, like the public confession, fit well with the modes of revivalism popular among lower-middle-class folk. Even the use of popular culture, begun in the Washingtonian phase of the movement, had its impact on later evangelical temperance crusaders. At the century's end Carry Nation's assaults on Kansas saloons were as theatrical as anything written by Timothy Shay Arthur. (She, along with her bar-smashing hatchet, became a sideshow attraction at county fairs.)

One important new tactic in the 1840s the Washingtonians neither initiated nor accepted with enthusiasm. It was political action of the sort Lyman Beecher and others proposed two decades earlier. In 1833 a group of lawmakers and public officials formed the Congressional

Temperance Society. Their avowed purpose was not to legislate alcohol out of existence but rather to provide a sterling moral example, as politicians rarely did. Yet the appearance of such a society was a sign that an influential anti-alcohol faction might possibly be put together in Congress. Its first president, Lewis Cass, had already used his political position as Secretary of War to remove liquor from the Army's rations. In 1833 the political question also surfaced within the convention that created the American Temperance Union. Gerrit Smith, an abolitionist later involved in the Liberty Party, introduced a controversial resolution declaring that "the traffic in ardent spirits" was "morally wrong" and that "the inhabitants of cities, towns, and other local communities, should be permitted by law to prohibit the said traffic within their respective jurisdictions." This was a direct statement of the prohibitionist position that characterized the movement by the end of the nineteenth century. The resolution passed.

In the 1830s and 1840s, however, many temperance people had their doubts about prohibition. Some feared casting aspersions on liquor dealers, a few of whom they thought to be pious, if misguided. There was also a feeling, common to many reformers, that electioneering appealed to base instincts and put expediency above virtue. Political action, furthermore, raised issues in temperance similar to ones that divided abolitionists. In particular, it compromised a commitment to "moral suasion" and the evangelical belief that true goodness could flow only from a converted heart. People had to want to behave properly, so the argument ran, and that came from enlightenment, not force. It took soul-searching for many temperance advocates to accept coercion, in the form of legislation, as a legitimate means of reform.

Still, prohibitionists had arguments in their favor. The liquor trade was licensed by the government and people were under no obligation to let their government license sin. Besides, most reformers agreed that if the public was godly, decent laws would follow as a matter of course. Prohibitionists felt that the process could be speeded up if temperance men engaged in political action, which would serve as a form of propaganda, and if alcohol, which corrupted many voters, were removed from the picture. That view gained renewed force in the

1840s and 1850s as reformers fretted about immigrants and their political power. A final argument—although few cared to put it so bluntly—was that prohibition promised to be successful.

Beginning in the 1830s, temperance voters agreed not to cast ballots for heavy drinkers, breaking the chains of party loyalty if need be. They also sought local option legislation, which gave communities the power to stop the traffic in liquor within their jurisdictions. The first statewide victory for temperance came in 1838, with a Massachusetts law banning the sale of distilled spirits in amounts of less than fifteen gallons, an act that removed hard beverages from taverns and kept them away from poor people, who could not afford such a quantity. The statute inspired civil disobedience from "rum-sellers" and much agitation for and against, during which many temperance people who had opposed political action fell into line behind the law. It was repealed in 1840, when Massachusetts prohibitionists shifted their attention to the towns, persuading about a hundred of them to go dry by 1845. In 1839 Mississippi passed a law like Massachusetts', although more modest. It forbade the sale of less than a gallon of liquor. After intensive lobbying on both sides, New York voters presented prohibitionists with a massive victory in 1846 and a defeat the following year. The U.S. Supreme Court gave the movement a boost in 1846 by deciding in favor of the right of states to deny licenses to sell distilled spirits. Reformers were not always so lucky in politics—a disastrous campaign set the cause in Georgia back almost a generation—but temperance battles at the ballot box and in the courts were fierce by the mid-1840s. By that time Maine had begun to lead the nation.

Much of what happened in Maine was due to two circumstances. The first was a strong antislavery movement. Abolitionists joined the fray, and their experience in building organizations and producing propaganda significantly increased temperance firepower in Maine. Prohibitionists had a second advantage in Neal Dow, a wealthy merchant and an ex-Quaker. Born in 1804, he converted to temperance in 1827 after exposure to Beecher and to Justin Edwards of the old American Temperance Society. By the early 1830s Dow was a total abstinence man and before the decade was out he took his principles into politics.

At about the time Massachusetts experimented with its fifteen-gallon law, Maine's legislature considered, then tabled, similar legislation. Meanwhile, Dow tried to move public opinion in Portland, his hometown. He and a coalition of groups, the Washingtonians among them, succeeded in 1842, when the Portland electorate voted by an almost two-to-one margin to stop the sale of alcohol. The ban was evaded and temperance men, led by Dow, agitated for statewide, and presumably more effective, legislation. In 1846 they got almost what they wanted: a law forbidding the sale of intoxicating beverages in less than twenty-eight-gallon lots. Enforcement, however, was the responsibility of town selectmen, who often looked the other way at infractions. Partly to remedy the situation, Dow ran for mayor of Portland; in 1851 he won. His office magnified his influence, and within a few months Dow and his supporters prodded the legislature into passing the so-called Maine Law of 1851. It prohibited the sale and manufacture of intoxicating beverages within the state.

Dow went on to have a long career in public life, although little of it in office. He was a tireless campaigner for prohibition in other states, as well as in Maine; he was a nativist, an abolitionist, a Republican, and, in the Civil War, the colonel of a regiment as sober as he could make it. His handiwork, the Maine Law, had even more impact. After its passage the American Temperance Union swung around to endorse prohibition. Within four years, thirteen states had their own versions of it and there were narrow defeats in others. By 1855 all of New England was dry; so, too, were New York and large parts of the Midwest. Those triumphs were swift and encouraging to prohibitionists, but temperance had achieved quieter, perhaps more impressive, objectives well before Maine saw the light. Per capita consumption of alcohol declined sharply between 1830 and 1850; and large parts of several states were dry before 1851 as the result of local-option laws.

Statewide prohibition legislation in the 1850s, however, was usually not well enough drafted or defended to survive court challenges. By the Civil War, Maine Laws had virtually disappeared outside New England, gone but, as it turned out, not forgotten.

Temperance politicking in the 1840s and 1850s had a testy but re-

ciprocal relationship with the electioneering style of the day. On the
one hand, temperance was a protest against the demagoguery of Jacksonian office seekers. It reeked with contempt for the besotted rabble
and those (usually Democrats) who sought votes by praising the "people," attacking the "aristocracy," and ignoring moral issues. On the
other hand, some temperance campaigners learned lessons from such
politicians and ended up teaching them a few. Rather than reviling
the masses for not electing their betters—the self-destructive course
of Federalists in the early 1800s—anti-alcohol politicians worked hard
to make a majority. They perfected their own brand of demagoguery,
with lurid propaganda against drink and "conspiracies" by "rum-
sellers." Realizing the effectiveness of public spectacles, they followed
the Washingtonians in imitating the parades and picnics of conventional party politics. They held cold-water Fourth of July festivities to
cloak their cause in the mantle of patriotism, as well as to keep their
supporters away from the standard celebrations, with their deadly combination of alcohol and oratory.

  In numerous local elections throughout the nineteenth and early
twentieth centuries alcohol mattered more than the national issues of
the day. At times it fractured parties; at other times it formed a sharp
division between them, as when wet Democrats ran against dry Republicans. In most instances temperance mingled with religion and
ethnicity, and it easily fused with other political crusades—with anti-
Masonry, nativism, antislavery, the Republican Party, and even woman's rights. Yet the crusade against alcohol had a vitality of its own,
separate from the fortunes of any party or any other cause, which is
partly why it stayed alive so long in American politics. More than
antislavery, it convinced reformers not to rely exclusively upon moral
suasion. The fifteen-gallon and Maine laws were proof that vices might
be legislated away more easily than sinners could be converted. By
the end of the antebellum period, moral issues—prohibition prime
among them—shaped party affiliations and how Americans voted.

  Besides venturing into politics, temperance made its way south of the
Mason-Dixon line; in 1841 77 percent of the nation's distilleries could

be found there. Although strongest in the usual havens for reform—
New England, New York, and the Midwest—temperance was among
the least sectional of the antebellum crusades. That is not accurately
reflected in statistics from the 1830s, which underestimate the appeal
of the cause in the South. Many Southerners were repulsed by the
antislavery activities of American Temperance Union leaders like Arthur Tappan and Gerrit Smith; they often pursued an independent
course, worked within their churches, or responded more enthusiasti-
cally to the organizations created in the 1840s, particularly the Washingtonians and the Sons of Temperance. In rural as well as urban areas
throughout the South, temperance organizations of one sort or another
popped up, inspired by a local clergyman, a traveling lecturer, or a few
neighborhood enthusiasts.

Temperance also made considerable headway in the West. In 1861
a woman in Eugene, Oregon, assured an absent friend that the local
society "is prospering finely since you left. Nearly all the drunkards
in town have joined." (She added, however, that "most of them are
now about as temperate as before they signed the pledge.") Even
California, in the rowdiest period in its history, had a strong anti-
alcohol movement. A visitor to San Francisco in 1853 could avoid the
city's fleshpots by staying at Hillman's Temperance House, with sixty
rooms for lodgers and capable of serving two hundred teetotaling din-
ers. At the same time, the Sons of Temperance claimed thirty chapters
in the state, including an Oriental Division. In part because of politicking by the Sons, California had a vote on a "Maine Law" of its
own in 1855. Although opinion ran against it by about a five-to-four
margin, the gold-mining districts turned out narrowly in favor of the
measure. That is impressive because of the rough-and-ready reputation of the Mother Lode country and because women, often the main-
stay of temperance agitation, were outnumbered by men ten or twelve
to one in the area. Thanks to the Sons, the Methodists, and a desire
for law, order, and respectability, more than eleven thousand men in
the mining counties went on record in favor of banishing alcoholic
beverages.

Temperance crossed racial lines as easily as geographic ones. Anti-alcohol sentiment appeared in free African American communities by the end of the eighteenth century. Organized efforts began in the late 1820s, when temperance societies for blacks appeared in New Haven and New York, with others following shortly thereafter in Brooklyn, Baltimore, Boston, and elsewhere. The Boston organization, founded in 1833, had a female auxiliary, and like their white sisters, African American women were tireless and effective advocates of temperance.

For the remainder of the antebellum period, the message continued to be spread through a variety of black-run organizations, some, such as the New England Colored Temperance Society (founded in 1836), specifically focused on drinking. Other means of promoting the cause, such as black conventions, churches, and newspapers, mingled anti-alcohol messages with commitment to a wider range of reforms. Leadership often came from men and women like J.W.C. Pennington, Samuel Ringgold Ward, Sarah Parker Remond, Frederick Douglass, and others who were also important black antislavery activists. In common with abolitionism, moreover, the African American crusade against intemperance often ran parallel to, and cooperated with, white efforts, but by the 1840s it, too, increasingly pursued an independent agenda.

To a greater degree than white temperance crusaders, black ones refused to separate their cause from a broader platform of social reform and racial uplift. Where "slavery to drink" might be a powerful metaphor for whites, for African Americans the connections between alcoholism and bondage were far more complex and deeply felt. By the late 1830s black reformers such as Lewis Woodson presented drinking as both a tool of slavery—as when masters "rewarded" their bondsmen with rations of alcohol—and as its own form of slavery, threatening to sap free black communities of resources that should be devoted to education, to fighting injustice, and to acquiring economic power. While black temperance reformers are open to the same charge as their white counterparts, namely, that they sought "social control" and the imposition of middle-class values on their poorer brethren, their branch of the movement rested on a stronger sense of community—of a more powerful bond—linking the fate of the reformer, the drinker, and racial progress. Although the evidence is fragmentary and indirect, it further suggests that African American efforts, like white ones, had an effect. In that hub of reform activity, Philadelphia, for instance, black arrests for drunkenness after 1860, as well as other indicators of alcoholism, were significantly lower than for whites.

The most intriguing question is what made temperance so attractive to such a diverse collection of people, men and women, Northerners, Southerners, and Westerners, urban and rural, rich and poor, black and white. The easy answer (and there is much to it) is that America had a drinking problem. Reliable figures are difficult to come by, but it seems that per capita consumption of alcohol was higher around 1810 than in the supposedly hard-drinking 1970s. One authority aptly describes the estimates for early-nineteenth-century drinking as "staggering." (By 1850 the use of alcohol declined to a rate perhaps lower than late-twentieth-century consumption, testimony to the effectiveness of reform.) Yet temperance was more than a response to rampant intoxication. The real rise in drunkenness must have gone back to the last half of the eighteenth century, when Americans improved their ability to make rum and whiskey, and more than a generation before the first anti-alcohol society was formed. Much the same thing happened in England, where gin put its baneful stamp upon the working classes long before temperance organizations materialized.

It took social and cultural pressures, combined with that prior increase in intoxication, to make some Americans see alcohol as a problem and temperance as a solution. For the gentlemen and clergy prominent in the early movement, the reform was a badge of their own respectability and of their disapproval of the behavior of poor people, set loose from traditional moral controls by economic and religious changes. Temperance presumably would reduce the nastiness of life in the burgeoning cities, elevate the tone of politics, and help preserve the old moral order. Changes in the nature of work, moreover, made it desirable for employers that the labor force have the discipline to stay in factories for long hours rather than pursue the traditional course of artisans, who enjoyed independence, conviviality, and tippling. Those moral, social, and economic calculations swayed some early temperance advocates, especially members of elites. For evangelicals, there was also the millennialistic and perfectionist hope for human progress and the creation of a nation of free moral agents.

If temperance sometimes seemed aimed by elites at poorer folk, the latter also found the movement compelling. For some it offered a prescription for respectability and success: a temperate, disciplined lifestyle and steady habits promised, and sometimes delivered, economic and emotional rewards. Men with a taste for liquor had even more straightforward reasons for joining, particularly after 1840, when the Washingtonians began to seek them out: temperance provided self-discipline, moral support, and a way of gaining control over a destructive impulse. It gave order to disorderly lives.

Temperance also provided a stage on which gender conflicts and anxieties could play and sometimes come to resolution, especially after 1840. The thousands of women attracted to the crusade found a public role that was less threatening to the social order than antislavery, woman's rights, and communitarianism. If anything, it claimed to defend the status quo against the forces of dissipation and to strengthen that bulwark of antebellum society, the family. Even though temperance attracted militant feminists, its respectability made it equally acceptable to conservative women who feared or rejected radical agitation but who nevertheless sought a place in public life.

Temperance could also be a reproach to males and a critique of their domination of women. Anti-alcohol propaganda, like the sentimental fiction American females read and wrote, consisted of a catalogue of the awful sufferings men inflicted upon their loved ones. It was almost always the father (or son, or brother) who brought grief to his wife (or mother, or sister) and his innocent children. If he was redeemed, it was often through the agency of a woman (or child, or both) whose natural goodness exorcized the demon rum. These melodramas had a ring of truth—American men were capable of swinish behavior—but such stories also sound like acts of protest by women, not simply against alcohol but also against the male world that glorified them, confined them to the home, and failed to live by its own preachings.

That simply makes more curious the matter of what drove thousands of reasonably sober men to sign the pledge after 1840. The evidence is fragmentary, but it gives some hints in their ages, which appear to have clustered in the early twenties, and in their occupations. Many belonged on the fringes of respectability, working in the lesser professions (including teaching), as petty entrepreneurs, or as artisans in skilled trades such as carpentry. These were men making their way in the world (upward, they hoped). An image of propriety could be very important in increasing their prospects. If that were not a consideration, self-control, which temperance required, was a valuable virtue for people whose success in an expanding economy depended on thrift and hard work. As we shall see, there were other crusades—notably health reform—offering much the same thing to youth wandering through the opportunities and temptations of antebellum America. In addition, temperance had counterfeminist as well as feminist implications. Organizations such as the Washingtonians and Sons of Temperance offered male camaraderie in an alternative to the saloon and reaffirmed patriarchical relationships by asserting the importance of the male as breadwinner and protector.

Whatever psychological and emotional needs they fulfilled, temperance organizations provided important services. The Sons of Temperance were especially strong in that respect, having as one of their primary objectives "mutual assistance in cases of sickness." In fact, they offered life, as well as health, insurance, and the San Francisco branch (and perhaps others) acted as an employment agency, posting the names of members who needed work. Those were no mean advantages in days when the government did little to help the ill, destitute, and unemployed. Post-1840 temperance societies also provided opportunities for sociability. The Sons of Temperance, with their rituals and regalia, satisfied the same impulses that drew American males into lodges like the Odd Fellows and countless similar voluntary organizations in antebellum America. Throughout the year there were various excuses for getting together—picnics, fairs, and Fourth of July celebrations. These were fine places to enjoy companionship and for decent women and men to court. (A North Carolinian described a neighborhood zealot as "a young widower" who "wanted a wife—and

he spoke to show how well he could speak rather than for any immediate practical effect in advertising the cause of temperance.") Besides saving drunkards, the movement redeemed the uncertainty and
loneliness of life in antebellum America. Only when it did that could
it become a genuine substitute for the solace of alcohol.

Despite the social and practical advantages of belonging to anti-
alcohol organizations, interest waxed and waned, both over time and
over the course of individual lives. Members acquired families and
ceased to participate actively; brethren fell from grace, some to be
forgiven, some to fall again. But at the core of the movement were
dedicated people who carried it through the years. They were a diverse lot: reformers who saw conquest of alcohol as an important part
of some broader program; religious men and women who felt abstinence was a divine command; and those who knew from personal
experience the evils of strong drink.

One of the impressive facts about temperance is its survival, especially
after the failure of Prohibition in the 1920s. The secret of temperance's
durability is probably its combination of clear focus and infinite adaptability. It has a definite demonology: alcohol and those who consume,
sell, and produce it. Battling them satisfies any number of motives. It
can be a religious imperative or a solution to personal difficulties. It
can be elitist or vulgar, dignified or boisterous, private or sociable.
It can be an explanation for poverty and failure or the key to a better
world. It can be a gesture of dismay at the modern world, as it was for
some of the early leaders and as it often is today; or it can reflect the
bourgeois virtues of discipline and self-control the modern order called
forth, as it did for middle-class and working people in the 1840s.

There is another important aspect to temperance besides its durability. It directed attention to the physical being. In that it foreshadowed several other, less conventional reforms and became part of a
large, important process in American social thought.

# SEVEN

# The Body and Beyond

The human body has always been a problem for Christians, who have been torn between glorifying it as God's handiwork and mistrusting its interference with spiritual life. At first glance, it seems that most antebellum reformers held the latter view. While their contemporary Walt Whitman praised "the body electric" in memorable poetry, they depicted humankind's physical state with disapproval. Temperance propagandists described the excesses of the flesh with disgust, as did anti-prostitution crusaders and others.

And yet antebellum reformers seldom entirely rejected the body in favor of the spirit. The point to temperance propaganda was not that humankind's physical nature ought to be despised but rather that men and women had to control it in order to be virtuous. In similar fashion, most antebellum reformers blurred the old distinction between body and soul and made each dependent on the other. Only on the periphery of reform or in such sentimental works as *Uncle Tom's Cabin* (1852) was there much trace of the romantic notion that so long as the spirit is free it makes no difference whether the individual is in chains. More often, reformers assumed that men and women could not behave in a morally responsible fashion unless their bodies were unfettered and uncorrupted.

That assumption marked a half step away from the religious

traditions that shaped antebellum reform and toward the kind of biological and materialistic modes of thought that permeated late-nineteenth-century social criticism. This was a transition from theological perfectionism, as preached by Charles G. Finney and others in the 1820s, to physical perfectionism, a belief that salvation was to be found in improvement of the body or of the species. By the early twentieth century the latter view took many forms, including eugenics and scientific racism. In the antebellum years, however, the most intriguing signs of the transition in social thought were not obviously racist or religious: they were in health reform, phrenology, and spiritualism.

Although different in many respects, the three—which I will label "body reforms" for want of a better term—had some things in common. Each appealed to a great variety of people, many of whom were not reformers and who had no interest beyond better health, getting ahead in the world, or contacting a dead loved one. Yet each became a genuine reform movement, with a vision of how humanity might be perfected and with organizations, lecturers, and publications to carry the message. Equally important, each attracted a considerable number of men and women who were centrally involved in such crusades as communitarianism, antislavery, woman's rights, and temperance. For them, body reforms gave a new vocabulary for expressing concerns that ran through most other causes of the day. The primary significance of the body reforms within antebellum reform, in fact, generally lies in the part they played in translating reform rhetoric from evangelical Protestant and political vocabularies into "scientific" ones.

Each of the body reforms was possible because in the early nineteenth century there were no academic and professional groups to determine what is respectable science and what is not. In the 1820s, 1830s, and 1840s, for instance, it was easy for a poor New England farmer named Samuel Thompson to acquire a considerable following for his belief that illness was the result of "clogging the system." (He unclogged it with botanical preparations, especially *Lobelia inflata*, an emetic.) The American Medical Association was not formed until 1847, and much time would pass before it was powerful enough to drive laymen like Thompson from the field. The situation was the same in all branches of science and in other professions as well. Every man, so it seemed, could be his own doctor, lawyer, or political oracle.

By present-day standards the results were appalling. Quackery flourished and the worst of fools and knaves announced they had unraveled the secrets of the universe. In truth, however, the situation was not entirely bad. Physicians trained in medical schools—and, for that matter, trained lawyers—often proved as destructive of health and happiness as were their amateur competitors. Fads like the Graham diet at times actually helped people with real illnesses without doing additional damage to them, a rare thing in the early nineteenth century. Besides, there was a certain consistency to the antebellum period. Any nation that gave a hearing to the Graham system, phrenology, and spiritualism clearly applied its democratic principles to matters of the intellect as well as to politics.

Sylvester Graham, the most famous health reformer of the antebellum period, had a career shortened by illnesses. His father, an elderly Connecticut clergyman, died when the boy was two years old. Poverty and a physical collapse prevented Sylvester from being ordained as a Presbyterian minister until the relatively advanced age of thirty-two. In 1830 he became a lecturer for the Pennsylvania Society for Discouraging the Use of Ardent Spirits. He was then thirty-six and had yet to show any sign of distinction. By 1832, however, he discovered the cause that made him something more than an obscure clergyman and temperance lecturer. But his time in the limelight was short: five years later he went into semiretirement, emerging briefly and then retiring again in the 1840s, for physical as well as psychological reasons. Nonetheless, he achieved a fame that eluded contemporaries who surpassed him in stamina and intellect: he had a cracker named after him.

An epidemic gave Graham his opportunity for notoriety. In the spring of 1832 Americans uneasily awaited the arrival of cholera from Europe, where it had been raging since the previous year. Graham had already ended his connection with the Pennsylvania Society, moved to New York City, and broadened his horizons. He had come to believe that alcohol was not the only substance damaging to the body, and he had begun to lecture on diet and hygiene. In March he announced a series of talks on cholera, and promptly attracted considerable attention and was plunged into controversy. Cholera had never appeared in the United States and authorities were not of one mind on how to prevent or cure it. Although physicians agreed with Graham that drunkards and unclean people were most susceptible, some doctors urged Americans to eat hearty, stimulating food to build their systems to withstand the disease. Graham dissented. He saw irritation of the stomach as the primary cause of all illness. A person who ate properly, he claimed, should not get sick. Eating properly, for Graham, meant a bland, plain diet of fruits, vegetables, and coarsely ground grain—no meat, spices, alcohol, coffee, or tea. The initial stage of cholera, characterized by vomiting and diarrhea, gave credibility to his belief that overstimulation of the stomach produced the disease. His self-promotion and his enemies, who attacked him in the press, spread his views to an anxious public whose resistance to new medical ideas was low.

It is not clear how Graham developed his theories. He confused the issue by insisting that they were completely his own. When accused of lifting them from European medical writers he proudly declared that "it is nearly twenty years since I have read any work on intellectual and moral philosophy." Ignorance may have been his best defense, but his ideas owed something to French physiological theory and to Dr. Benjamin Rush. Some of Graham's remarks on diet and sex, moreover, sound suspiciously like folk wisdom dressed up as science. Be that as it may, Graham elaborated, promoted, and gave coherence to concepts that were not entirely original.

Despite his emphasis on the stomach, Graham advised the public to pay attention to all aspects of hygiene, not just food. A consistent Grahamite would bathe (something Americans tended to avoid), exercise, wear loose-fitting clothing, and live in a well-ventilated house. Graham also warned against such bad habits as "indolence"; these, too, he felt could damage one's health.

And then there was sex. In 1834 Graham published his *Lectures on Chastity*. Although he was harshest in denouncing masturbation, he was vitriolic about sexual "excess" of any sort. He described "venereal indulgence" as sweeping over the body "with the violence of a tornado," even among married couples. Rather than regard that as a good thing, he warned: "too frequently repeated [it] cannot fail to produce the most terrible effects." These included insanity, debility, and death. Chilling as his words were, Graham was not the only nineteenth-century American to have dire things to say about sexuality. *Chastity* was just one among many similar books attacking masturbation and calling for sexual restraint, but unlike many of the others, it was part of a general scheme of hygiene. Graham's advice to any man "troubled by concupiscence" was virtually a summary of his whole regimen. Such a person should be "more abstemious, and less stimulating and heating in his diet, and take more active exercise in the open air, and use the cold bath under proper circumstances."

Deep psychological forces may have caused Graham to link sexual indulgence and eating habits as menaces to health, but he felt the two had something very obvious in common. Both came from "weaknesses" within human beings. Graham recast original sin into biological terms: it was raging and destructive bodily appetites, which the sanctified person had to resist. The road to heaven was paved with restraint in food and sex; those who yielded to temptation were doomed. Salvation was freedom from illness and infirmity; the hellfire Graham preached for lechers and gluttons was dissolution of their bodies. The Kingdom of God depended upon abstemiousness. According to the Grahamite American Physiological Society, "the millennium can never reasonably be expected to arrive, until those laws which God has implanted in the physical nature of man are, equally with his moral laws, universally known and obeyed." That was a curiously physical theology for a former clergyman. Although not openly in conflict with Protestantism, the message was subversive. It depended upon science and physiology rather than the Bible. The millennium and the perfection it promised did not require divine revelation, church attendance, or a conversion experience. All one had to do was follow rational laws of health, easily understood by common people, without help from clergy or physicians.

Whatever Graham's program cost a person in sensual pleasures, it repaid in autonomy. Mastery of the diet meant mastery of oneself and one's destiny. Like evangelical Protestantism, temperance, and many other antebellum reforms, the Graham regimen instilled discipline and a willingness to forgo gratification in its followers, virtues that led to survival, even success, in industrial and commercial societies. Self-controlled people who do not fritter away time or energy are not necessarily pleasant companions, but they are fine employees and businesspeople. They are not likely to be overwhelmed by the confusion of city life or by religious and political turmoil. They have no need to look beyond themselves for moral guidance, a considerable comfort in a day when other sources of moral authority seemed unreliable. Even in the hustle and bustle of New York City a Grahamite could prosper, be virtuous, and preserve many Protestant and rural patterns, including plain living. For women, works like Graham's that emphasized the need for sexual restraint by men offered something else: the prospect of greater control over reproduction and sexuality, as well as the repudiation of a double standard that demanded chastity for women while tolerating male indiscretions.

The regimen may have been a psychological help for Grahamites coping with a society in flux, but it had another advantage as well. It was healthy. Even though nineteenth-century Americans did not have the latter-day perils of additives and junk food, they ate badly. Wealthy and middle-class people gorged themselves on rich dishes. Poor people ate food that was ill preserved, ill prepared, and not always nutritionally sound. Graham's diet was extreme, but an improvement. He was similarly right to urge exercise and to attack Americans for their reluctance to let fresh air into their houses, trains, and public buildings. Bathing also proved to be a good idea once people got used to it.                              .

Concern for the well-being of the public appeared in many different places in antebellum America, ranging from advice books for homemakers to medical publications like a *Journal of Health*, begun in 1829 by prominent doctors in Philadelphia and possibly an influence upon Graham. Someone with Graham's magnetism and a more conciliatory personality might have tied this widespread sentiment into a unified movement. As it was, health reform remained amorphous and Graham's role was primarily that of inspiration and occasional nuisance.

There was, however, no shortage of institutions and publications to spread the gospel. Much of the activity was in Boston. In 1837 Grahamites in that city formed the American Physiological Society. It had a membership of more than two hundred before a year was out, and it soon began publication of the *Graham Journal of Health and Longevity*. In 1838, Bostonians were instrumental in calling the first Health Convention, which drew a mixed crew of reformers—including many abolitionists—from New England and New York. Yet the movement itself faltered after the financial panic of 1837. The second Health Convention, held in New York in 1839, was a success in terms of numbers attending, but it ran up debts that had to be paid by a wealthy Bostonian. There would not be a third one. Also in 1839 the *Graham Journal* ceased publication and the New England branch of health reform suffered its cruelest blow. The American Physiological Society sought, and failed, to receive incorporation from the commonwealth of Massachusetts. One politician declared "people might eat bricks, bran, or saw-dust, or anything they chose, but that subject was entirely beneath the notice of the legislature."

Fortunately for the cause, it did not depend on the Massachusetts legislature. Grahamism, along with the other body reforms, was national in scope. Although strongest in Boston and New York City, it had converts throughout New England and across the country. The *Graham Journal*, for instance, had an agent in Crawfordsville, Georgia, and the second Health Convention had delegates from as far away as the West Indies. Through the years, publications and local societies, many of them for women, kept health reform alive. In small towns and larger cities Grahamites set up stores and boardinghouses run on correct principles; these apparently acted as gathering points for crusaders of all sorts who happened to be in the neighborhood. By 1840 Grahamism had a major bastion in the West. Oberlin College, sympathetic to every antebellum reform, invited former *Graham Journal* editor and former Garrisonian abolitionist David Cambell to run the student commons. Many of Graham's teachings had been put into practice before Cambell and his wife arrived, but his appointment marked Oberlin's full, although brief, commitment to health reform. (Cambell resigned in 1841, after protests from parents, students, faculty, and townspeople, some of whom described the food as "inadequate to the demands of the human system as at present developed.") Despite setbacks, health reform endured, increased its audience, and went through schisms and many other changes after 1840.

Graham's part in this larger movement was small. During much of the greatest excitement in Boston he stayed in western Massachusetts, away from the center of things. When he did reappear, he often proved to be a divisive rather than unifying force. As the movement widened, his view contracted. Although he had always advocated a general plan of hygiene, he came to place more emphasis on diet than many health reformers thought was wise. That side of Graham is obvious in his *Treatise on Bread and Bread-Making* (1837) with its glorification of bygone days when mothers supposedly did all the family baking and used only coarse, wholesome flour. Some of that may have been nostalgia for an imagined past (Graham's mother probably was mentally unbalanced and had difficulty caring for him, her youngest child). Surely, it was a criticism of the way in which industrialization moved production of items like bread out of the household and into commercial enterprises. Whatever it represented, the *Treatise* neither endeared him to bakers nor restored him to the forefront of health reform. Even his return to the speaking circuit and his ambitious *Lectures on the Science of Human Life*, both in 1839, left him a leader more in name than in fact.

It was another native of Connecticut, Dr. William Andrus Alcott, who reached the broad constituency Graham felt he deserved. Four years younger than Graham, Alcott became a schoolteacher at eighteen. A serious illness inspired him to study medicine, which he did in the mid-1820s, receiving his training at Yale. For the next several years his life took twists and turns, in part because he was dogged by illness. In 1831 he came to Boston to edit an educational journal and a periodical for children; by then he was thirty-three and his career as a writer was under way. Before it was over he had published scores of books and hundreds of shorter pieces on almost every aspect of moral and healthful living.

Although sometimes at odds with Graham, Alcott was a devoted health reformer and first president of the American Physiological Society. Alcott stressed a strict vegetarian diet, with no tea, coffee, alcohol, or spices, but his interests were more catholic than Graham's and he was not so committed to bran bread as the cornerstone of health. He dispensed advice to young men, to young women, to mothers, and to anyone who would listen, on gymnastics, proper reading matter, manners, friendship, ventilation, sex, diet, education, and much more. The book-buying public was eager to be told how to live and behave, probably because families and churches were no longer conveying that information satisfactorily. Alcott sensed the market and spoke to it in language that was neither theological nor overly technical. His message may also have been effective precisely because it touched on so many things. A person could achieve full potential, Alcott implied, only by attending to all the details of life.

In spite of Alcott's success, health reform in the 1840s and 1850s went the way of most antebellum crusades. Rather than coalescing as it gained a hearing, it subdivided. Some members remained staunch Grahamites, with bran bread as their bible; others followed Alcott's broader path. Still others dwelt upon some particular aspect of health and hygiene. Exercise, especially, had zealous promoters. (Since the 1820s Americans had been influenced by German gymnastic practices and by European educational theories linking physical and mental development.) But it was hydropathy more than anything else that marked a new departure for health reformers after 1840.

Originating in Europe, hydropathy was a system of cleansing the body—and presumably curing it—by bathing and filling it with water in every imaginable manner. Like the Graham diet, the water cure was the bane of trained medical men and singularly attractive to all kinds of reformers, including numerous abolitionists. Also like the Graham diet, it probably did some good, especially because it was linked to a comprehensive, holistic regimen involving exercise, nutrition, temperance, and healthy living in general. Through following hydropathic precepts, individuals (with help from water-cure practitioners, publications, and establishments) could take responsibility for their own well-being. By 1845 the cause had its own periodical, *The Water-Cure Journal* (with a circulation of 10,000 by 1849), and it had a national organization four years later in the American Hydropathic Society. Hydropathy appealed strongly to women. It endorsed medical training for them and offered a sense of sisterhood, as well as an escape from husbands and families, in gender-segregated hydropathic resorts. It may also have offered relief from otherwise untreatable urogenital infections and reproductive problems.

No one better symbolized the transition from Grahamism to hydropathy than Mary Gove Nichols. In 1838 she ran a Graham boardinghouse in Boston and lectured to female audiences on physiology and related subjects. In the remaining forty-six years of her life she wrote fiction, divorced, had an affair, was drawn to communitarianism, advocated free love, advocated chastity, participated in séances, became a Catholic, claimed the power to heal, and moved to England. In the midst of that pilgrimage she was exposed to hydropathic theories; after studying at water-cure establishments in Vermont and New York in 1845, she became an evangelist for the cause.

Mary Gove Nichols never entirely lost her early health reform principles: what is significant is the way she, and others like her, subordinated and reshaped them. Hydropathy and the Graham diet were quite compatible (they often went together), but the water cure became the overriding concern of Nichols and many of her later colleagues. Hydropathy offered greater possibilities than Grahamism for binding its believers in literal, if temporary communities, not to mention greater entrepreneurial opportunities. Other than writing and lecturing there was little one could do to make a career out of extending Grahamite principles. To be sure, there had been many Graham boardinghouses, but those were small operations, unable to promise the dramatic results, or charge the higher rates, of water-cure resorts. Hydropathy could be practiced at home, but it also mandated building and operating fair-sized establishments, with facilities for patients and for students of the art. By the mid-1850s these numbered at least sixty-two, with more to come in the next decade. They dotted the landscape from coast to coast, springing up in such out-of-the-way places as rural Oregon and Sacramento, California—wherever there was clean water and a clientele searching for good health or a respite from family members.

Besides marking a new stage in health reform, water cures signaled the beginning of a quest for legitimacy. Mary's second husband, Thomas Nichols, went back in 1850 to complete conventional medical studies. Until their conversion to Catholicism in 1857 the Nicholses worked strenuously to make water-cure training more formal and respectable—more "professional." They founded the American Hydropathic Institute in 1851, which offered a full scientific, medical, and physiological curriculum. Similar efforts continued well after the Civil War, most notably in New York City by Dr. Russell Trall, whose Hygeio-Therapeutic College was incorporated in 1857 and was to be the hydropathic counterpart of conventional medical schools. The professional ambitions of the Nicholses and Trall were ironic in a movement originating with Sylvester Graham, who believed that people were healthiest when they avoided irritating foods and medical men.

The American Medical Association eventually achieved its monopoly at the expense of hydropathy (which declined in the 1870s) and other now discredited panaceas, of which there were hundreds. But many health reform ideas gained wide acceptance, even among Graham's archenemies in the medical profession. Doctors who scorned Graham's "quackery" often gave advice very much like his: they urged a moderate diet, cleanliness, sexual restraint, exercise, and avoidance of stimulants. They may have refused to go to his extremes or to accept the exaggerated claims reformers made for preventing and curing diseases, but on principles of health and underlying moral values, regular physicians and Grahamites were in greater agreement than their mutual hostility made it seem.

Health reform had widespread effects and a broad constituency, comprising reformers such as communitarians and abolitionists, some affluent people, and young men and young women who had more hope than social position. Exercise and fresh air became especially respectable and popular, even in social circles where bran bread was not—there is testimony to that in the multitude of parks created and gymnasia built in antebellum America. Through William Andrus Alcott, health reform also had an impact on the development of school systems. He promoted the idea that students should work in a hygienic environment, have periods of recreation, and be taught the elements of good health. These recommendations filtered into Horace Mann's landmark *Reports* to the Massachusetts Board of Education, and in 1850 physiology and hygiene became a required course of study in Massachusetts schools, as Alcott had hoped. Health reform also had a role in shaping some nineteenth-century religious sects, who combined its physical perfectionism with the older theological variety. In the case of the Seventh-Day Adventists, the connection was direct. The denomination's founder Ellen White was a Grahamite and a believer in hydropathy. A prominent layman, John Harvey Kellogg, ran a huge health care establishment at Battle Creek, Michigan, where he practiced many of the old physiological doctrines. Although bran bread failed to become a staple of the national diet, traces of Grahamism survive in what we are taught, how we live, and how some of us worship.

"For more than forty years," an exasperated phrenologist wrote in 1882, "we have been trying to convince the world, that in examination of the head we do not look for 'bumps.' " Even at that late date he was rankled by critics who pictured phrenologists as charlatans charging fees for feeling the skulls of ignorant men and women. Phrenology was something more than that. Like health reform, it was an assertion that biological "laws" could be used to uplift humankind. It was also a system of psychology, a form of career and marital counseling, and the nineteenth-century equivalent of educational testing.

Although it may have seemed like nothing more than groping for bumps, serious phrenology involved carefully charting the shape of a person's cranium. Rather than assume that the mind is a single entity, phrenologists divided it into thirty-seven "faculties." These corresponded to personality traits: an individual could have too much, too little, or just the right amount of each. Take, for example:

AMATIVENESS—the faculty of physical love lends attractiveness to the opposite sex and a desire to unite in wedlock and enjoy their company. *Excess*: Tendency to licentiousness. *Deficiency*: Indifference to the other sex.

Every one of the thirty-seven faculties was represented in an "organ," or position on the head, the size of which indicated its strength or weakness. (Amativeness was located at the base of the skull, between the ears.) To this point, phrenology was a science: that is, a serious attempt, given the state of knowledge in the nineteenth century, to understand how the mind functioned.

On a superficial level, phrenology was a variety of biological determinism—after all, there is not much people can do about the shape of their heads. Logic, however, never stopped the antebellum perfectionist impulse. In defiance of intellectual consistency, phrenologists argued that men and women could indeed take immediate steps to remedy defective organs. Once made aware of their characters through phrenological analysis, they could take advantage of assets and compensate for liabilities. More surprising, phrenologists further insisted that substandard "organs" could be improved by exercise, diet, education, new surroundings, or other means. Rather than assert that people were prisoners of bone structure, phrenologists assured them that they could be better than their skulls indicated. The goal of the science was to show individuals "what they are, and what they can be, as well as how to make themselves what they should become." Orson Fowler reduced that to a cheery cliché: "Self Made or Never Made."

The founder of phrenology might have blanched, had he lived to hear Fowler's words. He was a German physician named Franz Joseph Gall, born in 1758. From his days as a medical student, Gall had begun to note connections between facial types, configurations of the skull, and personal characteristics. Over the years he made thousands of meticulous observations. His was the first, best, and nearly the last de-

tailed empirical research done by a phrenologist. By 1802 Gall set off
to spread his findings across most of Europe, accompanied by his pupil
Johann Spurzheim. They eventually settled in Paris, where Gall acquired a distinguished clientele and, in collaboration with Spurzheim,
wrote large medical treatises on the nervous system and the brain. It
was Spurzheim who cast their work in popular form, coined the word
"phrenology," and claimed that it was a means of perfecting humankind, somewhat to Gall's disapproval.

Beyond a handful who had heard Gall's lectures in Paris, few Americans knew of phrenology until the 1820s. In 1822, however, a group
consisting largely of prominent Philadelphia doctors created the Central Phrenological Society, evidence of rising awareness in the medical
profession. Two years later, Dr. Charles Caldwell published the first
phrenological book written by an American. By the end of the decade
works by Spurzheim and especially by George Combe, a Scottish lawyer, were reaching a broad audience. But Spurzheim's trip to America
in 1832 did more than any other event to bring the subject before the
people. He charmed and impressed his hosts in New England, lectured, performed a public dissection of a brain, observed criminals and
inmates of asylums, and behaved like the medical celebrity he was.
Unfortunately, his organ of vitativeness ("love of life; a desire to exist") was not strong. He died in Boston after little more than two
months in the United States. Even in death he served science. A Harvard professor conducted a public autopsy of Spurzheim, coupling it
with a phrenological lecture and preserving the brain as a specimen.
Spurzheim would have wanted it that way.

Phrenology continued to gain a hearing throughout the 1830s.
Combe had already advanced the cause in the United States through
his influential *The Constitution of Man*, described many years after by
an American phrenologist as "not surpassed in scope and value by any
work in any language." His own eighteen-month tour of North America, begun in 1838, was a social success—he met presidents, past and
future, and befriended writers, bankers, medical men, and reformers.
The visit was especially opportune for phrenology. Combe drew attention to the subject while treating it in a manner dignified enough
to sustain his scientific credentials.

The impressive performances of Spurzheim and Combe gave phrenology credibility among ladies and gentlemen of intellect and standing. Horace Mann brought its principles to bear on educational practices and treatment of the insane. He was so much an enthusiast that he named a child after Combe. Phrenology also claimed a convert in Henry Ward Beecher, Lyman's son and, after mid-century, the best-known clergyman in America. While a student at Amherst in 1833, Beecher took on the task of attacking phrenology in a debate. After reading about it, he changed sides. The list of prominent supporters went on and on, and the very terminology of the "science" crept into the public discourse of the day. Good fiction and bad, essays, sermons, and political oratory contained references to its "faculties," "organs," and—yes—bumps.

Lecturers carried phrenology across the land, to rural folk as well as urban, to poor as well as rich, Southerners and Westerners as well as Northerners. Practitioners dispensed character analysis along the highways and byways of the nation (beware of the man who "has great development between and back of the ears and is short in front . . . he is not intelligent, but very passionate, selfish, base, and animal in his instincts"). Professionals helped individuals find occupations and spouses by means of its principles. Publications proclaimed the glory of phrenology, told people how to apply it, and offered further assistance for a fee.

In the midst of this activity, local phrenological societies formed, some of them with libraries, plaster casts, and real skulls available for study. These organizations often drew members of the local elite, and a few had considerable staying power. Many, nonetheless, met the fate of the Phrenological Society of Cincinnati, as described by an English traveler. Founded by "between twenty and thirty of the most erudite citizens," the society's "first meeting dissolved with every appearance of energetic perseverance in scientific research." One half the original number showed up for the second meeting "and they enacted rules and laws, and passed resolutions, sufficient, it was said, to have filled three folios." A third meeting was set, at which time subscriptions to the society were to be paid. Only the treasurer came.

Reluctant though Americans might be to pay membership dues,

they had given phrenology a fair hearing by 1840. But those who endorsed it divided into two camps. Some regarded phrenology as a serious science, to be investigated with care and precision. These men and women, quite intellectually responsible, had no means of setting professional standards, since phrenologists did not bother to hold a national convention or create a national organization—the American Phrenological Society—until 1849. By that time a second, much larger group predominated. It consisted of "practical" phrenologists, less interested in research than in giving character readings and in trying to solve immediate problems of human unhappiness. The split in the ranks eroded the discipline's scientific respectability but increased its constituency in the 1840s and 1850s, as phrenologists fanned out into the hinterland, unhampered by a code of ethics.

Of all the practical phrenologists, none was more practical than the Fowler brothers. Orson was an Amherst classmate of Henry Ward Beecher and he combined the passion of an evangelist with very secular abilities. Abandoning thoughts of becoming a clergyman, Orson and his brother Lorenzo became missionaries for phrenology in the 1830s. It was primarily their ambition and entrepreneurial skill that set them apart from the hundreds of men and women also taking to the field to promote the new fad.

In common with touring phrenologists, the Fowlers were as much showmen as reformers or scientists. They lectured to an audience and, simultaneously, engaged in a battle of wits with it, inviting it to debate and test the accuracy of phrenology. More than one practical joker, hoping for a demonstrably false analysis, took the challenge and presented an unsuspecting phrenologist with the village scoundrel, looking innocent for the occasion. Phrenologists reported their triumphs in these cases; literature and local lore recorded their failures. But where the majority of their competitors eked out a living on the road, the Fowlers set up headquarters in New York City in 1835 from which they constructed an enterprise of considerable vitality, run by themselves and assorted relatives.

The keystone of the operation was a publishing house, Fowlers and Wells, which began the *American Phrenological Journal* in 1837 and ground out countless books on the subject. The company also printed works on temperance and health reform (there were many in those crusades who endorsed phrenology): it took over *The Water-Cure Journal* in 1848 and kept Sylvester Graham's *Science of Human Life* and *Chastity* on its list at least into the 1880s. Not content with that, Fowlers and Wells acted as an agency for phrenological lecturers, ran a museum of cranial curiosities in New York, with branches in Boston and Philadelphia, and sold various artifacts—among them, plaster casts of famous heads, a model of the brain, and real human and animal skulls. At one time the company boasted of being the largest mail-order business in New York. The Fowlers earned a place in the annals of capitalism as well as of reform.

Despite their managerial talents, Fowlers and Wells and their colleagues would not have been successful if they had failed to address real concerns of nineteenth-century Americans. There are clues to phrenology's appeal in the fact that much of it was advice to people seeking the right mate, employee, or employer. In a period of social fluidity and high geographic mobility, it was difficult to know whom to trust. Phrenology provided answers. It let businessmen assess potential workers and clients and permitted men and women to calculate their prospects for future happiness together. Before phrenology, an enthusiast declared, "the wisest of men had no means of deciding, with anything like certainty, the talents or character of a stranger." In the same fashion it assisted individuals trying to choose from among the new opportunities opening up in the wake of economic development. The *American Phrenological Journal* received ample thanks from young men who had been unsure of a course to pursue, only to be set straight after phrenological analysis. Phrenology allowed Americans to make crucial predictions about themselves and others with nothing more than an easily acquired knowledge of basic principles, available by mail from Fowlers and Wells.

Unlike most antebellum pseudo-sciences, phrenology lived to a ripe old age. The publishing house of Fowlers and Wells lasted into the twentieth century; the *American Phrenological Journal* did not disappear until 1911. But a combination of internal weaknesses and external events sent phrenology into a decline decades earlier. Few "discoveries" were made after the 1840s: virtually all practitioners shunned research in favor of pronouncing the same principles over and over. Phrenology simply did not—could not—grow as a science. Meanwhile, more dynamic disciplines overshadowed it. By the end of the century serious scholars ignored Gall and Spurzheim and looked to William James, G. Stanley Hall, and other gifted psychologists for more exciting discussions of the human mind. The general public likewise found more reliable sources of information or became bored. Lack of innovation by relatively responsible operators like the Fowlers left a profitable field open for rascals who discredited the whole enterprise by mixing phrenology with fortune-telling, magic, and greed.

Although it ended as little more than a sideshow attraction, phrenology was both a reform movement and the beginning of a retreat from a belief in human perfectibility. That curious position is clearest when phrenology is set alongside the so-called American School of anthropology, current in the 1840s and 1850s. The "school" consisted mainly of several scientific treatises dealing with racial differences, which the authors measured partially in terms of the average cranial capacity of each "racial" group. Since people assumed that humans with the largest heads were smartest, the implications of these measurements were considerable. The American School "discovered" from analysis of its samples that white men were superior and other groups trailed behind. This was a strong and early example of enlisting "science" to serve racism and sexism, somewhat shunned at the time because it conflicted with the biblical version of creation (writers of the American School argued that the races did not stem from Adam and Eve but had separate origins). It may seem as if phrenology had much in common with the American School, an impression borne out by the latter's seminal work, Dr. Samuel George Morton's *Crania Americana* (1839), devoted to painstaking cranial measurements and descriptions of racial "characteristics." Morton permitted George Combe to add a chapter on phrenology. Yet that, and a mutual interest in skulls, was not enough to make the two men comfortable allies. Morton was wary of phrenology and ignored opportunities to try to "prove" its virtues. Combe was not entirely satisfied with the work or with Morton's attitude toward him.

The differences between the American School and phrenology were more serious than even Morton and Combe may have sensed. The American School sought to prove that the character of human beings was fixed for eternity: white people were white people, others were others, women were not men, and there was nothing to do except recognize the truth. That line of reasoning cut against phrenologists' doctrines and practices. Their role, as they saw it, was to help individuals understand their nature in order to make them better, not to keep them in their place.

Despite its hopefulness about the improvability of humankind, phrenology had a part in preparing the public to accept later nineteenth-century biological determinism. Indeed, the English patron saint of eugenics, Francis Galton, resorted to a phrenological examination at a dispirited point in his life. There was an ominous foreshadowing of the future in phrenological advice such as that Nelson Sizer gave to a potential suicide. "[Y]our organism," Sizer counseled, "not your fate, is at fault." Sizer meant that the person's problems were rooted in his or her physical being, but they could be solved. Later kinds of "science" rejected the last part of the sentence. Phrenologists, like health reformers, were sailing into uncharted waters when they pictured mortality and virtue as dependent on the body. Once that assumption was made, optimism about humankind became fragile. The appearance in 1859 of Charles Darwin's evolutionary theory, coupled with the failure of reform itself, made it easier to decide that biology is destiny after all, and thus beyond the efforts of do-gooders to change. In the antebellum years, however, phrenologists and Grahamites had no way of anticipating how biological thought could be turned against them and any scheme of social uplift. They believed that the body set limits on human potential; but they were reformers precisely because they believed those limits could be transcended.

In a different, but equally significant, manner, spiritualism also dealt with issues of body, soul, and human progress. These concerns, nonetheless, seldom troubled the two girls who began the antebellum craze of "spirit-rapping." They were Kate and Margaret Fox, aged about twelve and fifteen, daughters of a poor farming family living about thirty miles east of Rochester, New York. In the winter and spring of 1848 strange knocking noises kept everyone in the house awake at night. The girls made the sounds respond to their words and, by means of a code, to signal answers to questions. Neighbors gathered to hear the revelations. The knocks, the girls claimed, came from the spirit of a peddler, murdered in the house and buried beneath it years earlier. A hasty excavation of the cellar revealed no bones, although stories have it that some were found later.

Failure to find a skeleton in the family basement did not stop the Foxes. The sisters were believed and challenged, praised and denounced. Some neighbors avoided them and there was attempted exorcism. Despite that, the knocking persisted wherever they went. An older sister, Leah, took the girls to Rochester, where they gave demonstrations of "spirit-rapping." Soon Leah and an early disciple, Eliab W. Capron, were promoting Kate and Margaret skillfully, at first locally in the Burned-Over District, then in New York City, and eventually elsewhere in the United States and England. Belief in spirits was ancient, but this was different: a system of communication between living and dead, available for public observation.

In 1888 Margaret and Kate, both of whom had had bouts of alcoholism, confessed that the noises came from a cracking sound they made with the joints of their big toes. It began as a prank. Margaret later denied she and Kate were frauds. In 1849 and 1850, however, the girls put forth revelation after revelation from the great beyond. Soon word came of similar happenings in other places. The dead were suddenly garrulous, speaking out in séances and public gatherings, rapping and banging, bumping furniture, or merely holding private conversations with mediums. As with every antebellum crusade, spiritualism took strongest hold in the Northeast and Ohio. New York led the way in mediums (seventy-one to Massachusetts' fifty-five in 1859) and probably in numbers of believers. Within a few years, however, spiritualist periodicals spread the cause across the land (there were sixty-seven of them by 1857); and there was no shortage of seers bringing the spirit world to the cities and small towns of America.

Spiritualism crossed class lines as easily as geographic boundaries. A prominent New York jurist was a founder of the Society for the Diffusion of Spiritual Knowledge in 1854, and among the other early promoters was a former territorial governor of Wisconsin and United States senator from New York. Middle-class reformers, well-educated and distinguished people, were fascinated, but so were men and women who were ignorant, credulous, and poor. In the nineteenth century, as well as the twentieth, no group had a monopoly on hearing messages from other worlds.

As it grew, spiritualism, like temperance and phrenology, became a form of popular entertainment. Spiritualists baited their opponents, submitted to examination by "experts," and generally encouraged audiences to test them. In that respect they and phrenologists were not so different from P. T. Barnum, the showman, who dared the antebellum public to determine if his exhibits were marvels of nature or hoaxes. There were, of course, those who scoffed at spiritualists, and even acts of mob violence against them. But the worst that usually could be demonstrated was that the rappings might have been produced fraudulently, not that they were.

The staunchest critics of spiritualism were ministers. Clergy were appalled at the high number of unchurched men and women, religious liberals, and—later—sexual radicals drawn to the movement. Such people were bound to preach dangerous doctrines. Sometimes they did. On the rare occasions spiritualists talked about God, they described him or her as an amorphous entity, pervading all existence and not intervening in human affairs. Spiritualist theology collapsed God, nature, and humankind into a harmonious unity, while insisting that people kept distinct personalities after death—an example of American individualism conquering metaphysics. In the phrase of one leading spiritualist, God was the "Supernal Soul of Nature"—a far cry from the omnipotent being of Calvinism and one of the most cumbersome labels ever given a deity. Some spiritualists described Christ as no more than an extraordinarily capable medium, declared that hell did not exist, and dismissed Protestant doctrines of predestination, atonement, and salvation. Sin, in the words of Andrew Jackson Davis, was "an atavism, merely." Rather than be unorthodox and leave it at that, a few spiritualists were aggressively hostile to organized religion. Davis spoke of going to church as a matter of putting innocent young minds "in the pen, with those domestic animals known as *cat*-echism and *dog*-matism." The "contact," he concluded, "is contaminating to the last degree."

Ministers fought back, but they were not entirely correct to believe that spiritualism was antithetical to Christianity. Anti-religious spiritualists were balanced by those who believed that Christianity and spiritualism reinforced each other. Even where spiritualists were unorthodox, their heresies were not unique in antebellum America. Well before the Fox sisters' rapping sounds, some Americans had accepted the teachings of Emanuel Swedenborg, an eighteenth-century Scandinavian mystic who conversed with spirits. (For a variety of reasons, however, Swedenborgians usually disavowed spiritualism.) Universalists had previously abolished hell; Transcendentalists had formed a conception of God as amorphous as that of spiritualists; and members of several sects had pretty much done away with the concept of sin.

It is, nonetheless, futile to argue whether spiritualism and Protestantism were enemies. For some people they were, for others they were not. Furthermore, Americans had an ability to keep what they believed at a séance separate from what they professed in church on Sunday. They did not exert themselves to find inconsistencies. Thousands of men and women came to spiritualism for reasons distinct from their theology. For some, it was a chance to see a show and, in the bargain, to ponder life and death. For others, it offered solace. Many and touching are the stories of conversations people had with departed parents, spouses, and children.

Because spiritualism frequently was a private experience, undertaken for intensely personal motives, it was difficult to form institutions to propagate the faith. People preferred lectures and séances to rules, regulations, and meetings. Local and state societies appeared and disappeared. Conventions, summer camps, and spiritualistic Sunday schools came and went. Communitarian societies were founded on spiritualistic principles and vanished quickly. Like the phrenologists, spiritualists were late in creating a national association and had trouble keeping it going. The National Organization of Spiritualists—later called the American Association of Spiritualists—lasted only from 1864 to 1873. Institutional weakness, as well as the large element of entertainment and fraud involved in spirit-rapping, make it hard to think of spiritualism as an antebellum reform.

It was primarily through the efforts of Andrew Jackson Davis that spiritualism became a reform movement, although an odd and limited one. Like the Fox sisters, Davis began his contacts with the spirits in rural New York, where, as a boy, he had experiences with "animal magnetism," or hypnotism. Instead of rappings, he heard voices and carried on conversations with dead people, including Swedenborg. By 1847 the "Poughkeepsie Seer," age twenty-one, was in New York City, explaining the origins of the universe, suggesting how society might be improved, and, in a trance, dictating his discoveries. The title of his book was no more modest than its nearly eight-hundred-page length: *The Principles of Nature, Her Divine Revelation, and a Voice to Mankind.* The reviews were mixed. A few took it for what it claimed to be. Others dismissed it as nonsense and accused Davis of plagiarizing the work of his long-deceased spirit friend Swedenborg. All this was happening months before the Fox family lost sleep over noises in the night.

Davis claimed that Kate and Margaret Fox demonstrated the validity of his work, but he and the sisters moved in different circles. The girls had little interest in ideas or in changing the world. Davis, on the contrary, believed that higher spheres were trying to help humans transform this one and he did his part to assist them. He endorsed virtually every contemporary reform, including antislavery, temperance, and woman's rights. He and his followers, furthermore, took action of their own to hasten the dawn of the new day. They created "Harmonial Brotherhoods" to discuss and implement his teachings; and in 1863 Davis organized the Children's Progressive Lyceum, a spiritualist alternative to Sunday schools that by 1871 had branches in seventeen states and in Britain. Also in 1863 he began the Moral Police Fraternity, an attempt to use spiritualist principles to eliminate crime and poverty in New York City. It failed. Davis's commitment to reform remained strong after the Civil War and was a factor in 1878 when he broke with the mainstream of spiritualism, which he saw turning to magic and superstition.

Over the years Davis spun out his thoughts, and other people's, in a comprehensive "Harmonial Philosophy." Its intellectual origins were not extraterrestrial: a smattering of mesmerism; a big helping of Swedenborg; maybe a dash of Fourier; and surely a pinch of folklore. Added to that were his belief in science and natural law. Probably not even Davis was aware of all the influences that went into Harmonial Philosophy.

It is perhaps as well to let the roots of Davis's theories remain tangled and obscure. What mattered was the message. On one level, it was positive and unmystical. Davis did not counsel readers to lie back and listen to spirits. He urged them to think, to study, to receive wisdom from all sources, dead or alive, and to act. Spiritualism was not supernatural, in Davis's mind, but another kind of knowledge to be used for the benefit of mankind, as were science and technology.

Davis was clearer about his enemies than he was about his sources. He was opposed to religious sectarianism, the clergy, conflict between North and South, "the confusion among the political parties now so numerous," and unfair accumulation of property. That list is strikingly close to ones most other antebellum reformers would have made. He, and they, were against the disruptive and divisive forces then at work in the United States. He (and, again, they) wanted to expand freedom and erase political, religious, and many social distinctions. He wanted to preserve morality and make *"our country the best place in the world* for the industrious." He wanted perfect human beings and the millennium.

Even if a job that big required help from the great beyond, the good society Davis described in *The Harmonial Man* (1853) was not especially unearthly. The "Harmonial Republic" rested on "ORGANIC LIBERTY, which brings to every man his natural Rights and attractive Industry!" It was to be protected by *"Free speech . . . Free schools for the masses . . . Freedom of the press . . . Free churches and honest teachers . . .* And Nature's own religion." The government's role in such a society

would be limited and mostly protective: it would "permit no monop-
olizing of the land by the few, to the injury of the many," and it would
ensure that "Industry is Happiness." Most of those points brought
nods of agreement from reformers and a substantial number of non-
reformers. When the spirits gave such advice they told Americans to
live up to their own ideals.

In spite of Davis's efforts, much of spiritualism's significance for
reform came through its influence on men and women involved in
other crusades. The Reverend John Pierpont defended it as firmly as
he did phrenology and antislavery, while William Lloyd Garrison received an important communication on abolitionist tactics through a
medium in contact with a departed colleague. Robert Dale Owen, son
of Robert Owen and a reformer in his own right, was so impressed
with spiritualism that in 1859 he published a 528-page defense of it.
Hundreds of antebellum reformers, although not so verbose, were just
as taken by it, and for many of the same reasons they found Grahamism and phrenology appealing. All three causes provided support
for the notion that the nineteenth century was a special moment in
history; each was a sign of progress in understanding mankind and the
universe. Reformers also discovered in spiritualism a variant of their
own message that human beings had the power to transform themselves and, moreover, an obligation to do so. Since people remained
for eternity as they were in life, Owen concluded that spiritualism
proved "We are architects of our own destiny: we inflict our punish-
ments; we select our own rewards." More than a generation before,
the same faith sent Americans into communitarian societies (including
his father's) and into the antislavery and temperance movements.

Spiritualism also made its mark by erasing the old Christian line
between body and soul. "Matter is the foundation of Mind," Davis
declared. "Mind is the spiritualization of Matter." There, once again,
was the belief that no clear distinction exists between humankind's
moral and physical selves, a familiar enough notion in health reform
and phrenology, but evident in temperance, antislavery, and communitarianism as well.

Spiritualism similarly played a variation on another common theme in antebellum reform: a desire to create a world of harmony and order. In most reforms that meant eliminating the source of disorder, whether it was slavery, bad diet, alcohol, or politics. Spiritualism's answer was to assert that the world was harmonious. Despite chaos and uncertainty in the present, existence was a continuum, not bounded by the human body, space, or time.

On a more mundane level, spiritualism attracted reformers because it provided solace. Seldom, if ever, did a spirit do anything except encourage a reformer or suggest new directions. One young man claimed to be guided in his activities by Thomas Jefferson, whose postmortem opinion of slavery was nearly that of a Garrisonian abolitionist. The same young man later received advice on building a communitarian society from the spirits. Martin Luther was especially helpful with that endeavor. The young man's heavenly collaborators may also have endorsed sexual experimentation.

Clearly there was an unconscious element of self-serving in such dealings with the dead, as well as self-delusion. But reformers mistrusted older moral authorities—notably, clergymen and politicians—while wanting to find an anchor for moral certainty. Unless one based everything on individual conscience or traditional religion (and some reformers did), the only solution was to find a new dispensation. Physiological laws and voices from the spirit world were non-theological revelations and served as well as any others to reinforce the reformer's sense of what was right and wrong.

The issues between the "body reforms" and American Protestantism were never clearly joined, and the languages of "science" and religion mingled as often as they conflicted. Grahamites, phrenologists, and spiritualists frequently denied any quarrel between their crusades and Christianity. Clergy, for their part, spoke both for and against each cause. In a sense, that was appropriate, for the three movements each rephrased Protestant moralism, millennialism, and perfectionism in "scientific" and physical terms. The Kingdom of God became good health, understanding oneself and one's fellow humans, and communicating with the rest of the universe.

That, nonetheless, represented a significant change. Communitarianism, antislavery, and temperance, as well as the body reforms, inched away from formal religion and arguments based on the Bible (Sylvester Graham, a former minister, seldom referred to it). Each was part of a much larger nineteenth-century search for new, secular modes of understanding the world, rooted in an analysis of "human nature" and "science." A small but telling sign of the power of the latter was the frequent comparison spiritualists made between their contact with the dead and the recently invented telegraph. The Graham diet, phrenology, and spiritualism scarcely seem scientific by twentieth-century standards, but, like much of antebellum reform, they were often rationalistic and egalitarian. They insisted that by following easily understood rules every man and woman could achieve health and happiness, even reach past the fact of death. When reform made those promises it was both asserting its claim on this world and moving into religion's territory.

There were difficulties and unrealistic expectations when reformers cast their solutions in physical terms. It was misleading to think that perfection was an individual matter, gained through understanding the relation between body and soul. Better diet, phrenological principles, and spiritualism might lead to personal happiness, but they were little help with the deeper, less tractable problems of nineteenth-century America: poverty, economic uncertainty, and crime among them.

# EIGHT

# Dangerous Classes

Much twentieth-century reform aimed at doing things for the casualties of urban and industrial life, whether through settlement houses, consumer-protection legislation, Social Security, welfare, or other means. There was little sentiment for anything like that in antebellum America. Most commonly, reformers wanted either to stop a sinful practice, such as slave-holding or drinking, or else to help people help themselves without "charity." There was confidence that individuals could accomplish almost anything if they really wanted to, including overcoming alcoholism, ill health, and (with phrenology) the deficiencies of their own brain. If a person could do all that, surely he or she could conquer poverty. The notion was naïve. It was also not universal. Some middle-class reformers attempted to assist unfortunate and suffering Americans through voluntary associations; still others tried to improve the lot of working people. They were never as numerous or nationally organized as temperance advocates or abolitionists, but their endeavors show antebellum reform directly confronting the new industrial order. Working men and women themselves, moreover, were anything but silent sufferers and passive recipients of charity. Through their own actions they also confronted the new industrial order, sometimes with beliefs, goals, and tactics similar to those of other, more middle-class reformers, and sometimes in distinctly different ways.

• • •

The chief problem of antebellum cities was poverty, and neither it nor dealing with it began in the nineteenth century. Boston in 1664 opened a public almshouse to care for the indigent. Other cities slowly followed suit. Beginning in the late eighteenth century, private charity—spurred by the humanitarian doctrines of the day and by Christian piety—assumed a significant role in providing services for the needy. Within a few decades Americans formed a variety of voluntary agencies to help their destitute fellow citizens, always drawing a distinction between the deserving and the undeserving poor, the latter being idlers or criminals who got nothing but contempt. By the end of the first quarter of the nineteenth century, according to one historian, more than a hundred relief organizations had appeared in New York City alone, many of them short-lived and designed to meet particular crises. Americans generally assumed, however, that poverty was part of the social order and could never be eradicated, that neither the state nor individuals had an obligation to alleviate it, and that poor people were usually the cause of their own troubles. Those attitudes did not vanish after 1815, but they mingled with newer ones, particularly when evangelical Protestantism entered the picture. As we shall see in the next chapter, they also became bound up with institutional approaches to social problems.

As early as 1810, local Bible, tract, and missionary societies were making efforts to reach heathens in the cities as well as those in the West and in foreign lands. These organizations established urban missions and assigned particular neighborhoods to volunteers, who then called upon residents, distributing literature to them and inquiring about their spiritual state. Among the earliest was a Female Missionary Society in New York City in 1816, with similar organizations following in cities as distant as Boston and Charleston, South Carolina. Whatever else these visitations did, they exposed middle-class and wealthy Americans to the realities of squalor and vice. Many responded with efforts to treat worldly as well as spiritual problems. Among the enterprises arising out of this missionary zeal was, for instance, the Society for the Prevention of Pauperism in the City of New York.

Founded in 1817, its prime movers had ties to the evangelical "benevolent empire." Even the Episcopalian and two Quakers among its active leaders had been involved with such organizations as the American Bible Society. The society investigated both economic and moral aspects of slum life, suggested changes in city-run institutions, and opened savings banks to encourage thrift. It also sent out home visitors, corresponded with similar groups in other cities, and gathered statistics. One of its schemes involved selling firewood cheaply to poor families.

Contact with slum dwellers may have inspired well-to-do Protestants to create more organizations, but it did not necessarily lead them to feel empathy for their clients. If anything, the contact confirmed some charity workers in their dismal expectations about poor people. In 1821 women running a mission in a black district thought it a major triumph "that the torch of an incendiary has not been applied" to their building. Through the early 1820s people involved in urban charitable societies remained conservative and cautious—appropriately enough, given the significant wealth some possessed. They tended to see moral failings as the root cause of squalor and to insist that religion, temperance, and thrift were the cures (although firewood helped). They did not wish to upset relations between classes, and few expected to end poverty. If deserving poor people could be made pious and comfortable, the thought was, they would be less dangerous to themselves and to social stability.

By 1830 several things made poverty appear in a different light to Protestants. After 1819 there had been much pressure on states to stop imprisoning people for debt, a counterproductive practice that prevented debtors from paying their obligations and brought misery upon their families. Even Jacksonian Democrats, disdainful of moral crusades such as temperance, could defend debtors, some of whom were well-off speculators and many of whom voted. The cause was prevailing in the 1820s and agitation for it increased general awareness of the plight of the honest poor. At the same time, poverty in the cities appeared to be worsening, largely the result of urban population growth in the 1820s and the arrival of large numbers of immigrants, many of them destitute. In New York, Boston, Philadelphia, and other urban areas the extremes of wealth and deprivation were obvious and offensive in a supposedly democratic and bountiful nation. The oft-quoted French observer Alexis de Tocqueville remarked of his visit in 1831–32: "I look upon the size of certain American cities, and especially on the nature of their population, as a real danger which threatens the future security of the democratic republics of the New World . . ." He recommended creating an armed force "independent of the town population and able to repress its excesses." Native-born reformers shared his fear for the fate of the nation unless something was done to make the masses virtuous, contented, and American.

Charles G. Finney's brand of revivalism directed this growing perception of poverty into a new, activist campaign to bring Protestant benevolence into the city. Finney himself came to New York City in 1829 at the urging of—and with financial assistance from—Arthur Tappan and Anson Phelps, merchants heavily involved in tract distribution. He inspired them and all other reform-minded urban Protestants to renew their efforts to reach the unregenerate. Even among non-evangelical sects there was a sharp rise in city missionary activities after Finney's arrival on the scene. Indeed, an effect of evangelical activity was to spur Catholics to create charitable agencies of their own to keep church members out of the clutches of Protestant missionaries. Not all such efforts, of course, aimed at poverty or even necessarily at poor people. Many sought to suppress vice and immorality, and to provide support for virtuous young men and women in resisting the temptations of urban life. Their goal was as much to foster self-control as to exert social control over the poor. Even so, there were important and striking ways in which middle-class Protestants thrust themselves into the lives of their poor neighbors, especially through home visiting to dispense religious literature, advice, and assistance.

The home visitors of the 1830s never lost their sense of social distance from the people they met, but they were deeply touched by the misery they saw. Unlike their predecessors of the 1810s and 1820s, they had come to the task feeling that poverty and sin might be eradicated. Millennialism and perfectionism prepared them to believe that the whole nation might be converted; prosperity in the 1820s had made them think opportunities were limitless. In the slums, however, they found depravity and degradation more stubborn and crushing than they had imagined. They began dispensing larger amounts of support to the poor in the 1830s.

Optimism faded. Some urban ventures made more enemies than converts. The New-York Magdalen Society, for instance, was the center of a controversy within a year of its founding in the 1830s. It hired an enthusiastic young agent, the Reverend John McDowall, to help it save prostitutes from lives of penury and sin (and to save young men from "fallen women"). His first report scandalized New Yorkers with its claim that there were "not less than TEN THOUSAND" prostitutes in the city, not to mention kept women and ruined servant girls. The outcry against McDowall's accusations was so embarrassing that the society disbanded. A group of pious women, including Mrs. Finney, continued its work for many years, in a new guise and with greater discretion.

Poverty and not public hostility, however, was the real challenge to millennial expectations. After a few years of contact with the slums, missionary workers grew depressingly aware of the extent of destitution and vice. They lost confidence that they could eradicate it or the patterns of life it produced. As they became less hopeful, some fell back into their old habit of chiding poor people for being the authors of their own misery through intemperance and licentiousness. The Panic of 1837 made matters worse. Prompted by financial difficulties, which compromised every variety of antebellum reform, and by rising fears of disorder from the lower classes, many middle-class people withdrew from programs to aid the needy and accepted the solution we will deal with in the next chapter, the public almshouse. The ranks of paupers swelled at the very moment sympathy and aid for them dwindled.

Although the Protestant attack on poverty stalled in the late 1830s, it would never die, and its system of home visiting had important implications both for feminism (as some women came to see problems in terms of gender rather than class) and for the development of notions of "scientific charity" in the 1870s. Urban missionary activity, moreover, had effects having little directly to do with overcoming poverty. By insisting that it was as important to do God's bidding in the slums as in the West or in foreign lands, urban evangelicals did not reject the city as a hopeless cesspool of sin, as some of their peers did. (Finney himself left New York to preside over Oberlin College.) By the mid-1830s missionary and tract workers also brought to debates over poverty a hopefulness that something might be done about it. Their millennial faith was sorely tried by reality, but it was an admirable starting point and a countercurrent to the view of others, newly buttressed by British utilitarian thought, that charity itself encouraged poverty and dependence. Urban missionaries, moreover, saw firsthand the social factors that kept people from escaping the slums: unhealthy food and housing, bad family life, evil companionship, unemployment, and ignorance. The notorious first report of the New-York Magdalen Society, for instance, explained that much prostitution was "the result of sheer necessity, poverty rather than [preference]." That simple observation was an admission that degradation could be the product of economic and environmental forces.

Somewhat subdued, Protestant charitable endeavors continued past the Panic of 1837 and eventually converged with twentieth-century types of social welfare. The New York Association for Improving the Condition of the Poor provided an example of how the transition occurred. Formed in 1843 to relieve the New York City Tract Society of administering alms, it resembled earlier organizations by gathering data on health, education, and crime, and by using the old system of home visitors. But its volunteers functioned somewhat more like twentieth-century case workers, dispensing relief to particular clients and acting as intermediaries between them and the city's charitable and governmental services. As time went on, the association's approach became still more "scientific" and its staff less amateur. It tried to make charity rational and systematic, and lobbied for government help in such matters as education and the treatment of juvenile delinquents. The association also focused attention on tenement housing

and saw the slums as a menace to "public health." (That argument
became fashionable after the Civil War, when it played to middle-class
urbanites who cared more about epidemics and disease than about the
poor.)

Despite its "modern" approach, the association—which lasted into
the twentieth century—took decades to shake off its antebellum and
Protestant presuppositions about poverty. For years it counseled paupers to solve their own problems by righteous living and by going
West. Its longtime agent Robert Hartley coupled detailed investigations of slum conditions with sour remarks about the less worthy indigents, whom he called the "debased poor" and whom others referred
to as the "dangerous classes." If anyone mistook the association for a
secular social-service agency, Hartley's words would have dispelled the
illusion. One can hardly imagine a twentieth-century social worker, no
matter how desperate for funds, making the poetic appeal in Hartley's
eighth annual report (1851):

> *Give alms: the needy sink with pain;*
> *The orphans mourn, the crushed complain.*
> *Give freely: hoarded gold is curst,*
> *A prey to robbers and to rust.*
> *Christ, through his poor, a claim doth make,*
> *Give gladly, for thy Saviour's sake.*

It is not entirely clear whether Hartley was more concerned about the
recipient's soul or about the donor's.

By the late nineteenth century, the Protestant charitable apparatus
(and the Catholic one as well) grew to formidable proportions, even
though the government assumed many of its functions. Its beginnings,
however, were in the late eighteenth and early nineteenth centuries,
and for a time it was the best provider of essential services for the
destitute. Yet in the antebellum years it was difficult for evangelicals,
or any middle-class people, to see poverty very broadly or very intensely. Although the cities might have looked awful to them, their
own style of life was improving. Men and women of goodwill could

honestly believe that free land, moral uplift, and divine intervention would cure whatever ills there might happen to be. Given that perspective, charity workers deserve respect for their ability to learn and to adapt. Some of their number, like Hartley, could go a half step toward the view that prevailed for much of the twentieth century: the belief that social conditions, not just personal morality, have to be changed and that the state has a responsibility to do the job.

When antebellum reformers spoke sympathetically of poor people, they had in mind the helpless and virtuous ones—widows, orphans, and men ill or injured through no fault of their own. The honest workingman, according to reformers, had little to worry about. If he was temperate, thrifty, and careful about having children, he could, they thought, live in simple comfort. When they spoke of the "problems" confronting wage earners, it was often to promote their own causes (temperance was the key to success, abolition of slavery would elevate the condition of free workers, and phrenology could assist in finding a job). When middle-class reformers such as the abolitionists talked about conflict between capital and labor, they generally claimed it could be resolved once both sides realized each had an interest in the other's well-being. That analysis was superficial and not always persuasive to workingmen and -women. Beginning in the 1820s, an assortment of artisans, visionaries, politicians, and opportunists put together a series of working people's organizations to deal with industrial problems. In many respects these stand at the opposite extreme from Protestant missionary activities. Although the two kinds of endeavor used some of the same images and figures of speech, they shared virtually no personnel, drew leadership from different classes, and disagreed over the effectiveness of religion as a means of change. These organizations of working people, moreover, represented only a small fraction of the ways in which common men and women dealt with a new society they were helping bring into being. Such people also had—as a generation of late-twentieth-century scholars demonstrated—their own dense world of street life and public rituals, family relationships, ethnic and work cultures, neighborhoods, popular amusements, and institutions, most of which lay outside conventional notions of reform (and therefore outside this book). In the end, this world of working-class life probably did more than antebellum protest organizations, which proved fragile, to provide the base from which common people accommodated to, changed, shaped, understood, and found alternatives to the urban and industrial order. In the story of working people's organizations, nonetheless, there are commonalities and counterpoints to the rest of antebellum reform, as well as paths not taken and alternatives that failed.

By the mid-1820s there were hundreds of local labor societies. They appeared among skilled workers and offered a variety of mutual benefits and social opportunities, as well as allowing masters and journeymen to set rules and regulations for their craft. There was, then, nothing exceptional about a journeyman carpenters' association that went on strike in Philadelphia in 1827. Its demand was common in the 1820s and for the next two decades: it sought a ten-hour, rather than sunrise-to-sunset, workday. The response of fellow artisans, however, was unprecedented. The walkout, which failed, illustrated to them the need for skilled workers in every craft to pool funds and coordinate activities—otherwise it was difficult to win against determined employers. The result was the Mechanics' Union of Trade Associations, the first citywide federation of workingmen's groups. The fifteen or so member trades, seeking strength in numbers, pledged to aid one another in future disputes.

The Mechanics' Union was an important move toward solidarity among artisans, but for several years it was also an isolated venture. Lawsuits, politics, and an economic downturn took most of labor's resources between 1828 and 1832. Workingmen's groups put up candidates for office and struggled for survival. By 1833, nonetheless, trades' associations began to appear in New York and in cities as farflung as Boston, Baltimore, Washington, and Louisville. They sponsored newspapers, lobbied for legislation, and gave financial support to striking unions. Even though many labor groups remained independent of them, these trades' associations signaled a mobilization of a significant fraction of the workforce. Along with their growth came increases in the number of local unions and strikes. By the mid-1830s more than a hundred thousand (perhaps up to three hundred thousand) men and women belonged to a labor organization.

Much of the energy of the 1820s and 1830s came from artisans, or mechanics, as they were also known. Frequently used loosely, the terms apply to people who were knowledgeable in a craft requiring special training and equipment (shoemaking, for instance). Within each trade, artisans divided into masters (who were self-employed and hired assistants), journeymen (who were proficient in the craft and usually owned their tools, but who worked for wages), and apprentices (who were learning the craft under a master's supervision). Although differing among themselves in wealth and education, artisans in general were a labor elite. Their skills gave them a measure of independence in choosing when and how to practice their trade. They also had self-respect, a high rate of literacy, and a tradition of political involvement going back to before the Revolution. These characteristics made them the segment of the labor force quickest to perceive and to oppose threats to their interests.

After 1800 economic change upset their world of small shops. Master mechanics took advantage of cheaper transportation and increased production to reach wider markets, thanks to the spread of canals, turnpikes, steamboats, and, eventually, railroads. Such masters were more capitalists than workingmen, and their interests often clashed with those of the journeymen they hired, especially when they sought low wages and high output. When they could, ambitious master artisans replaced skilled help with unskilled and human beings with machines. Journeymen faced the possibility of dropping into the ranks of common laborers, with none of the autonomy and hoped-for advancement they once enjoyed. They resisted, and some of the fiercest antebellum labor conflict, including the Philadelphia carpenters' strike, was not across class lines (as people perceived them), but rather between masters and journeymen in the same trade.

Antebellum labor reform, however, was not just a response to the plight of the journeymen. Workers in many occupations were doing poorly, even in good years; and still others found their style of life

altered for the worse by the rise of the factory system. The antebellum
economy, for example, offered little security and low pay to the unskilled men who dug canals and built railroads, the stevedores who
loaded and unloaded ships in river towns and seaports, the sailors (a
high proportion of them African American) whose work was crucial for
American commercial expansion, and the men and women who became machine operatives in early factories. They nonetheless seldom
formed unions, were looked down upon by the craftsmen who did,
and remained on the periphery of the antebellum labor organizations.
In labor unrest, as in antebellum reform generally, it took more than
the existence of a problem to produce a movement.

Workingmen's societies, in fact, did best in periods of prosperity,
when skilled employees were in the strongest bargaining position, and
among people (such as carpenters) who were unlikely ever to become
factory hands. Workingmen's organizations were also stimulated—not
always for the better—by ideas and tactics from other antebellum crusades. With all manner of causes clamoring for attention, labor would
have found it difficult not to enter the public arena, or, for that matter,
to keep middle-class reformers out of its organizations and affairs.

Finally, the Jacksonian political style inspired workingmen's groups.
They divided over Jackson himself, but his call for common people to
participate in politics reinforced a long-standing tradition of artisan
activism that included strong engagement in Revolutionary-era politics. The Jacksonian attack on "monopolies" likewise resonated with
older republican ideology and encouraged them to mount their own
campaigns against the economic privileges enjoyed by their employers
and men of wealth.

The situations that triggered particular strikes varied and, overall,
the grievances of the mechanics were several and complex, as were
their capabilities and hopes. They were squeezed by inflation and their
employers; they knew how to build organizations and were politically
conscious; they felt skilled labor was not receiving the respect it deserved and that long workdays and harsher conditions further debased
it; and they saw the emerging capitalism of their day as a menace to
their traditional prerogatives and to American liberty. They also shared

antebellum reformers' confidence that the world could be made a better place. A variety of languages served to articulate the artisans' worldview, including one of "equal rights" derived from the Revolution, refashioned in the antebellum period to include property, and applied occasionally to women, though seldom extended by whites to African Americans.

In the summer of 1828 the Philadelphia Mechanics' Union of Trade Associations took off in a new direction. It resolved "to form a ticket for Assembly and City Councils to be supported by Mechanics and Working Men in the next General Elections." This inaugurated the first effort to draw substantial numbers of American workers into a labor party, distinct from, and in competition with, all other political organizations. The union made nominations of its own (its candidates lost) and endorsed sympathetic candidates put up by both major parties, some of whom won. It had become a full-fledged political organization and within two years others like it appeared throughout Pennsylvania, New Jersey, New York, and New England. Working Men's parties achieved impressive victories in Newark, New London, and Wilmington, Delaware, and they made considerable splashes in New York City and in New England. A few were spurious creations, assembled by politicians courting the labor vote, but many originated with artisans and addressed the issues they took most seriously.

The New York City Working Men's Party grew out of a series of mass meetings held in the spring of 1829 to resist an alleged plot by masters to extend the workday. (Ten hours was customary among the city's artisans.) A Committee of Fifty was appointed to coordinate future protests. In October it issued a ringing report containing many of the egalitarian ideas of Thomas Skidmore, a Connecticut-born machinist who appalled conservatives with his belief in equality of property. The document began with the premise that "all human society . . . is constructed radically wrong" and ended with a call for nominations for upcoming state and municipal elections. The ticket, with less than a month to campaign, did remarkably well. A carpenter won a seat in the legislature and other candidates, including Skidmore, fell only a few votes short. The election revealed a significant amount of discontent, much of it roughly following class lines.

During its glory days in 1829 and 1830 the party was a forum for a variety of capable and articulate people, not all of them artisans. The best known were Skidmore; George Henry Evans, editor of the largest labor journal of the time, the *Working Man's Advocate*; and Robert Dale Owen, fresh from the failure of his father's communitarian society at New Harmony and convinced that education, rather than redistribution of property of the sort Skidmore wanted, was what common people most needed. After its spectacular beginning, the party broke into bitterly hostile factions. By 1831 each was insignificant.

Partisan activity in New England took a slightly different form and met much the same fate. The initial issue there, as in New York, was the ten-hour day. New York artisans, however, sought to preserve it, while New England artisans had been trying for years to get it. As part of the drive, a convention in Boston in the spring of 1832 brought forth the New England Association of Farmers, Mechanics, and Other Working Men. Its most distinctive feature was comprehensiveness. In part designed to be a central union for the region, it opened membership to groups usually excluded, notably factory hands and (as the name indicated) farmers. The association also dabbled in politics, building on the scattered efforts of earlier New England Working Men's parties. In addition to campaigning in local elections, the association endorsed a candidate for governor of Massachusetts in 1833 and 1834 (he did poorly) and suggested that labor ought to build an independent national political organization.

That did not occur. Before 1834 was over, the association was defunct and there were few legitimate Working Men's parties of any sort left. They were weakened by personal and ideological conflict and frustrated by their inability to wean the mass of workers away from traditional party loyalties. The major parties, in turn, damaged Working Men's parties by infiltrating them, taking over their issues, and slandering them. By the mid-1830s some workers turned to Jackson's Democrats, others to their rivals. Labor was back to the strategy of voting to reward its friends and punish its enemies, however difficult it might be to tell them apart.

While they lasted, nonetheless, Working Men's parties fostered wide-ranging, often radical debate and consistently made several demands; these likewise appeared among the resolutions of trades' associations and were at the heart of labor reform. The ten-hour workday was always high on the artisans' list of priorities. Anything more lengthy, they argued, deprived them of good health, a proper family life, and opportunities for self-improvement and political participation. Artisans also urged abolition of imprisonment for debt and demanded that the legal and electoral systems and the militia be made fair to common folk. They sought passage of mechanic's lien laws: these entitled workers to make claims against the estates of deceased or bankrupt employers in order to recover back wages. Like the Jacksonians, artisans waged war on monopolies, by which they meant any sort of legally sanctioned economic privilege, including corporation charters. They regarded these as conferring benefits on a handful of idle and wealthy individuals and called for open competition, with the government granting no special favors. On no issue, however, were Working Men's parties more insistent than on the need for free public schools. Artisans believed that equal access to knowledge erased invidious social distinctions, provided all with a fair chance to rise in the world, and swept away the baneful effects of ignorance and prejudice. "In obtaining an equal system of education," the Philadelphia party declared in 1830, "we will rid ourselves of every existing evil." That faith was pervasive, powerful, millennial, and misplaced.

In the view of many late-nineteenth- and twentieth-century observers, the mechanics' programs looked mild. Many items were merely demands for fair play; most bespoke a firm confidence in self-advancement and in individual initiative. The stands against monopolies and in favor of public education, for instance, reflected the traditional hope of journeymen that they might themselves become masters, employers, and petty capitalists. Among the formal resolutions of the Working Men's parties there were no calls for anything resembling the modern welfare state, nor was there much evidence of a desire to change society, root and branch, except in the case of genuine radicals like Skidmore. Artisans wished to avoid being reduced to common laborers, feared betrayal of the egalitarian promises of the Revolution, and thought America might well be coming to resemble Europe, with its extremes of wealth and poverty. "Equal rights," in its most conservative definition, did not include women and African Americans; with talent and hard work, honest mechanics could continue to become small-scale entrepreneurs and active, respected citizens. In common with evangelicals, artisans recognized the misery around them, denounced it harshly, and yet were optimistic about the ability of individuals to surmount it.

There was, nonetheless, a radical streak to labor reform in the 1830s. Artisans expressed disenchantment with "the two great political parties which have heretofore misruled and misguided the people" (a feeling many middle-class reformers shared). Spokesmen for workers declared that the partisan organizations of the day were in the clutches of "aristocrats" and rotten to the core. Cautious labor leaders as well as radicals painted grim pictures of a political structure corrupt almost beyond redemption and of a nation blighted by poverty, degradation, and exploitation. To talk in those terms, even if occasionally, was to deny the optimism that likewise appeared in workingmen's pronouncements and to invite disaffection with the economic system.

Labor reform did indeed attract legions of men and women with ideas about restructuring the social order. Abolitionists, temperance workers, and most conventional reformers may have shunned workingmen's organizations, but utopians came to them—of these, Frances Wright and Robert Dale Owen were the most famous. They rubbed shoulders with artisan radicals like Skidmore, who questioned the right of individuals to accumulate great wealth and who talked of the exploitation of labor by capital. Even the *Working Man's Advocate*, edited by Skidmore's moderate rival George Henry Evans, was inaugurated with a masthead proclaiming: "All children are entitled to equal education; all adults to equal property; and all mankind to equal privileges." (The middle phrase disappeared after the second issue.) For artisans to give such views a hearing in the 1830s indicates at least ambivalence about capitalistic individualism. There was a radical edge to the expectation that workingmen could triumph "over every species of injustice and oppression."

If Working Men's parties occasionally used the language of class conflict, they were nonetheless broad in their social composition. Artisans accepted as a brother or sister anyone who supported their programs, and, as a consequence, the parties included masters, journeymen, politicians, men who never worked with their hands, utopians like Owen, extremists, conservatives, practical unionists, and crackpots. Despite that diversity, many of these people shared characteristics setting them apart from other antebellum reformers. They differed, for instance, in status and theology from the directors of the Protestant "benevolent empire." Although Working Men's parties sometimes put wealthy non-worker candidates up for office, few labor leaders had the social prominence or financial resources of an Arthur Tappan. An impressively large proportion did not share Tappan's theology either. More than any other crusade, with the possible exception of spiritualism, labor reform provided a haven for atheists, deists, and opponents of formal religion like Owen and Wright. That was testimony both to the secular nature of workingmen's groups and to an undercurrent of freethinking among the artisans themselves.

Virtually unique to the labor movement were ties between it and English radical traditions, a bond going back to the eighteenth century and personified by Tom Paine. Owen, Evans, William Heighton (a founder of the Mechanics' Union), and Thomas Brothers (a Philadelphia hatmaker and radical journalist) were British-born and versed in the literature of European socialism and working-class protest. The same sort of books and pamphlets they cited were reprinted in labor newspapers and quoted by native workingmen. Artisans had their international connections, just as evangelical abolitionists, pacifists, and temperance reformers did, although at different levels of society and political consciousness.

The ideological and sociological mix of the Working Men's parties led some historians to question whether they really represented labor. Certainly they did not reach down to the lowest levels of the workforce (the American labor movement seldom has). Equally true, ambitious men, with money and leisure, found it possible to capture mechanics' organizations and use them to promote some other party or cause. Yet in terms of issues, candidates for office, and access to positions of authority, Working Men's parties at their worst did better by artisans than did the Whigs and Democrats. Never after 1834 would America come so close to having a viable labor party.

Labor reform, of course, did not die with the Working Men's parties in the early 1830s. As before, local unions and trade associations agitated for social causes and provided a home for utopians, even while pressing hard on economic issues. On all fronts they had successes. Wages seem to have risen by 1837 (so had prices) and the ten-hour day became commonplace for artisans in the East. In 1840 President Van Buren established it on federal projects. State governments began to meet a few of the demands of workingmen's groups by abolishing imprisonment for debt and by making changes in the militia and in educational systems. In spite of the failure of independent political action, labor appeared to be making gains by the mid-1830s.

There was every reason to believe that better organization could accomplish still more. For a brief period, beginning in 1834, there was a first attempt at a countrywide federation of workers' groups, the National Trades Union. Seeking to "unite and harmonize the efforts of all the productive classes of our country," the union was a step toward consolidating and giving central direction to the labor movement. Before it met an untimely end with the Panic of 1837, it had begun to tighten its authority and had suggested such strong measures as general strikes in support of member unions. One such strike in Philadelphia in 1834 focused upon the ten-hour workday and involved skilled, unskilled, and female workers. Perhaps inspired by the union, at least five trades attempted to form their own national organizations in the 1830s.

The bottom dropped out in 1837. The Panic and the subsequent half decade of depression threw a third of the labor force out of work. Pay fell by a third, or perhaps a half. Workingmen's organizations collapsed.

Hard times only partially explain the falling off of labor reform in the late 1830s. It also suffered from institutional and ideological liabilities. The legal status of unions, boycotts, and strikes was dubious, and labor leaders lived under the shadow of possible prosecution for conspiracy. That threat eased somewhat in 1842, with a landmark pro-union Massachusetts Supreme Court decision in *Commonwealth* v. *Hunt*. Employers, nonetheless, continued to coerce workers who tried to engage in collective action. Even without any sort of persecution it would have been difficult to fashion an effective nationwide labor movement in the antebellum years. Industry itself tended to be local or regional and small-scale. Trade associations had trouble coordinating terms of employment in different areas—there were too many producers with whom to deal. Workers, meanwhile, made use of cheap transportation, as their employers did, and slipped from place to place, seeking different conditions and better opportunities on their own.

Labor organizations created further troubles for themselves. They admitted people with clashing economic interests (notably masters and journeymen) and with different ideologies, ensuring a high level of internecine warfare. They also accepted assumptions that undermined the class consciousness and commitment to collective action a labor movement has to have. Like Ben Franklin, a patron saint of the artisans, they believed that education, hard work, and thrift brought success. Such a view assumed that social mobility was a real possibility and that achievement was an individual matter. Why, then, take the risks of joining the movement when initiative and better schooling could lift one, or one's children, into the ranks of lesser capitalists? For a fraction of the artisans, the hallmarks of middle-class antebellum reform—temperance, evangelical Protestant morality, self-control, and education—offered respectability and hope for success without collective political action.

As the economy revived in the early 1840s, so did labor reform, although with alterations in goals and tactics. Some reformers turned toward individualistic and self-help panaceas, including temperance, as cures for working-class ills. By contrast, several onetime labor reformers committed themselves to communitarianism, especially the Fourierist variety, with its elaborate mechanisms for allocating work and its promise of keeping America from following Europe's descent into inequality and class conflict. Others thought the answer was to set up producers' cooperatives so craftsmen could reap the full profit of their labor. Land reform also had advocates. George Henry Evans emerged from retirement to propagandize for it through his National Reform Association, founded in 1844. Evans argued that the solution to labor's difficulties was to give public lands to settlers. Free farms in the West, he reasoned, would draw excess population from the East and raise wages for those who remained. If anything, the idea of homesteading gained more popularity among farmers and middle-class folk than among workers (by 1860 Northern Republicans and Democrats both endorsed it and in 1862 it became law). In any event, land reform's message for labor, like that of evangelical Protestant respectability, cooperatives, and communitarianism, was to tell it to find salvation by avoiding direct conflict with capital and with the factory system.

That may have been appealing advice, but it was not practical for the mass of workers. The majority of labor reformers lost or muted their millennial zeal in the 1840s and directed their attention to achievable short-range objectives (a change many other antebellum crusaders went through in the following decade). Trades' associations, dormant since the Panic, reappeared around 1847, when they again flourished for a few years. Individual unions, meanwhile, concentrated on wages and working conditions more often than they had in the 1830s.

Labor's great collective effort in the 1840s was scarcely new, let alone radical. It was to bring the ten-hour day to artisans and factory workers who had not gained it in the 1830s. Lobbying organizations appeared locally in Massachusetts by 1842. Female mill operatives of the kind we met in Chapter 5 were especially dedicated campaigners for the reduced workday, as well as for regulations protecting child labor. The cause had a boost with creation, in 1844, of the New England Working Men's Association, designed to coordinate efforts throughout the region. Its effectiveness, however, was immediately compromised by conflict between Fourierists, land reformers, and those who favored leaving extraneous crusades alone. Leaders such as William Field Young, editor of an association paper, *Voice of Industry*, revealed another kind of weakness by promoting a confusing mix of radical-sounding rhetoric, millennialism, and evangelical exhortations for hard work and forgiveness of oppressors.

By the time the association fell apart in 1848, the ten-hour movement was safely in the hands of other groups throughout New England and, slightly later, in the mid-Atlantic states. The campaign was intense and significant for speaking to the condition of factory hands more than previous organizational drives had done. A few legislatures responded, beginning with New Hampshire's in 1847, but these victories were as modest as the demand. The earliest laws left workers free to contract voluntarily for longer hours, an option employers strongly encouraged.

In the 1850s labor organizations once again followed the business cycle—up in 1850–51, down in 1854–55, up again, then down sharply in 1857. The most successful unions of the period were, as usual, in the skilled trades and they had many of the features of their twentieth-century counterparts. They collected dues, provided benefits for members, bargained with employers, used strikes (about four hundred in 1853–54 alone), and sometimes won. In general, they were more tightly organized than earlier unions and less involved in politics or in wide-ranging social crusades.

Perhaps the most impressive development in the 1850s was the re-emergence of national trade associations. More than a dozen of them formed between 1850 and 1860. Many were short-lived and ineffective, but they represented an awareness that workers had to have standard agreements throughout the industrial regions, lest producers use goods from cheap-labor areas to drive down wages elsewhere. Three of the nationals, moreover, broke with the older mode of organizing. These trade associations—for molders, machinists, and cotton mule spinners—consisted for the most part of men who worked in factories at a single stage in the manufacturing process, rather than making a finished product. For them to put together a national union was a tacit admission that the division of labor was here to stay and that many wage earners no longer had the independence or skills that had once been the pride of the artisans.

Another kind of division also characterized antebellum working people's movements. One student of the subject concluded that, prior to the Civil War, probably fewer than a dozen strikes left any record of attempts to include African Americans. To some extent, that reflected the small size of black communities in the North and the virtual exclusion of blacks from most of the trades that nurtured artisan radicalism. Yet in some respects the very things that supported labor militance in the antebellum years may well have at least maintained, perhaps reinforced, racial divisions. The language of protest, with its images of slavery and freedom, was only one of several ways by which white workers defined and measured their identity—their whiteness —positively against what they saw as the blackness and servility of African Americans. Emancipation, new kinds of immigration, and industrialization changed the terms of competition for jobs after the Civil War and recast the issue of race; but even in its most sweeping and radical moments, antebellum labor reform seldom confronted the deepest divide of all in American society or conjured visions of a world in which racial as well as economic justice would prevail.

Time gave a vindication of sorts for the labor leaders of the 1850s. Their type of unionism outlived their organizations, survived the Civil War, and eventually succeeded in raising pay, improving conditions, helping brethren through hard times, and holding on to a dues-paying membership. Their practicality, however, was at the expense of the old radical spirit of men like Thomas Skidmore, which was mostly gone by 1860. (Immigrants would bring it back later in the century.) Also largely gone was the view—which caused so much trouble for the Working Men's parties—that all who toiled with their hands were brothers and sisters. It was replaced by a sense that each segment of the workforce had to look out primarily for its own welfare, while the devil took the hindmost (or the least skilled).

The worldview in much of antebellum labor reform was alien to later generations. People who believed in practical, "bread and butter" unionism of the sort that prevailed by the end of the nineteenth century faulted workingmen's associations of the 1830s for their political involvement and utopian binges, as if idealism and imagination were sins in labor organizations. Radicals, on the other hand, criticized antebellum labor leaders for failure to develop a clear sense of class consciousness and class conflict, for believing in private property, and for frequently excluding women and more consistently excluding African Americans.

By whatever latter-day standards one uses, labor reform and evangelical Protestant charity before 1850 seem imperfect responses to urbanization and industrialization. Both, however, define the outer limits of most Americans' ability to treat directly the problems posed by economic change. One cause was secular, the other religious; one had roots among artisans, the other was middle- and upper-class. Both had a brief millennial fling—a temporary belief that the Kingdom was about to come and that poverty could be abolished along with the rest of the world's evils. Neither was adequate to the job, and each, by the 1850s, settled in for trench warfare against the disruptive effects of cities and factories, organized to endure and to fight for tightly defined objectives, with lowered expectations.

The story was much the same for many other antebellum reformers. Few ever aimed at a total transformation of society (communitarians and nonresistants were the prime exceptions). In their most enthusiastic moments—which likewise had become less frequent by 1850— they talked about the march of civilization and painted pictures of a millennium soon to come. What they had in mind, nonetheless, looked like what America would have been if it lived up to its own Protestant and democratic pieties. On that score, the pattern was not peculiar to antebellum reform but rather of the nature of American reform, which frequently asserts widely held values and tries to reconcile reality with them. Rather than transcending society, it is frequently a mechanism through which the public debates, modifies, and enforces rules.

That poses problems, however, for those whose values are different, who are outside the debate, and against whom the rules are made.

# NINE

# Institutions and Uplift

One of the basic problems in combating sin is to identify the sinners. Some reforms, such as the Graham diet and phrenology, answer that we are all sinners and direct their efforts primarily to curing the reformer. Most causes, however, identify others as culprits and aim at them. For antebellum reformers this act of labeling groups or individuals as evil or misguided took many forms and served many functions, including setting limits on pluralism in an increasingly pluralistic nation. It also encouraged approaches to social problems that isolated, rather than incorporated, the objects of reform, especially after the Civil War, when their numbers increasingly included people whom middle-class whites regarded as unalterably different from themselves: African Americans, Asians, Jews, and Southern and Eastern Europeans.

American culture is filled with images of outsiders, ranging from alienated heroes to despised social groups. Perhaps the most ironic of these is the Indian, who has the best claim, by length of residence, to representing the true American way of life. Indians never were a major concern of pre–Civil War reform but white attitudes toward them illustrate a point about social crusades and the objects of their attention.

Beginning in the late eighteenth century, missionary societies sent agents to proselytize red, as well as white, heathens in the West. Their goal was to do more than gather converts. As a Methodist preacher admitted in 1857, missionaries sought "to teach the Indians to live like white people." To many present-day Americans, those words have a distasteful air of paternalism and colonialism. Yet there were worse ways of dealing with people different from one's own kind: at least the missionary assumed that Indians were capable of becoming brethren in Christ and of mastering the arts and refinements of whites. Others were not so charitable, nor always were missionaries themselves. But whether whites advocated conversion or extermination, they imagined the Indians' "savagery" as the antithesis of "civilization." Only a few radicals (including Tom Paine in the eighteenth century) reversed the equation and calculated the decadence of white civilization against the virtues of Native Americans. Theirs were lonely voices. For the most part, whites measured their own "progress" and "superiority" against Indian culture and its forced retreat across the American landscape.

Other "outsiders" served similar functions in nineteenth-century America: "normal" people projected hopes and fears onto them and used stereotypes of them to mark the difference between what was good and bad. That is a common enough psychological process; and in the antebellum years, blacks, foreigners, and subversives (including reformers) represented the same kind of negative reference points that Indians often did. Hatred and prejudice lay behind those feelings, but their function was to help groups of whites clarify in their own minds what was American and right by contrast with what was un-American and wrong.

Much the same thing went on among reformers. They expressed their sense of righteousness by describing unrighteous people. With hindsight, many of their judgments seem appropriate: if one has to have an opposite, it might as well be a slaveholder, a warmonger, an oppressor of women or workers, a drunkard, or a glutton. Yet the comparison with anti-Indian, anti-black, and anti-immigrant sentiment is a warning. There are dangers in drawing sharp, highly moralistic social boundaries like the ones often marked out by pre–Civil War reformers. If too restrictive and rigidly enforced, they stifle diversity without promoting justice and virtue.

In the early nineteenth century, reformers usually relied on moral suasion rather than compulsion and believed that sinners could be accepted into the circle of righteousness after repentance. At least some of the "others" might become "us," they argued. Things took a more repressive and pessimistic turn in the late 1830s, when temperance workers used legislation to force conformity to their view of drinking. Slightly earlier, other reformers were developing different means of coercing people in the name of social progress. In the process, they took halting steps away from the voluntaristic and individualistic paths charted by some antebellum crusaders and toward using the state as an instrument of reform. This was a move toward institutional, hierarchical, exclusionary, and coercive approaches to social change. It was, in other words, a move toward the future.

After the War of 1812 state and local officials began to examine poverty, dependency, and crime within their jurisdictions. The Massachusetts legislature led the way in 1820 with a comprehensive study of indigence and its treatment. New York followed in 1823. Cities also inspected their welfare apparatus. These investigations were in part inspired by sudden urban growth and by a depression that began in 1819; but even when they were undertaken in a mood of urgency, they displayed some of the same millennial confidence that Protestant charity workers radiated. Pauperism, the New York report declared, "may, with proper care and attention, be almost wholly eradicated from our soil."

It is no wonder that there were similarities in tone between governmental investigations and the rhetoric of evangelical Protestantism that we heard in the previous chapter. Private and public benevolence closely entwined in antebellum America and continued to be interconnected to the end of the nineteenth century. State and municipal administrations, however, often dispensed aid in a different manner from that of private charities. Although the latter ran some asylums (orphanages, for instance), they more commonly gave assistance directly to individuals living in their own homes. Antebellum public officials spent proportionally less money on such "outdoor relief," as it was called. After 1820 they often preferred putting burdensome human beings in institutions, including placing paupers in almshouses (also known as poorhouses) where they learned steady habits and were removed from vice and temptation.

The antebellum proliferation of a wide range of custodial institutions—orphanages, juvenile homes, penitentiaries, and mental hospitals, as well as poorhouses—is striking and greater than the population increase or the level of disorder warranted. In justifying such institutions, reformers themselves tended to lay responsibility on urban overcrowding, intemperance, the arrival of "worthless foreigners" (in the phrase of one report), and the moral failings of individuals. Even as they shifted away from the older view that social ills were a matter of divine judgment about which little could be done, reformers lacked the twentieth-century sense that poverty, crime, and mental disorders might be structural, that is, have social and economic causes.

Reformers participated in international debates over social problems and spoke with a distinctively American and evangelical inflection. While Americans defined and discussed these issues on the local level, for example, Great Britain considered them matters of national policy in Parliamentary debates in the 1820s and 1830s and afterward. This pattern of regarding crime and social welfare as municipal or state problems persisted in the United States throughout the nineteenth century and into the twentieth. Also in Britain the writings of Thomas Malthus, Adam Smith, and others raised the prospect of doing away entirely with relief for the needy, on the ground that it discouraged working and actually produced indigence. One Philadelphian echoed these views in 1825 when he informed the legislature that poor laws "destroy or diminish the virtue and industry of the labouring classes." Few American reformers, however, went that far, even though most made a moral distinction between the worthy poor—such as widows, orphans, the elderly, and men incapable of working—and the unworthy poor, who simply chose not to work. The worthy were to be separated from the latter and, as it turned out, sometimes from the rest of society through life in the poorhouse.

Although Americans and Europeans addressed common issues and examined each other's proposals and solutions, the choices antebellum

Americans made in dealing with poverty, insanity, and crime (and, for that matter, education) were distinctively their own and of considerable consequence for future generations. In the chillingly apt phrase of one of the most astute students of the process, American social welfare policy for over a century would live "in the shadow of the poorhouse."

That is not to say the poorhouse was the only way reformers dealt with poor people. It was not even necessarily the dominant form of assistance, when all public and private charity is weighed. At the height of the almshouse much relief still went to people in their own homes rather than within its walls—for New York State in 1850, for example, the best estimate is that outdoor relief cost $314,517 as opposed to $492,100 for almshouses, with the latter serving roughly 40 percent fewer clients. More significant than the exact ratio of one kind of relief to the other, however, is the fact that antebellum municipalities and reformers turned to such institutions to solve what they regarded as problems and, in the process, changed the institutions as well as their own understanding of poverty, crime, and insanity. Eighteenth-century almshouses, for instance, were rare and usually served as places of last resort for the most helpless of the poor. Otherwise, families cared for their own; able-bodied vagrant paupers were set to work or hurried out of the jurisdiction, to become somebody else's headache. For the rest, it was a matter of indenturing children, providing outdoor relief, and selling others to bidders who supported them in return for their labor. In the early nineteenth century, however, the almshouse became a major way for governments to deal with indigents. For a decade, the Philadelphia and Chicago city fathers refused to give any outdoor relief whatsoever.

The virtues of nineteenth-century almshouses, in the minds of their proponents, were several: they handled, supposedly at low cost, individuals whom families and neighbors no longer cared for in a mobile, heterogeneous society; the stigma of living in the poorhouse discouraged the unworthy from seeking assistance; and the institution exemplified the habits and skills of useful, virtuous lives. In the latter respect, they were both a negative commentary on their inmates, who could not function independently, and a model of how the poor ought to behave. Eighteenth-century almshouses had not been burdened either with such a large clientele or with such grand expectations.

Another kind of institution aimed primarily at urban problems, the prison, also flourished and was transformed in the antebellum years. Since the late eighteenth century American and European philanthropists had been trying to make jails more humane. They had some effect in the United States, particularly in Pennsylvania, where Quaker benevolence was a force, and in New York. But it was after 1800 that prisons became a major issue, agitated effectively by new organizations like the Boston Prison Discipline Society, founded in 1825 by an agent of the American Bible Society. Such groups helped shape the many jails and penitentiaries built after 1810. Especially influential—and hotly debated—were the systems implemented by New York at Auburn and Ossining (Sing Sing) between 1819 and 1825 and by Pennsylvania at Pittsburgh and Philadelphia between 1826 and 1829. The plans differed in detail and supporters quarreled over the merits of each; but the hallmark of both was almost total isolation of prisoners from one another and from the outside world. New York made provision for interaction among inmates through prison labor, although with virtually no verbal communication between them. In Pennsylvania, prisoners were kept in solitary confinement so absolute that they were not even to know the identities of fellow convicts. Nearly a dozen states imitated one or the other system before the Civil War, although mostly for men. Facilities for female prisoners, and concern for their welfare, remained minimal until after 1840, when their proportion of the convict population increased noticeably and women reformers sought amelioration for their plight.

There were cheaper ways of dealing with criminals than erecting expensive stone fortresses and separate cells for each inmate. The object, however, was not entirely economy, or to ease the suffering of the prisoner, the goal of eighteenth-century humanitarianism: it was to make the convict into a model citizen. Antebellum prison reformers assumed that the environment, not flaws in a person's character, produced sin. (Their view was close to that of Robert Owen and many communitarians, who also thought of moral behavior as a product of the conditions under which human beings lived.) Reformers attempted—with much success—to persuade ordinarily parsimonious state legislatures that if criminals were taken out of the milieu that created them, they would be amenable to good influences. Convicts could ponder their errors and gain the self-discipline they had not learned from their families and communities. Alexis de Tocqueville and Gustave de Beaumont, in America to gather information on its prisons, claimed that the philanthropists they met "consider man, however far advanced in crime, as still susceptible of being brought back to virtue." The penitentiary "seems the remedy for all the evils of society."

As reformers learned more about the dependent classes, they came to see differences and to realize that even the best almshouses and prisons were not beneficial for every inmate. The insane and children, in particular, had a difficult time when thrown in with hardened rogues. Concerned men and women considered what sort of treatment might be more appropriate for them. The answer was new, special asylums. Just as some reformers' interests clustered around antislavery, pacifism, and woman's rights, the commitments of others focused on almshouses and prisons, and then broadened to include more novel institutions.

The first facility for juvenile delinquents, the New York House of Refuge, opened its doors to wayward boys and girls on New Year's Day, 1825. For over a decade the city's Common Council had been concerned about mayhem from youthful vagrants and with the difficulties of placing them in existing institutions. It took the Society for the Prevention of Pauperism—among whose members was the mayor—to come up with a solution. Drawing on one person's knowledge of European experiments with problem children, a committee appointed by the society compiled a report that led to the creation of a Society for the Reformation of Juvenile Delinquents. Its mandate was to raise money for a "prison" for minors. Endorsing the idea, the Common Council donated the land upon which an outmoded federal arsenal stood. The United States Government then sold the building itself to the society for $2,000. For its part, the society provided management and much of the money, at least until 1829, when public funding became a dependable source of revenue.

Boston built its House of Refuge in 1826 and Philadelphia built one in 1828. By the late 1850s these institutions appeared in cities as widely scattered as New Orleans, Chicago, and Providence. Massachusetts, in 1848, and New York, in 1849, opened the first state-supported reform schools. Even with public financing, however, they continued —in the tradition of the New York House of Refuge—to receive generous assistance from charitable groups and individuals. In 1860 three of the major facilities for delinquents were still private corporations with some state regulation.

Many features of these houses and reform schools are open to harsh criticism, particularly their use of solitary confinement and corporal punishment. The earliest and best, however, were remarkable for their attempts to help delinquents. Officials believed that young wrongdoers were best "subdued by kindness." Discipline was never lax and moralizing was often heavy-handed, but these institutions aimed at teaching self-control and clean living to children who had known little of either. The Boston house encouraged a sense of responsibility by involving inmates in judging their own and one another's conduct, and by rewarding improvement in behavior. Formal instruction in the houses ranged from the most elementary homemaking skills to conventional schooling, both of which were alien to many of the children. When a youth showed signs of being able to function as an independent, law-abiding human being, he or she was bound out as an apprentice to learn a trade. Through the 1840s reformers were confident that the majority of their wards were amenable to such therapy. A hymn written in honor of the Massachusetts State Reform School assumed that if this "sweet retreat"

> . . . *may win from folly's wiles,*
> *The little wanderer's feet;*
> *Then from this guardian home will rise*
> *The good and great, refined and wise.*

That did not always happen. The houses suffered from overcrowding, too much illicit advice communicated from older to younger inmates, and too few outside jobs for them. By the 1860s the rate of "cures" was so disappointing that reformers wondered whether the failure might not lie with the clients rather than the institutions. Although it eventually became respectable to blame underage criminals (or their "race" or heredity) for their criminality, dissatisfaction with the houses had been mounting through the 1850s. Private benevolent societies were particularly eager to come up with alternatives and to reach children before they were caught up in public institutions. As early as 1832, with the founding of the Boston Asylum and Farm School for Boys, philanthropists sought idle and rowdy minors who, if not helped, were likely candidates for the houses. Of most consequence were the New York City labors of Charles Loring Brace, a former divinity student and assistant to an urban missionary. His Children's Aid Society (1853) inspired public and private charities across the land. It was a well-diversified enterprise providing everything from education to lodging for city children, all the while being run on "scientific principles" and teaching self-reliance, hard work, and thrift.

That was a difficult performance for cost-conscious public officials to match, and few had the inclination to try. The states, nonetheless, became aware of deficiencies in the houses and they made innovations of their own in the 1850s. Several began "reform schools" to take minor offenders and those from rural areas. Massachusetts' Reform School for Girls (1855) and Ohio's Reform Farm (1857) experimented with a different mode of organization, a "family system" in which delinquents were placed in a country atmosphere, in smaller groups approximating a normal household. After initiation of the "family system" there were few changes in the handling of young offenders until the end of the nineteenth century, when separate juvenile-court systems were begun. In the twentieth century, the most important reforms repudiated what was done earlier in the name of reform—especially the nineteenth-century eagerness to put minors in institutions.

The record may well justify twentieth-century skepticism about antebellum solutions. As time went on, the Houses of Refuge bore less and less resemblance to the good intentions of the men and women who created them, a pattern they shared with penitentiaries. Over-crowding and understaffing made it difficult to give personal attention to delinquents. The houses became dumping grounds for people too young for regular jails and too tough to be on the loose. And even the most perceptive and innovative of pre–Civil War figures came up with counterproposals of limited effectiveness, at best. Charles Loring Brace, for instance, recognized the failure of custodial institutions to cure delinquency. Yet among his favorite alternatives was placement of New York vagabonds on western farms. The plan neither succeeded in "draining the City of vagrant Children," as he hoped, nor served as much of a solution to the problems of poverty and juvenile crime.

The development of mental hospitals followed a parallel course to that of penitentiaries and Houses of Refuge. All derived from the notion, relatively new in the antebellum period, that asylums could be a tool of social and individual advancement. All stemmed from recognition that different categories of poor and dependent people required different treatment. Yet even more clearly than the Houses of Refuge, mental hospitals demonstrate how reformist goals could be betrayed by asylums as well as embodied in them. After lobbying by the Boston Prison Discipline Society and a young legislator named Horace Mann, the Massachusetts General Court in 1830 authorized construction of a hospital for lunatics, to be located at Worcester. The facility, which opened its doors in 1833, was not the first public insane asylum, but it was the most modern and influential in its day. The other four in existence in 1833 were obscure and in slave states, where social services were ill maintained.

The superintendent at Worcester, Samuel B. Woodward, was an able administrator and publicist. He and his supporters proclaimed the asylum to be a model for the rest of the nation. It took time to convince legislatures—only two states followed Massachusetts' example in the 1830s. The pace quickened in the 1840s, and again in the 1850s. By the Civil War, twenty-eight states, four cities, and the federal government had public mental institutions. That was an impressive amount of asylum building in view of the obstacles, foremost of which was the reluctance of antebellum lawmakers to spend money on the needy and on non-voters. Indeed, their willingness to construct mental hospitals is far more surprising than their willingness to invest in prisons, because the sense of urgency about insanity was less than about crime. Both seemed to be dramatically on the rise (madness probably was not); but a walk through any American city would convince a taxpayer that there was more to fear from thugs than from the insane.

Proponents of asylums won many of their victories by skillful agitation. Unlike many antebellum reformers, they trusted politicians and the political system and used both effectively. Although religiously inspired, they were more orthodox and less offensive in their theology than, for instance, William Lloyd Garrison. They, moreover, mingled their religious imperatives with the language of "science," which promised certain results. Often comfortable and secure in status (a modest inheritance financed Dorothea Dix's career), they had respectability and a moderate demeanor that reassured, rather than alienated, influential people. So cautious was Dix that she refused to take a stand against slavery, making her one of the few New England reformers welcome in the South.

Dix and her colleagues had a conservative side to their ideas as well as their tactics. They often blamed the strains of "civilization" for causing increasing amounts of insanity. The idea was common in both Europe and the United States, but it could lead in different directions. For romantic radicals it implied a need for humans to liberate themselves from institutions and dogmas and return to a free, natural existence. That was not what asylum-builders had in mind. To the contrary, their concern was with freedom itself, which they regarded as excessive in nineteenth-century America. Pursuit of economic advantage, political turmoil, and the hustle and bustle of cities were more than fragile minds could bear. Reformers wished to see mental institutions instill in patients the motivation necessary for survival in a confusing world of choices and fluidity. That meant learning Protestant morality, cleanliness, thrift, discipline, continence, and temperance. In teaching those habits, mental hospitals both fulfilled a need created by the failure of families and churches and reproved an egalitarian, capitalistic society for driving people mad. At the same time, of course, the ideal asylum would be producing precisely the kind of orderly, disciplined individuals necessary for the smooth functioning of the factories and cities of an egalitarian, capitalistic society.

The metaphysics of asylums probably had less effect on penny-pinching legislators than the claims of professionals like Woodward that madness was curable. Europeans had long insisted that it was, and Americans were no less optimistic. Woodward believed "judicious treatment" of "recent cases of insanity" would result in "as large a proportion of recoveries . . . as from any other acute disease of equal severity." Worcester, according to him, was able to discharge between 80 and 90 percent of those whom it got in the early stages of lunacy. Not to be outdone, his fellow superintendents presented similar figures, and two, in the 1840s, claimed 100 percent success. The statistics clearly were exaggerated: patients were counted as "cured" more than once, and there were other failures in record keeping.

Still, the first asylums may have done well by their inmates. The institutions were small (Worcester originally had room for 120 patients), life in them was highly structured, and treatment was always moralistic, and sometimes personal and gentle—a kind of therapy that can be effective in treating some mental disorders. A twentieth-century authority calculated that the real cure rate probably was over 50 percent, a fine showing by present-day standards. Yet even that rate might have been unacceptably below the expectations of reformers. Although sober, respectable men and women, they (no less than the wildest perfectionists) wanted to believe that no human was beyond redemption. With the proper application of scientific principles, the asylum—like the penitentiary and the House of Refuge—could take society's outcasts and make them well-functioning, virtuous, and productive. As late as 1856, a New York State report maintained that "Insanity is not only a disease susceptible of treatment, but of actual cure."

Because mental hospitals fulfilled a variety of functions and because their very existence helped define "insanity" as a "problem," they created a demand for their own services. There was a growing willingness to identify strange behavior as lunacy and the asylum as the solution. Although antebellum families were no less adept than twentieth-century ones at denying the problematic nature of a relative's behavior, the asylum offered hope that a troublesome loved one could be made sane again. Many inmates were harmless, if difficult, and in earlier years would have been kept in private homes or left to wander. Some were senile, imbeciles, or syphilitics who were untreatable, even by reform rhetoric. Soon the hospitals were crowded; cities constructed their own institutions rather than ship lunatics to state facilities, located in the countryside. Those institutions became filled. Small hospitals gave way to large ones; the superintendent became a bureaucrat rather than a healer; and restraints and force replaced individual attention and kindness. As conditions deteriorated, optimism about curability faded. A report undertaken in 1854 for the Massachusetts legislature and written by a medical authority spoke of "inherent elements of poverty and insanity."

That position, later to become orthodox and to be cloaked in the language of biological science, shifted responsibility for insanity from the environment to the brain and justified the failure of mental hospitals to help transform their inmates. Like penitentiaries and Houses of Refuge, they were losing their reformist mission in the 1850s and becoming storage bins for society's outcasts.

There is a long postscript to the story of antebellum asylum building. In 1844 managers of mental hospitals formed the Association of Medical Superintendents of American Institutions for the Insane, which promoted the superintendents' viewpoint through conferences and a periodical, the *American Journal of Insanity*. By 1870 there was a National Prison Congress and in 1872 a series of international meetings began. Asylum administrators of all sorts gathered into organizations, attempted to set standards, and acted as members of a group with distinct interests to promote and defend. In so doing, they were part of a trend toward professionalization and bureaucratization that went against the anti-hierarchical cast of much antebellum reform and was destined to become even stronger within American reform after the Civil War.

At the same time that superintendents' professional identity was becoming clearer, however, clients, state legislatures, and superiors put it in jeopardy. Ex-inmates published sensational exposés of maltreatment and wrongful incarceration in mental institutions—one became the basis of a popular song, "The Maniac," in 1840. The outcry in response to such works resulted in proposals for personal-liberty laws protecting the rights of men and women committed to asylums. Little legislation ever passed, but the prospect was enough to make administrators cautious. More of a threat to them were the very processes of professionalization and bureaucratization of which they were a part. By the 1850s cities and states were moving to consolidate public welfare activities, then administered and financed haphazardly. In 1863 Massachusetts founded its Board of State Charities, the closest thing at the time to a state welfare department. By the early 1870s many states in the Northeast and Midwest had similar agencies. The people who staffed them were usually professionals, like the asylum managers, but their goals were to cut costs, improve efficiency, and bring all public services under their jurisdiction. That necessarily worked against the autonomy of superintendents of particular institutions. City and state boards, furthermore, were signs that the original reformist expectations were disappearing in favor of the view that social problems had to be managed rather than cured. Board members were often less interested in trying to eliminate poverty, crime, and insanity—the dreams of the 1820s, 1830s, and 1840s—than they were in eliminating welfare. Yet neither they nor (predictably) the superintendents challenged the notion that incarceration was the best treatment for deviance. That would remain an article of faith until well into the twentieth century, when, in another turn of the wheel, new kinds of reformers and cost-cutters promoted "deinstitutionalization" as a progressive cause, just as their professional forebears had promoted institutionalization.

Grim as asylums were, they attempted positive things, especially at first. No one can read of conditions in nineteenth-century slums and of cruelty toward the insane without feeling that many delinquents and mad persons were better off inside institutions than out. Even prison reform may have been a pleasant reality for convicts like those in Connecticut who were moved in the 1820s from an abandoned copper mine to a new state penitentiary. There were, moreover, other, lesser-known varieties of asylums in the antebellum period, some of them remarkable for their accomplishments and decency. Particularly impressive were the endeavors of Thomas Gallaudet with deaf-mutes and of Samuel Gridley Howe with the blind in his Perkins Institute, founded in 1832. Their work, and that of the earliest mental hospitals and Houses of Refuge, gave ample evidence that human sympathy toward disadvantaged "others" was very much a part of asylum building. But there were harsher aspects to it, and features that were downright insidious.

By nature, asylums are repressive and, if anything, reformers made them more so by insisting on completely cutting inmates off from their previous environment. Of course, there are forms of behavior no society can tolerate, and many men and women put away in prisons and mental hospitals would have been dangerous if left loose. In less extreme cases, however, the condition being "cured" was more benign and did not require incarceration. Concepts of what is criminal or deviant are social and cultural constructs, varying over time and from group to group. What one person or generation considers wrong or crazy may be acceptable to the next. Without meaning to, a nineteenth-century German medical student provided a perfect illustration of the point. He discovered an epidemic of madness in Europe and America and presented his findings under the descriptive title "On the Democratic Disease, a New Form of Insanity." By his way of reckoning, in the United States the lunatics were indeed running the asylum.

Since criminality and madness can be defined in different ways, later critics charged that the real purpose of nineteenth-century asylums was to discipline Americans to middle-class standards of decorum and instill the regimentation and values of an industrial order. Certainly, the potential existed for using asylums to achieve personal ends or to satisfy individual or class prejudices. Admissions standards were loose enough to allow public officials and relatives much latitude in determining who belonged in an institution. In 1826, for instance, Massachusetts permitted the Boston House of Reformation to take "all children who live an idle or dissolute life, whose parents are dead, or if living, from drunkenness, or other vices, neglect to provide any suitable employment, or exercise any salutary control over said children." That left a fair amount of room for value judgments. Within the asylum, superintendents had an equivalent amount of discretion. Release from a House of Refuge—where juveniles served indeterminate sentences—or from a mental hospital usually depended on the inmate's ability to convince the administration that he or she was now prepared to conform to the expectations of decent folk.

The result was a system in which standards could be applied arbitrarily in the case of individuals and systematically against the interests of particular classes and ethnic groups. Catholics objected strenuously to Protestant evangelizing in the institutions. (In 1863 New York they organized a reformatory to keep their delinquents away from Charles Loring Brace and out of the clutches of the House of Refuge.) Inequities also clearly existed in admissions to public institutions. Very early on, immigrants and poor people were overrepresented—partly because of genuine criminality and insanity, the result of poverty and life in a foreign land. But the disparity also reflected the ability of middle-class Protestants to afford private care and good lawyers, each of which helped, and continue to help, keep privileged people out of public institutions. It was, moreover, easier to label an immigrant or a pauper as deviant than a person of standing. John Randolph, of the Virginia Randolphs, could act bizarrely, keep his freedom, and have a political career. If an Irish laborer muttered to himself and appeared "superstitious" or quarrelsome, he was a candidate for incarceration. Once in the asylum, he was in the custody of people who did not like his religion, did not understand or sympathize with him, and considered him unacceptably "different" even when he was behaving himself.

Little of the old reformist desire to perfect human beings survived in prisons, Houses of Refuge, and mental institutions after the 1850s. What remained was the idea of isolating and regimenting people in order to cure them.

Of all the institution building that went on in the antebellum period the most far-reaching and valuable was the construction of free public schools. They were not as repressive or demeaning as asylums, childhood folklore to the contrary. They were promoted to bring people into the mainstream of American life rather than isolate them from it, as did asylums. Both types of institution, however, achieved reformist goals through indoctrination and discipline. Each tried to create a new person, incapable of immorality; both affirmed the primacy of particular values and norms in a disunited society.

Education was not an antebellum invention. The Puritans of New England held the traditional Protestant conviction that all believers ought to be able to read the Bible, and they had begun common schools in the seventeenth century. In the eighteenth century such influential figures as Benjamin Franklin and Thomas Jefferson wrote of the need for education and assisted efforts to improve it. Schools, nonetheless, were poorly conducted and attendance was spotty until the middle of the nineteenth century, even in New England. Although there were local variations, in many places children of the wealthy were taught in private institutions or at home by special tutors; others paid fees to go to public schools or were designated "charity" cases, a label offensive to parental pride.

Between the 1830s and the Civil War a great change occurred, with Massachusetts leading the way. Enrollments in Bay State schools had been expanding well before 1837, when the legislature created a Board of Education. Its first secretary was Horace Mann, then forty-one years old, experienced as a legislator, and long interested in asylums. For more than a decade Mann used his post to promote a number of innovations. The cause of school reform in Massachusetts was also aided by the state government's willingness to formulate educational policy and to implement it against the wishes of reluctant communities. Indeed, one of the most persistent themes in American educational his-

tory is the battle between those who wish to assert central control over
schools and those who speak for local control, whatever the locality
may be.

The list of the Massachusetts achievements in the antebellum
period—before, during, and after Mann's secretaryship—is impressive.
Among the items on it are the first Board of Education, the first public
high school (1821), the first normal (or teacher training) school (1839),
and the first compulsory school attendance law (1852). Mann and Massachusetts, nonetheless, were not the sum total of educational reform.
Visionaries experimented with pedagogical theories of their own or
ones borrowed from Europeans. (The communitarian societies at New
Harmony and Brook Farm were notable in that respect.) Other states
besides Massachusetts formed common-school systems. Almost everywhere, the training of teachers became more formal and the profession
rose in status and salary. All these developments were complicated
and uneven, both between states and within them, particularly between rural and urban schools. Yet whatever the situation was in any
particular place, one thing was apparent: by 1860, Americans were
committed to free public education, at least through the primary levels.
They were willing to pay a large share of their taxes for school systems
staffed by professionals and, increasingly, administered by bureau-
cracies.

Later generations accepted public education as one of the glories of
the United States, conveniently forgetting how stiff opposition to it
was in the mid-nineteenth century. Attacks came from local interests
mistrustful of the state government, from old-fashioned teachers, from
Catholics and immigrants who regarded the schools as middle-class
Protestant propaganda machines, from working people dependent on
their children's income, and from wealthy conservatives who saw no
sense in trying to teach the rabble. Battles did not cease once school
systems were organized, as parents, school boards, religious and ethnic
groups, and professionals argued over curriculum and control. Yet educational reformers had a number of advantages in any conflict. Among
antebellum crusaders they were the closest thing to political insiders;
for instance, Horace Mann and Henry Barnard, Commissioner of Ed-

ucation for Connecticut (later United States Commissioner of Education), were Whig politicians and ex-lawmakers. Schools, like asylums, benefited from having supporters who knew their way around the state capitol.

Educational reformers, in addition, received backing from an odd and effective assortment of groups, including many communitarians and phrenologists, who thought learning was the key to progress. Evangelical Protestants realized that public education would be, from their viewpoint, morally sound and an ally for their own Sunday schools and Bible and tract societies. The more prosperous and skilled segments of the working class likewise demanded free schools. Since the eighteenth century, artisans had regarded education as crucial for exercising and defending citizenship and would have agreed with Mann when he wrote that public schools are "the great equalizer of the condition of men." Mann and many working people alike could hope that education would save America from the European class system.

Although educational reform was broadly based in its support, a crucial element behind it was the solid, respectable urban professional and middle classes, the kind of people who fled city school systems over a century later. They were not in such financial need that they had to have free schooling for their children, but they, too, found attractive things in the rhetoric of Mann and his colleagues. It reassured them that social tensions could be resolved easily and without radical change. Education, Mann told them, "does better than disarm the poor of their hostility toward the rich; it prevents being poor." That idea was both comforting and a secular refashioning of millennial optimism and American exceptionalism: anyone could be improved; the nation had wealth enough for everybody.

School reform, however, played equally well to the darker moods of middle-class men and women. Since the eighteenth century, Americans had fretted over what would become of the Republic if its people declined in virtue. Many middle-class Protestants saw that happening all around them: politics was in the hands of demagogues; foreigners and paupers made the cities unpleasant and threatening for respectable folk. Schools were the answer. In Mann's words, they were the means for decent Americans to "free ourselves from the low-minded and the vicious; not by their expatriation, but by their elevation." Education would teach good behavior and make the dangerous classes trustworthy.

Curriculum reflected those goals. "Our system," Mann wrote, "inculcates all Christian morals." Although public schools had to steer clear of denominational issues, they often had readings from the Scriptures (required in Massachusetts in 1855). (Their Bible and theology were Protestant, which angered Catholics.) Everything, nonetheless, had a moral purpose, even exercise and play, which were supposed to create sound bodies that were, antebellum Americans assumed, less likely to sin. Textbooks taught virtue as much as literacy. A popular reader of the 1840s, for instance, had a lesson entitled "Danger of Bad Habits." It warned that "vice is not a thing to be trifled with." (Another section praised the mother, then added that "next in rank and in efficacy to that pure and holy source of moral influence is that of the schoolmaster.") There was no room here for doubt or disobedience. The child learned self-control, punctuality, all the Protestant and patriotic verities, and intolerance for different styles of life.

The schoolmen were proud of their work. In the 1850s the Boston School Committee, with the Irish clearly in mind, described its noble task as "taking children at random from a great city, undisciplined, uninstructed, often with inveterate forwardness and obstinacy, and with the inherited stupidity of centuries of ignorant ancestors; forming them from animals into intellectual beings, and . . . from intellectual beings into Spiritual beings." Schools—just like asylums—were institutions to instill a sharply defined set of values to every class and ethnic group.

Public education failed to create cultural homogeneity. That was not for lack of effort, but rather because of the overwhelming regional and sociological complexity of the United States and because of the weakness of the classroom when it came into conflict with the student's family life and peers. If the repressive side of such institutions has been emphasized recently (as it is here), the reasons are several.

As time went along, Americans became more and more aware of the gap between what the nation's much-vaunted educational system was supposed to be and what it was. From being pictured in the nineteenth century as the cradle of democracy, public schools came to be attacked by twentieth-century critics as elitist, racist, incompetent, and a threat to mind and body. Prisons and asylums similarly degenerated and failed to match the expectations their proponents raised.

Some of the attack on school systems and custodial institutions, however, could come only with a historical perspective unavailable in the antebellum period: an awareness that bureaucratic structures can perpetuate themselves even when they do not work properly, and that they can impinge on personal freedom and suppress cultural diversity (little valued in nineteenth-century America). By the twentieth century, professional managers—asylum directors, school administrators, and the like—had to battle public suspicion that their chief interest was finding people to fill their institutions and that they sought to contain, rather than solve, problems.

Antislavery was the most significant and temperance the largest and most enduring of the antebellum crusades. Communitarianism, non-resistance, and workingmen's movements were the most radical. Yet school reform brought together the greatest number of strands and, in some respects, was the epitome. Nearly all reformist groups endorsed it: evangelical Protestants, utopians, artisans, and even pseudo-scientists like the phrenologists. It drew upon and wove together the various languages that permeated antebellum reform. It addressed classical republican fears about the decline of civic virtue. It combined optimism about human nature with a "scientific" desire to shape it by rational means. It had the millennial and perfectionist impulses of evangelical Protestantism—all could be taught, all uplifted. It affirmed that America was, and could remain, unique and free of Europe's ills.

It ended with less hope and a bureaucratic structure.

# Afterword:
# A Matter of Time

Reformers are not the best judges of their place in the great scheme of things. True enough, antebellum crusaders assessed their social origins fairly well: they characterized themselves as hardworking Christians of modest means, neither very rich nor very poor. On non-sociological matters, they were less astute. Like most American reformers, they often envisioned themselves as part of a grand procession stretching across the centuries—soldiers in the long march of Protestantism, republican principles, Science, Reason, Progress, American Destiny, or Democracy. At other moments they—also like later reformers—regarded themselves as outsiders whose critical distance from their society enabled them to see its flaws and to beckon it upward. In both instances the basic assumption was that reformers were special people, either detached from their time and place or else having a peculiar position within it. There is truth to that notion, and historians frequently echo it. Certainly, commitment to a cause separates radicals and reformers from an apathetic or hostile majority. One of the attractions of antebellum reform clearly was the way its organizations and meetings provided moralistic men and women with little islands of righteousness amid what they thought was a vast churning ocean of depravity, acquisitiveness, and disorder.

Yet there are flaws to the idea that reformers and radicals are greatly different from their non-reformist contemporaries. Antebellum reform was very much a product of its milieu: it could not have existed without contemporary developments in printing and transportation or without a standard of living capable of supporting a life devoted to a cause. It also reflected widespread concerns about the family, self-control, arbitrary power, cultural diversity, economic opportunities, vice, and political turmoil. Above all, it provided men and women with one out of many possible means for comprehending, coping with, shaping, and occasionally denying the larger nineteenth-century processes of urbanization, industrialization, population growth, and immigration.

It is not enough to root antebellum reform in economic, demographic, social, and technological changes. To leave it there is to miss the importance of the way reformers perceived problems, strategies, tactics, and solutions. That is where culture enters the picture—it limits the responses people can make to a social situation and it determines the particular configuration of ideas, emotions, attitudes, insights, metaphors, and blind spots characteristic of reformers and radicals in a given age. The style of antebellum reform, in its initial stages, was very much that of evangelical Protestantism, with a leavening of classical republican rhetoric from the American Revolution, a measure of individualism, and a dash of economic or scientific thought, especially in communitarianism, labor reform, health reform, and asylum-building. In the 1820s and 1830s most reformers thought they were attacking sins, not social problems, and they urged individual repentance rather than legislation and coercion. By the 1840s that had begun to change, understandably so because reform is never homogeneous or static. Moral commitments can lead in several directions and tend to be modified by events, successes, failures, and even by fatigue and frustration. In the case of antebellum reformers, dissatisfaction with religion and churches prompted exploration of such "sciences" as health reform, phrenology, and spiritualism, which often dressed Protestant pieties in non-theological language. The ineffectiveness of voluntarism and moral suasion pushed reformers into advocating governmental action, including temperance laws and construction of asylums to turn deviants into model citizens. A mode of reform that in the 1830s sought to transform the world was itself greatly transformed by 1860.

Occasionally scholars argue about whether certain American social movements were backward- or forward-looking. Antebellum reform was both. It attempted to preserve and extend old virtues—orderliness, plain living, freedom from external restraints, and so on—but it also made shifts in emphasis and added such newer goals as strict self-control. If reformers could not entirely accept the behavior of their contemporaries, they nonetheless did not entirely reject the values and accomplishments of the social order emerging in the United States. Like most of their non-reformer peers, they were simultaneously awed and disquieted by the rising glory of the United States and by humankind's marvelous mechanical and electrical inventions. Only a few visionaries, usually in less popular causes—communitarians, feminists, Christian anarchists, labor reformers, and African Americans who saw into the heart of injustice and inequality—posed a deep threat to the emerging social, political, and economic order. The chief effect of other crusades—notably temperance, phrenology, and asylum- or school-building—was to encourage people to adjust to, rather than resist, the brave new world of the nineteenth century. Most antebellum reformers were, at heart, trying to adapt old and respectable verities, plus a few new ones, to an age of cities, steam power, rowdy politics, and get-rich-quick schemes. To their way of thinking, that did not require stopping progress in its tracks. Proper morality, they assumed, would ensure that God's (or Nature's) plan would continue to unfold. For them, reform explained what was wrong with individuals and the nation, what might go wrong in the future, and how to avoid it without sacrificing the historic mission of Americans to increase and be prosperous.

It is one of the minor tragedies of antebellum reform that few noticed its death or mourned its passing. Millennialism and the ability to believe in several causes simultaneously began to slip quietly away in the 1850s. By the 1870s they were all but gone. Perhaps the analogy is wrong. Eras do not die like living creatures; they merge and blend into one another. Antebellum reforms set the tone for a great deal of what came afterward: the search for secular and scientific modes of social thought; the quest for equality for women and African Americans; the professionalization of reform; and much more. But the future belonged to new sorts of people: to those who accepted the human body as a positive good; to those who tolerated diversity and believed that morality was not absolute; to those who had faith in improvement and adjustment rather than in the millennium; to those who saw economic and urban problems as economic and urban problems, not moral failures; and to those who believed that men and women are not masters of their destiny and that social change does not depend on overcoming the sinfulness of the human heart.

Above all, the future of reform belonged to institution users—to men and women who regarded bureaus, agencies, and the government in general as instruments of social policy. I have in mind, of course, the stream of liberalism that flows from Progressivism through the New Deal to the "Great Society" of the 1960s. It was at once more practical than antebellum reform and less radical. It seldom sought to transform America; more often, it tried to make the system run better. Except in rare radical moments (there were some in the 1960s), hope for a new heaven on earth, commitment to an oppositional style of life, and repudiation of sin and governmental coercion—characteristics of some of the greatest of antebellum reformers—were ground up by the very machinery of modern times that produced antebellum reform. If they were to reappear, it was uncertain whether or not they would rise in the guise of radicalism or reform, or even what those terms would mean in such a world.

# Bibliographical Essay

This bibliography is intended as a guide for general readers who want to look more deeply into the world of antebellum reform. It is also partial acknowledgment of my debt to the richness of the literature, including many excellent, more specialized studies not cited here. The publication dates of the titles that follow are reminders that had I known what fine work lay just around the corner in 1978, I probably would have been too intimidated to write *American Reformers*.

## GENERAL WORKS
The classic on antebellum reform is Alice Felt Tyler, *Freedom's Ferment: Phases of American Social History from the Colonial Period to the Outbreak of the Civil War* (Minneapolis: University of Minnesota Press, 1944). After more than a half century, its faults are obvious: it rambles, largely ignores such "fads" as phrenology, and is dated and simplistic in its interpretation. It is also a marvelous compendium that probably will never be supplanted for the mass of information it presents and for its charm. Another synthesis appeared as revisions to this work were being completed: Steven Mintz, *Moralists and Modernizers: America's Pre–Civil War Reformers* (Baltimore: The Johns Hopkins University Press, 1995).

Although the writing of social history has changed much since the publication of Whitney Cross, *The Burned-over District: The Social and Intellectual History of Enthusiastic Religion in Western New York, 1800–1850* (Ithaca: Cornell University Press, 1950), its analysis of reform holds up well. As few other studies have done, *Burned-over District* depicts the social and cultural matrix of reform and demonstrates the interconnections between crusades. It should, however, be supplemented by Michael Barkun, *Crucible of the Millennium: The Burned-Over District of New York in the 1840s* (Syracuse: Syracuse University Press, 1986), and by a forthcoming study, John W. Quist, *Restless Visionaries: The Social Roots of Antebellum Reform in Alabama and Michigan* (Baton Rouge: Louisiana University Press, 1997), as well as by the general works on evangelical Protestantism cited in the next section.

Several works provide valuable surveys of the culture out of which antebellum reform grew and of which it was a part. See, for example, Richard D. Brown, *Modernization: The Transformation of American Life, 1600–1865* (New York: Hill and Wang, 1976); Robert L. Hampel, "The Contexts of Antebellum Reform," *American Quarterly* 33 (Spring 1981): 93–101; Lawrence Frederick Kohl, "The Concept of Social Control and the History of Jacksonian America," *Journal of the Early Republic* 5 (Spring 1985): 21–34; Jean V. Matthews, *Toward a New Society: American Thought and Culture, 1800–1830* (Boston: Twayne, 1991); Anne Norton, *Alternative Americas: A Reading of Antebellum Political Culture* (Chicago: University of Chicago Press, 1986); and Lewis Perry, *Boats Against the Current: American Culture Between Revolution and Modernity, 1820–1860* (New York: Oxford University Press, 1993). Robert H. Walker, *Reform in America: The Continuing Frontier* (Lexington: The University Press of Kentucky, 1985), is an attempt to provide a classification of American reform. Robert H. Abzug, *Cosmos Crumbling: American Reform and the Religious Imagination* (New York: Oxford University Press, 1994), is the first installment of a promised two-part work that focuses on the religious core of reform. *The Antislavery Debate: Capitalism and Abolitionism as a Problem in Historical Interpretation*, edited by Thomas Bender (Berkeley: University of California Press, 1992), contains a high-powered discussion of the rise of humanitarian sentiment in the eighteenth and nineteenth centuries that forms an important part of the background of the reform movements discussed in this book.

## 1. THE MISSIONARY IMPULSE

The interrelations between Protestant churches and reform can be traced in John R. Bodo, *The Protestant Clergy and Public Issues, 1812–1848* (Princeton: Princeton University Press, 1954); Charles C. Cole, Jr., *The Social Ideas of the Northern Evangelists, 1826–1860* (New York: Columbia University Press, 1954); and Clifford S. Griffin, *Their Brothers' Keepers: Moral Stewardship in the United States, 1800–1865* (New Brunswick, N.J.: Rutgers University Press, 1960). Bertram Wyatt-Brown, *Lewis Tappan and the Evangelical War against Slavery* (Cleveland: Case-Western Reserve University Press, 1969), gives a clear sense of how the "benevolent empire" functioned. Finney is well treated in William G. McLoughlin, *Modern Revivalism: Charles G. Finney to Billy Graham* (New York: Ronald Press, 1959).

Timothy L. Smith, *Revivalism and Social Reform: American Protestantism on the Eve of the Civil War* (Nashville: Abingdon Press, 1957), was an influential corrective to misconceptions about the evangelical sects. More recent general works are Nathan O. Hatch, *The Democratization of American Christianity* (New Haven: Yale University Press, 1989); William G. McLoughlin, *Revivals, Awakenings, and Reform: An Essay on Religion and Social Change in America, 1607–1977* (Chicago: The University of Chicago Press, 1978); and James H. Moorhead, "Between Progress and Apocalypse: A Reassessment of Millennialism in American Religious Thought, 1800–1880," *The Journal of American History* 71, no. 3 (December 1984): 524–42. On millenarianism, see *The Disappointed: Millerism and Millenarianism in the Nineteenth Century*, edited by Ronald L. Numbers and Jonathan M. Butler (Bloomington: Indiana University Press, 1987). Richard J. Carwardine, *Evangelicals and Politics in Antebellum America* (New Haven: Yale University Press, 1993), is an important treatment that can be complemented by Daniel Walker Howe, "The Evangelical Movement and Political Culture in the North During the Second Party System," *Journal of American History* 77, no. 4 (March 1991): 1216–39, a helpful, suggestive essay tracing the connections between evangelical Protestantism and politics. Two studies trace the role of evangelical Protestantism in the breakup of the Union in 1860: C. C. Goen, *Broken Churches, Broken Nation: Denominationalism, Schisms and the Coming of the Civil War* (Macon: Mercer University Press, 1985), and Mitchell Snay, *Gospel of Disunion: Religion and Separatism in the Antebellum South* (New York: Cambridge University Press, 1993).

## 2. HEAVEN ON EARTH

Of the general histories of communitarian ventures, I have found most interesting three by participants (including a modern one): William A. Hinds, *American Communities and Co-operative Colonies*, 2nd ed. (Chicago: C. H. Kerr and Company, 1908); Rosabeth Moss Kanter, *Commitment and Community: Communes and Utopias in Sociological Perspective* (Cambridge: Harvard University Press, 1972); and John Humphrey Noyes, *History of American Socialisms* (Philadelphia: J. B. Lippincott, 1870). Also informative are Michael Fellman, *The Unbounded Frame: Freedom and Community in Nineteenth-Century American Utopianism* (Westport: Greenwood Press, 1973); Mark Holloway, *Heavens on Earth: Utopian Communities in America* (New York: Dover Books, 1966); and Edward K. Spann, *Brotherly Tomorrows: Movements for a Cooperative Society in America, 1820–1920* (New York: Columbia University Press, 1989).

Karl J.R. Arndt, *George Rapp's Harmony Society, 1785–1847* (Philadelphia: University of Pennsylvania Press, 1965), is a thorough treatment of a major strand of German pietistic communitarianism. On the Shakers, see Priscilla J. Brewer, *Shaker Communities, Shaker Lives* (Hanover: University of New Hampshire Press, 1986), as well as the works by Foster and Kern cited below.

As might be expected, Oneida has attracted a great deal of attention. Important for themes developed in this book are Maren Lockwood Carden, *Oneida: Utopian Community to Modern Corporation* (Baltimore: The Johns Hopkins University Press, 1969); Robert David Thomas, *The Man Who Would Be Perfect: John Humphrey Noyes and the Utopian Impulse* (Philadelphia: University of Pennsylvania Press, 1977); and, especially, Louis Kern, *An Ordered Love: Sex Roles and Sexuality in Victorian Utopias: The Shakers, The Mormons, and the Oneida Community* (Chapel Hill: University of North Carolina Press, 1981), and two works by Lawrence Foster, *Religion and Sexuality: Three American Communal Experiments of the Nineteenth Century* (New York: Oxford University Press, 1981), and *Women, Family, and Utopia: Communal Experiments of the Shakers, the Oneida Community, and the Mormons* (Syracuse: Syracuse University Press, 1991). Victor Hawley, *Special Love/Special Sex: An Oneida Community Diary* (Syracuse: Syracuse University Press), features an excellent commentary by Robert J. Fogarty. Although it covers a period beyond the scope of this book, it provides wonderful insight into sexual tensions within Oneida. Also on the later period see Robert J. Fogarty, *All Things New: American Communes and Utopian Movements, 1860–1914* (Chicago: University of Chicago Press, 1990).

Adin Ballou and Hopedale loom large in Lewis Perry, *Radical Abolitionism: Anarchy and the Government of God in Antislavery Thought* (Ithaca: Cornell University Press, 1973), and receive full treatment in Edward K. Spann, *Hopedale: From Commune to Company Town* (Columbus: Ohio State University Press, 1992). Charles Crowe does well by his subject in *George Ripley: Transcendentalist and Utopian Socialist* (Athens: University of Georgia Press, 1967). For sheer charm, my favorite account of Ripley's creation remains F. Lindsay Swift's *Brook Farm: Its Members, Scholars, and Visitors* (New York: Macmillan, 1900).

Paul E. Johnson and Sean Wilentz, *The Kingdom of Matthias: A Story of Sex and Salvation in Nineteenth-Century America* (New York: Oxford University Press, 1994), tells a fascinating story (in which the great African American abolitionist Sojourner Truth plays a part) and is a reminder of the sinister possibilities in evangelical and communitarian impulses.

## 3. EARTH AS HEAVEN

On Owen and the Owenites, see Arthur E. Bestor, Jr., *Backwoods Utopias: The Sectarian and Owenite Phases of Communitarian Socialism in America, 1663–1829* (Philadelphia: University of Pennsylvania Press, 1950); J.F.C. Harrison, *Quest for the New Moral World: Robert Owen and the Owenites in Britain and America* (New York: Scribner, 1969); and Carol A. Kolmerten, *Women in Utopia: The Ideology of Gender in the American Owenite Communities* (Bloomington: Indiana University Press, 1990).

In the first edition of *American Reformers* I bemoaned the relative lack of scholarship on Fourier's influence in America. That is no longer true, thanks to Carl J. Guarneri's fine *The Utopian Alternative: Fourierism in Nineteenth-Century America* (Ithaca: Cornell University Press, 1991). See also *The Utopian Vision of Charles Fourier: Selected Texts on Work, Love, and Passionate Attraction*, edited by Jonathan Beecher and Richard Bienvenu (Berkeley: University of California Press, 1971); and Nicholas V. Riasanovsky, *The Teachings of Charles Fourier* (Berkeley: University of California Press, 1969). The Modern Times community is the subject of Roger Wunderlich, *Low Living and High Thinking at Modern Times, New York* (Syracuse: Syracuse University Press, 1992). See also Christopher Clark, *The Communitarian Moment: The Radical Challenge of the Northampton Association* (Ithaca: Cornell University Press, 1995).

## 4. ANTISLAVERY

The study of antislavery took a new turn with Gilbert H. Barnes, *The Anti-Slavery Impulse, 1830–1844* (New York: D. Appleton-Century, 1933), which stressed the connection between evangelical Protestantism and abolitionism. James Brewer Stewart, *Holy Warriors: The Abolitionists and American Slavery* (New York: Hill and Wang, 1976), remains a lively, valuable general study. Among influential, but more specialized, works are Lawrence J. Friedman, *Gregarious Saints: Self and Community in American Abolitionism, 1830–1870* (New York: Cambridge University Press, 1982); Louis S. Gerteis, *Morality and Utility in American Antislavery Reform* (Chapel Hill: University of North Carolina Press, 1987); Aileen S. Kraditor, *Means and Ends in American Abolitionism: Garrison and His Critics on Strategy and Tactics, 1834–1850* (New York: Pantheon Books, 1967); John R. McKivigan, *The War Against Proslavery Religion: Abolitionism and the Northern Churches, 1830–1865* (Ithaca: Cornell University Press, 1984); and Donald G. Mathews,

*Slavery and Methodism: A Chapter in American Morality, 1780–1845* (Princeton: Princeton University Press, 1965). I said what I had to say about antislavery in Ronald G. Walters, *The Antislavery Appeal: American Abolitionism after 1830* (Baltimore: Johns Hopkins University Press, 1976).

There are a number of fine biographies of abolitionists, and a healthy trend in the field has been to produce valuable ones of second-level figures. Among those of major figures several stand out as particularly significant. They include Bertram Wyatt-Brown's biography of Lewis Tappan (previously cited); the biographies of the Grimké sisters and Frederick Douglass cited below; James Brewer Stewart, *Wendell Phillips: Liberty's Hero* (Baton Rouge: Louisiana State University Press, 1986); and Robert H. Abzug, *Passionate Liberator: Theodore Dwight Weld and the Dilemma of Reform* (New York: Oxford University Press, 1980). Edward Magdol, *The Antislavery Rank and File: A Social Profile of the Abolitionists' Constituency* (New York: Greenwood Press, 1986), is an effort to look beyond the leadership to discover an antislavery constituency. Leonard L. Richards, *"Gentlemen of Property and Standing": Anti-Abolition Mobs in Jacksonian America* (New York: Oxford University Press, 1970), looks at the other side.

Classic treatments of the early stages of antislavery are Winthrop D. Jordan, *White over Black: American Attitudes toward the Negro, 1550–1812* (Chapel Hill: University of North Carolina Press, 1968), and the work of David Brion Davis, especially *The Problem of Slavery in Western Culture* (Ithaca: Cornell University Press, 1966), *The Problem of Slavery in the Age of Revolution* (Ithaca: Cornell University Press, 1975), and *Slavery and Human Progress* (New York: Oxford University Press, 1984).

On African American abolitionists, see Benjamin Quarles, *Black Abolitionists* (New York: Oxford University Press, 1969); William S. McFeeley, *Frederick Douglass* (New York: Norton, 1991); Waldo E. Martin, *The Mind of Frederick Douglass* (Chapel Hill: University of North Carolina Press, 1984); and Shirley Yee, *Black Women Abolitionists: A Study in Activism, 1828–1860* (Knoxville: University of Tennessee Press, 1992).

On women abolitionists, especially useful works are Blanche Glassman Hersh, *The Slavery of Sex: Feminist-Abolitionists in America* (Urbana: University of Illinois Press, 1978); *The Abolitionist Sisterhood: Women's Political Culture in Antebellum America*, edited by Jean Fagan Yellin and John C. Van Horne (Ithaca: Cornell University Press with the Library Company of Philadelphia, 1994); Gerda Lerner, *The Grimké Sisters from South Carolina: Pioneers for Woman's Rights* (New York: Schocken Books, 1968); and Katharine Du Pre Lumpkin, *The Emancipation of Angelina Grimké* (Chapel Hill: University of North Carolina Press, 1974).

The transition of abolitionism into politics is traced in Eric Foner, *Free Soil, Free Labor, Free Men: The Ideology of the Republican Party before the Civil War* (New York: Oxford University Press, 1970); William E. Gienapp, *The Origins of the Republican Party, 1852–1856* (New York: Oxford University Press, 1985); and Richard H. Sewell, *Ballots for Freedom: Antislavery Politics in the United States, 1837–1860* (New York: Oxford University Press, 1976).

## 5. WOMEN AND A WORLD WITHOUT WAR

Peter Brock, *Pacifism in the United States from the Colonial Era to the First World War* (Princeton: Princeton University Press, 1968), is an exhaustive treatment of the subject that needs to be supplemented by three more recent studies: Charles Chatfield, *The American Peace Movement: Ideals and Activism* (New York: Twayne, 1992); Charles DeBenedetti, *The Peace Reform in American History* (Bloomington: Indiana University Press, 1980); and Valarie H. Ziegler, *The Advocates of Peace in Antebellum America* (Bloomington: Indiana University Press, 1992). Lewis Perry, *Radical Abolitionism: Anarchy and the Government of God in Antislavery Thought* (Ithaca: Cornell University Press, 1973), gives a sensitive account of nonresistance. Elihu Burritt's career can be followed in his own words and in those of Merle Curti in Curti, *The Learned Blacksmith: The Letters and Journals of Elihu Burritt* (New York: Wilson-Erickson, 1937).

Fine works about nineteenth-century women's activism began appearing at a rapid rate about the time *American Reformers* first appeared, and they reshaped the way we think about reform, politics, and gender. There is a helpful overview in Anne Firor Scott, *Natural Allies: Women's Associations in American History* (Urbana: University of Illinois Press, 1992).

Among the most relevant specialized studies for antebellum reform are Barbara J. Berg, *The Remembered Gate: Origins of American Feminism, The Woman and the City, 1800–1860* (New York: Oxford University Press, 1978); Ellen Carol DuBois, *Feminism and Suffrage: The Emergence of an Independent Women's Movement in America, 1848–1869* (Ithaca: Cornell University Press, 1978); Lori D. Ginzberg, *Women and the Work of Benevolence: Morality, Politics, and Class in the Nineteenth-Century United States* (New Haven: Yale University Press, 1990); Nancy A. Hewitt, *Women's Activism and Social Change: Rochester, New York, 1822–1872* (Ithaca: Cornell University Press, 1984); Keith E. Melder, *Beginnings of Sisterhood: The American Women's Rights Movement, 1800–1850* (New York: Schocken Books, 1977); Teresa Anne Murphy, *Ten Hours' Labor: Religion, Reform, and Gender in Early New England* (Ithaca: Cornell University Press, 1992); and the pioneering Mary P. Ryan, *Cradle of the Middle Class: The Family in Oneida County, New York, 1790–1865* (Cambridge: Cambridge University Press, 1981); Mary P. Ryan, *Women in Public: Between Banners and Ballots, 1825–1880* (Baltimore: The Johns Hopkins University Press, 1990); and Kathryn Kish Sklar, *Catharine Beecher: A Study in American Domesticity* (New Haven: Yale University Press, 1973). The valuable work of Anne M. Boylan is available in succinct form in her articles, especially "Women and Politics in the Era Before Seneca Falls," *Journal of the Early Republic* 10 (Fall 1990): 364–82; and "Women in Groups: An Analysis of Women's Benevolent Organizations in New York and Boston," *The Journal of American History* 71, no. 3 (December 1984): 497–523.

The study of women's work and working women's activism owes much to Thomas Dublin, *Women at Work: The Transformation of Work and Community in Lowell, Massachusetts, 1826–1860* (New York: Columbia University Press, 1979), now extended in his *Transforming Women's Work: New England Lives in the Industrial Revolution* (Ithaca: Cornell University Press, 1994). Also extremely important are Mary H. Blewett, *Men, Women, and Work: Class, Gender, and Protest in the New England*

232     BIBLIOGRAPHICAL ESSAY

*Shoe Industry, 1780–1910* (Urbana: University of Illinois Press, 1988); and Christine Stansell, *City of Women: Sex and Class in New York, 1789–1860* (Urbana: University of Illinois Press, 1987).

6. STRONG DRINK

Without intemperance, there would have been no temperance movement, so a useful starting point is with studies of American drinking habits, which include Edward Lender and James Kirby Martin, *Drinking in America: A History* (New York: The Free Press, 1982), and W. J. Rorabaugh, *The Alcoholic Republic: An American Tradition* (New York: Oxford University Press, 1979).

As an interpretation of the motives behind anti-alcohol campaigns, Joseph R. Gusfield, *Symbolic Crusade: Status Politics and the American Temperance Movement* (Urbana: University of Illinois Press, 1966), attracted both followers and detractors, but remains influential. Several subsequent studies, however, have greatly increased our appreciation for the diversity of temperance and for the various roles it played in antebellum society: Jack S. Blocker, *American Temperance Movements: Cycles of Reform* (Boston: Twayne, 1989); Jed Dannenbaum, *Drink and Disorder: Temperance Reform in Cincinnati from the Washingtonian Revival to the WCTU* (Urbana: University of Illinois Press, 1984); Barbara Leslie Epstein, *The Politics of Domesticity: Women, Evangelism, and Temperance in Nineteenth-Century America* (Middletown: Wesleyan University Press, 1981); Robert L. Hampel, *Temperance and Prohibition in Massachusetts, 1813–1852* (Ann Arbor: UMI Research Press, 1982); and Ian R. Tyrell, *Sobering Up: From Temperance to Prohibition in Antebellum America, 1800–1860* (Westport: Greenwood Press, 1979).

Joseph F. Kett, "Temperance and Intemperance as Historical Problems," *The Journal of American History* 67, no. 4 (March 1981): 878–85; and James R. Roher, "The Origins of the Temperance Movement: A Reinterpretation," *Journal of American Studies* 24 (August 1990): 228–35, give helpful overviews of the literature, while four other articles are reminders of the diversity of temperance's appeal: Robert L. Hampel, "Diversity in Early Temperance Reform: Another Look at the Massachusetts Society for the Suppression of Intemperance, 1813–

1825," *Journal of Studies on Alcohol* 43 (May 1982): 453–68; Edith Jeffrey, "Reform, Renewal, and Vindication: Irish Immigrants and the Catholic Total Abstinence Movement in Antebellum Philadelphia," *Pennsylvania Magazine of History and Biography* 112, no. 3 (1988): 407–31; Stanley K. Schultz, "Temperance Reform in the Antebellum South: Social Control and Urban Order," *The South Atlantic Quarterly* 83 (Summer 1984): 323–39; and Donald Yacovone, "The Transformation of the Black Temperance Movement, 1827–1854: An Interpretation," *Journal of the Early Republic* 8, no. 3 (Fall 1988): 281–97.

## 7. THE BODY AND BEYOND

Three books are good starting points for understanding nineteenth-century American health reform: Harvey Green, *Fit for America: Health, Fitness, Sport and American Society* (Baltimore: The Johns Hopkins University Press, 1986); Stephen Nissenbaum, *Sex, Diet, and Debility in Jacksonian America: Sylvester Graham and Health Reform* (Chicago: Dorsey Press, 1980); and James C. Whorton, *Crusaders for Fitness: The History of American Health Reformers* (Princeton: Princeton University Press, 1982).

Two studies, appearing almost simultaneously, greatly expanded our knowledge of the water cure and its implications for gender relations: Susan B. Cayleff, *Wash and Be Healed: The Water-Cure Movement and Women's Health* (Philadelphia: Temple University Press, 1987), and Jane B. Donegan, *"Hydropathic Highway to Health": Women and Water-Cure in Antebellum America* (New York: Greenwood Press, 1986). Also see Martha H. Verbrugge, *Able-Bodied Womanhood: Personal Health and Social Change in Nineteenth-Century Boston* (New York: Oxford University Press, 1988).

The standard book on phrenology, although due for replacement, is John D. Davies, *Phrenology, Fad and Science: A Nineteenth-Century American Crusade* (New Haven: Yale University Press, 1955). It can be supplemented by the lively, popularly written Madeline B. Stern, *Heads & Headlines: The Phrenological Fowlers* (Norman: University of Oklahoma Press, 1971). The most helpful study of spiritualism remains R. Laurence Moore, *In Search of White Crows: Spiritualism, Parapsy-*

*chology, and American Culture* (New York: Oxford University Press, 1977).

## 8. DANGEROUS CLASSES

For addressing issues in this chapter and the next, two crucial works are Paul Boyer, *Urban Masses and Moral Order in America: 1820–1920* (Cambridge: Harvard University Press, 1978), and Michael B. Katz, *In the Shadow of the Poorhouse: A Social History of Welfare in America* (New York: Basic Books, 1986). On the mission movement and poverty, also see Raymond A. Mohl, *Poverty in New York, 1783–1825* (New York: Oxford University Press, 1971), and Carroll Smith Rosenberg, *Religion and the Rise of the American City: The New York City Mission Movements 1812–1870* (Ithaca: Cornell University Press, 1971). A useful case study of welfare is Priscilla Ferguson Clement, *Welfare and the Poor in the Nineteenth-Century City: Philadelphia, 1800–1854* (Rutherford: Fairleigh Dickinson University Press, 1985).

Few fields have generated as much intellectual excitement as have studies of nineteenth-century working-class life. Many such works, however, deal with the richness of workingmen and -women's culture and the complexity of their lives, issues I have largely ignored in order to focus on reform organizations. Bruce Laurie, *Artisans into Workers: Labor in Nineteenth-Century America* (New York: Hill and Wang, 1989), provides an excellent overview. Among the more specialized works of importance for this chapter and for the field itself are Alan Dawley, *Class and Community: The Industrial Revolution in Lynn* (Cambridge: Harvard University Press, 1976); Paul G. Faler, *Mechanics and Manufacturers in the Early Industrial Revolution: Lynn, Massachusetts, 1780–1860* (Albany: State University of New York Press, 1981); Ronald Schultz, *The Republic of Labor: Philadelphia Artisans and the Politics of Class, 1720–1830* (New York: Oxford University Press, 1993); and Sean Wilentz, *Chants Democratic: New York City and the Rise of the American Working Class, 1788–1850* (New York: Oxford University Press, 1984). For major studies on working women and their forms of activism, see the titles by Dublin, Blewett, and Stansell cited in the bibliographical note for Chapter 5.

A provocative analysis of the relationship between class and race, with interesting things to say about popular culture, is David R. Roediger, *The Wages of Whiteness: Race and the Making of the American Working Class* (London and New York: Verso, 1991). Also useful in understanding how antebellum Americans perceived work is Jonathan A. Glickstein, *Concepts of Free Labor in Antebellum America* (New Haven: Yale University Press, 1991).

9. INSTITUTIONS AND UPLIFT

The historical literature on asylums and deviants has been strongly influenced by Michel Foucault and by American scholars in other fields, particularly sociologists and psychologists such as Howard Becker, Erving Goffman, and Thomas Szasz. Of works by historians relating to this chapter, Michael B. Katz, *The Irony of Early School Reform: Education and Innovation in Mid-Nineteenth Century Massachusetts* (Boston: Beacon Press, 1968), and David J. Rothman, *The Discovery of the Asylum: Social Order and Disorder in the New Republic* (Boston: Little, Brown, 1971), set in motion debates that were not resolved almost thirty years later. Gerald Grob, *Mental Institutions in America: Social Policy to 1875* (New York: Free Press, 1973), is more detailed, cautious, and balanced than Rothman's account. For narrower studies that give important glimpses into asylums, see Ellen Dwyer, *Homes for the Mad: Life Inside Two Nineteenth-Century Asylums* (New Brunswick: Rutgers University Press, 1987); Lynn Gamwell and Nancy Tomes, *Madness in America: Cultural and Medical Perceptions of Mental Illness Before 1914* (Ithaca: Cornell University Press, 1995); and Nancy Tomes, *The Art of Asylum-Keeping: Thomas Story Kirkbride and the Origins of American Psychiatry* (Philadelphia: University of Pennsylvania Press, 1994).

Joseph M. Hawes, *Children in Urban Society: Juvenile Delinquency in Nineteenth-Century America* (New York: Oxford University Press, 1971); Peter C. Holloran, *Boston's Wayward Children: Social Services for Homeless Children, 1830–1930* (Rutherford: Fairleigh Dickinson University Press, 1989); Robert M. Mennel, *Thorns & Thistles: Juvenile Delinquents in the United States, 1825–1940* (Hanover: University Press of New England, 1973); Eric C. Schneider, *In the Web of Class: Delinquents and*

*Reformers in Boston, 1810s–1930s* (New York: New York University Press, 1992); and Steven L. Schlossman, *Love and the American Delinquent: The Theory and Practice of "Progressive" Juvenile Justice, 1825–1920* (Chicago: University of Chicago Press, 1977), trace the progression from the House of Refuge to the juvenile court system.

In addition to Rothman's chapters on prisons, and the survey by Blake McKelvey, *American Prisons: A History of Good Intentions* (Montclair: Patterson Smith, 1977), there is Adam Jay Hirsch, *The Rise of the Penitentiary: Prisons and Punishment in Early America* (New Haven: Yale University Press, 1992), and, on the reform of women's prisons, Estelle B. Freedman, *Their Sister's Keepers: Women's Prison Reform in America, 1830–1930* (Ann Arbor: University of Michigan Press, 1981). Louis P. Masur, *Rites of Execution: Capital Punishment and the Transformation of American Culture, 1776–1865* (New York: Oxford University Press, 1989), treats changing views and practices regarding capital punishment. A theoretically and linguistically dense effort to relate the first two terms in its title is Thomas L. Daum, *Democracy and Punishment: Disciplinary Origins of the United States* (Madison: University of Wisconsin Press, 1987).

Carl F. Kaestle has provided surveys of the history of education in *Pillars of the Republic: Common Schools and American Society, 1780–1860* (New York: Hill and Wang, 1983) and "Ideology and American Educational History," *History of Education Quarterly* 22, no. 2 (1982): 122–37. See also Lawrence A. Cremin, *American Education: The National Experience, 1783–1876* (New York: Harper and Row, 1980), and more specialized studies by Carl F. Kaestle and Maris A. Vinovskis, *Education and Social Change in Nineteenth-Century Massachusetts* (Cambridge: Cambridge University Press, 1980), and Edith Nye MacMullen, *In the Cause of True Education: Henry Barnard and Nineteenth-Century School Reform* (New Haven: Yale University Press, 1991). For a methodical critique of Michael B. Katz's interpretation, see Maris A. Vinovskis, *The Origins of Public High Schools* (Madison: The University of Wisconsin Press, 1985).

# Index

abolitionism, *see* antislavery movement

Adams, John, 7

Adams, John Quincy, 7, 65

African Americans, 108–9, 186, 189, 197, 198, 221, 222; in antislavery movement, 78, 81–82, 85, 86, 97, 100, 102; labor reform and, 195; in temperance movement, 136, 141–43; voting rights granted to, 111

Alcott, Bronson, 54

Alcott, William Andrus, 154–55, 158

almshouses, 179, 200–3

Alphadelphia Phalanx, 71

Amana community, 40–42

American and Foreign Anti-Slavery Society, 92, 93

American Anti-Slavery Society, 49, 80–81, 86, 87, 92–94, 101, 118

American Association of Spiritualists, 169

American Bible Society, 31–33, 130–31, 177, 202

American Board of Commissioners for Foreign Missions, 31, 33

American Colonization Society, 79, 96

American exceptionalism, 26

American Hydropathic Institute, 157

American Hydropathic Society, 156

*American Journal of Insanity*, 209

American Medical Association, 148, 157

American Peace Society, 117–18, 120, 121, 123

*American Phrenological Journal,* 162, 163

American Physiological Society, 151, 152, 155, 162

American Revolution, 24, 29, 30, 45, 78, 115–16, 184, 186, 220

American School of anthropology, 164–65

American Sunday School Union, 31, 33

American Temperance Society, 129–30, 132, 138

American Temperance Union, 130, 132, 133–37, 139, 141

American Tract Society, 31–33

anarchism: Christian, 49, 85, 88, 91, 92, 118–21, 123, 221; communitarian, 67, 73–74

Andover South Parish Society for the Reformation of Morals, 31

Andrews, Stephen Pearl, 74

"animal magnetism," 169

Anthony, Susan B., 109

anthropology, 164–65

Anti-Dueling Society, 30

anti-licentiousness campaigns, 103, 106

anti-Masonry, 7, 9–11, 140

antislavery movement, xiii, xiv, 6, 8, 9, 11, 13–15, 17, 18, 77–103, 125, 126, 144, 148, 173, 175, 203; communitarianism and, 49, 74–75, 77; evangelicals and, 23, 28, 32, 33–37, 55; health reform and, 153, 155, 157; labor reform and, 182, 189; mob violence against, 86–88, 107; peace movement and, 118, 123–24; schism in, 87–94; spiritualism and, 171, 172; temperance and, 134, 137–42; territorial expansion and, 95–98; women's rights and, 85, 88–90, 103, 106–9, 111–12, 123

*Appeal to the Coloured Citizens of the World* (Walker), 78

Army, U.S., 137

Arthur, Timothy Shay, 134, 136

Asians, 197

Association of Medical Superintendents of American Institutions for the Insane, 209

asylum-building, 206–13, 215, 217, 220, 221

Bagley, Sarah, 114

Ballou, Adin, 49–51, 54, 55, 63, 120, 124

Baptists, 22, 23, 25, 29, 30, 33, 45, 93

Barnard, Henry, 214–15

Barnum, P. T., 167

Beaumont, Gustave de, 203

Beckwith, George C., 121

Beecher, Catherine, 107–8, 113

Beecher, Henry Ward, 161, 162

Beecher, Lyman, 22, 23, 27, 31, 128, 129, 132, 136, 138, 161

Beissel, Johann Conrad, 41, 42

Bible, the, 28, 35, 173, 216

biological determinism, 165
Birney, James G., 91–92, 95
birth control, 57, 113
Bishop Hill community, 44
blind, asylums for the, 211
*Blithedale Romance, The* (Hawthorne), 53–54
Boston Asylum and Farm School for Boys, 205
Boston Female Anti-Slavery Society, 107
Boston House of Reformation, 212
Boston Prison Discipline Society, 202, 206
Boston School Committee, 216
Brace, Charles Loring, 205, 206, 212
Brisbane, Albert, 68, 70–72
Brook Farm, 49–56, 60, 70–73, 214
Brooks, Preston, 100
Brothers, Thomas, 190
Brown, John, 100–1
bureaucratization, 209–10
Burritt, Elihu, 121–24

Caldwell, Charles, 160
Calvin, John, 26, 27
Calvinism, 26–29, 35, 167
Campbell, David, 153–54
capitalism: abolitionism and, 85; secular critique of, 64
Capron, Eliab W., 166
Cass, Lewis, 137

Catholics, 5, 9–10, 31, 34, 156, 157, 212; charitable agencies of, 178, 181; communitarianism and, 44; public schools and, 214, 216; temperance and, 135
Central Phrenological Society, 160
Channing, William Ellery, 51
charitable endeavors, 176–82
Chase, Salmon P., 96, 99
Child, Lydia Maria, 14, 108
child labor, 193
children, institutions for, 203–6, 212
Children's Aid Society, 205
Children's Progressive Lyceum, 169
cholera epidemic, 149–50
Christian anarchism, 49, 85, 88, 91, 92, 118–21, 123, 221
civil rights movement, xvii, 18
Civil War, xiv, 4, 16–17, 92, 101, 123–24, 139
Cobbett, William, 126–27
colonization, 79
Combe, George, 160–61, 164–65
common-school systems, 214
*Commonwealth v. Hunt* (1942), 192
communitarianism, 13, 15, 24, 37, 39–75, 103, 144, 148, 173, 196, 203, 217, 220, 221; abolitionism and, 49, 74–75, 77; education and, 49, 52, 103,

communitarianism (*cont.*)
214, 215; Fourierist, 52, 53, 56,
60, 67–74; health reform and,
156, 157; labor reform and, 74,
103, 189–90, 193–94; New
England, 49–54; Owenite, 62–
67; pacifism and, 120; pietistic,
41–49; spiritualism and, 168,
172; women's rights and, 106
complex marriage, 56–57, 60
Compromise of 1850, 96–98
Congregationalists, 22, 26–27,
30, 31, 33, 117, 128
Congress, U.S., 8, 65; abolitionism and, 81, 86–87, 95–99
Congressional Temperance Society, 136–37
Connecticut Missionary Society,
30
Connecticut Society for the Reformation of Morals, 30, 34,
128
Constitution, U.S., 99; Fourteenth Amendment, 111; Fifteenth Amendment, 101, 111
contraception, 113
Cragin, Mary, 56
cult of domesticity, 105, 113
Cummins, Henry, 14–15
Curtis, Burrill, 52
Curtis, George William, 52

Darwin, Charles, 58, 165
Daughters of Temperance, 136

David, Paulina Wright, 111
Davis, Andrew Jackson, 167–71
deaf-mutes, asylums for, 211
Declaration of Independence,
127
Deism, 24
Democratic Party, 7, 140, 191,
193; abolitionism and, 91, 92,
96, 98, 99; Jacksonian, 34, 131,
177, 185, 187–88
Democratic–Republican Party, 7,
31
Depression, xiv
determinism, biological, 165
Dew, Thomas R., 9
disunionism, 94
Dix, Dorothea, 207
Dodge, David Low, 116–19
domesticity, cult of, 105, 113
Douglas, Stephen A., 98
Douglass, Frederick, 81, 82, 100,
109, 142
Dow, Neal, 138–39
Draper, Ebenezer, 50
Draper, George, 50
Dunkers, 41
Dutch Reformed Church, 33

economic development: antebellum, 5–6; *see also*
industrialization
education, 180; communitarianism and, 49, 52, 103, 214, 215;
for girls, 113; health reform

and, 158; public, 8, 188, 213–
17, 221
Edwards, Justin, 129–30, 132,
138
egalitarianism, 64, 78
Emancipation Proclamation,
101
Emerson, Ralph Waldo, 51
Enlightenment humanitarianism,
78, 115
environmentalism, 63
Ephrata community, 41–44,
48
Episcopalians, 33, 177
Erie Canal, 5
eugenics, 148, 165
evangelical Protestants, xv, xvii,
8, 11, 15, 16, 21–37, 152, 189,
212, 220; in antislavery movement, 82, 84, 85, 90; charity
of, 176–78, 181, 196, 199;
communitarianism and, 39,
45–47, 51, 55, 58; labor reform
and, 192–94; missionary societies of, 30–35; pacifism of, 88,
119; public education and,
215, 217; in temperance movement, 23, 28, 30, 31, 33, 35–
37, 129–30, 144
Evans, Frederick W., 46, 67
Evans, George Henry, 187, 189,
190, 193
evolutionary theory, 165
exceptionalism, American, 26
exercise, 155, 158

Federalist Party, 7, 128, 129, 140
Female Labor Reform Associa-
tions, 114
Female Missionary Society, 176
Finney, Charles G., 22–23, 27–
29, 34–36, 46, 55, 178, 180
Finney, Mrs. Charles G., 179
Fourier, Charles, 60, 61, 67–71,
73, 75, 170
Fourierism, 52, 53, 56, 60, 67–
74, 193, 194
Fowler, Lorenzo, 162
Fowler, Orson, 159, 162
Fowlers and Wells publishing
house, 162–63
Fox sisters, 166, 169
Franklin, Benjamin, 13, 27, 29,
192, 213
free love, 57, 156
Free-Soil Party, 7, 96, 98, 99
French Revolution, 68
Fretageot, Marie D., 66
Fruitlands community, 54
Fugitive Slave Act (1850), 97–
100
Fuller, Margaret, 51, 112

Gall, Franz Joseph, 159–60,
164
Gallaudet, Thomas, 211
Galton, Francis, 58, 165
Garnet, Henry Highland, 100
Garrison, William Lloyd, 13, 14,
55, 77, 79–82, 87–94, 99–101,

Garrison, William Lloyd (*cont.*) 116, 118–20, 123, 126, 171, 207
Garrisonians, 90–92, 94–96, 109, 111, 121, 153, 172
German pietism, *see* pietistic communities
Giddings, Joshua R., 97–98
Gorsuch, Edward, 97
Graham, Sylvester, 149–57, 163, 171–73, 197
Great Awakening, 21, 24
Great Society, 222
Greeley, Horace, 68, 71, 72
Grimké, Angelina, 89–90, 103, 107, 108, 112, 114, 118
Grimké, Sarah, 89–90, 107, 108, 112, 114, 118
Grimké, Thomas, 118

Hague Conference (1899), 117
Hall, G. Stanley, 164
Hamilton, Alexander, 7
*Harbinger* (journal), 52, 56
*Harbinger of Peace* (journal), 118
Harmony Society, 41–44, 48, 53, 65
Hartley, Robert, 181, 182
Harvard University, 52
Hawthorne, Nathaniel, 52–54
health reform, xiii, 14, 36, 103, 106, 145, 148–58, 220; phrenology and, 163
Heighton, William, 190

Hicks, Edward, 115
Higginson, Thomas Wentworth, xiii, xix
Hinds, William, 53
Hofstadter, Richard, 125
Holley, Myron, 91
homesteading, 193
home visitors, 178–80
Hopedale community, 49–51, 53–55, 60, 73, 77, 120
House of Representatives, U.S., 86
Houses of Refuge, 203–6, 208, 211–13
Howe, Samuel Gridley, 211
humanitarianism, Enlightenment, 78, 115
Humphrey, Heman, 131
hydropathy, 155–58
Hygeio-Therapeutic College, 157
hypnotism, 169

immediatism, 18, 80, 85, 90, 96
immigrants, 4–5, 8, 10, 177–78, 195, 197, 198, 200; institutionalization of, 212; public schools and, 214, 215; temperance movement and, 138
Independent Order of Good Templars, 136
Indians, 115, 197–98
industrialization, 5, 6, 85, 154, 196

Industrial Revolution, 61, 74, 113

insane, institutions for the, 201, 203, 206–13

Jackson, Andrew, 7–8, 86, 87, 185, 187

James, William, 164

Jefferson, Thomas, 7, 31, 172, 213

Jerusalem community, 48

Jews, 197

Johnson, Richard M., 8

*Journal of Health*, 152

juvenile delinquency, 180, 203–6, 212

Kansas–Nebraska Act (1854), 98

Kelley, Abby, 92

Kellogg, John Harvey, 158

Know-Nothing Party, 7, 10, 12

Ku Klux Klan, xviii

labor reform, 46, 183–96, 217, 220, 221; communitarianism and, 74, 103, 189–90, 193–94; peace movement and, 122; political action and, 186–91; women and, 113–14

Ladd, William, 117–18, 120, 121

land reform, 193, 194

Lane Theological Seminary, 23, 28, 81

League of Universal Brotherhood, 121–22

Lee, Ann, 45–47

*Liberator, The*, 77–78, 82, 101, 112

Liberia, colonization of freed slaves in, 79

Liberty Party, 7, 23, 91–92, 94–96, 98, 137

Lincoln, Abraham, 7, 101, 123, 131

London Peace Society, 117

Lovejoy, Elijah, 87

Lowell (Massachusetts) strikes, 113–14

Luther, Martin, 172

Lutheran Church, 43

Macdaniel, Osborne, 70

McDowall, John, 179

Maclure, William, 66, 67

Maine Laws, 139, 141

male continence, 57–58

Malthus, Thomas, 200

Mann, Horace, 158, 161, 206, 213–16

manumission, 79

Masons, opposition to, *see* anti-Masonry

Massachusetts Anti-Slavery Society, 91

Massachusetts Board of Education, 158, 213
Massachusetts Board of State Charities, 210
Massachusetts Peace Society, 116, 118
Massachusetts Reform School for Girls, 205
Massachusetts Society for the Suppression of Intemperance (MSSI), 128, 133
Massachusetts State Reform School, 204
Massachusetts Supreme Court, 192
Mather, Cotton, 29, 30
Mathew, Theobald, 135
Meacham, Joseph, 46
Mechanics' Union of Trade Associations, 183, 186, 187, 190
Mencken, H. L., 24
mental institutions, 206–13
Merwin, Abigail, 55
Methodists, 22, 23, 26–27, 29, 30, 33, 93, 127, 141, 198
Mexican War, 95–96, 115, 121
middle class, 181, 197, 211; charitable activities of, 178–79, 181; homesteading and, 193; labor reform and, 185; morality of, 84; public schools and, 214–16; spiritualism and, 167; temperance and, 131, 146; women of, 104–5, 108, 112–13, 115

millenarianism, 24–25
millennialism, 18, 25–26, 34, 172, 178, 193, 194, 221; abolitionism and, 92; communitarianism and, 44, 46; peace movement and, 119
Miller, Peter, 42
Miller, William, 25
Millerites, 25
missionary societies, 30–35, 176, 180; communitarian, 49; Indians and, 182–83
Missouri Compromise, 98
mob violence, 9–12, 115; against abolitionists, 86–88, 107
Modern Times community, 50, 61, 74
Monroe, James, 65
Moral Police Fraternity, 169
moral suasion, 94, 100, 199
Moravians, 33
Morgan, William, 9
Morton, Samuel George, 164–65
Mott, Lucretia Coffin, 109–10

Nation, Carry, 125, 136
nationalism, 32
National Negro Convention movement, 82, 100
National Organization of Spiritualists, 169
National Prison Congress, 209
National Reform Association, 193

National Trades Union, 191
nativism, 10–12, 139
New Deal, xiii, 18, 222
New-England Anti-Slavery Society, 80
New England Association of Farmers, Mechanics, and Other Working Men, 187
New England Colored Temperance Society, 142
New England Non-Resistance Society, 49, 120, 121
New England Working Men's Association, 193
New Harmony, 64–67, 71–73, 187, 214
New Lanark (Scotland), 62
New View of Society (Owen), 63
New York Association for Improving the Condition of the Poor, 180
New York City Tract Society, 180
New York City Working Men's Party, 186
New York House of Refuge, 203–4, 212
New-York Magdalen Society, 179, 180
New York Peace Society, 116, 118
New York Society for Promoting Communities, 65
New York Tribune, 68
Nichols, Mary Gove, 156–57

Nichols, Thomas, 157
nonresistance, 88, 101, 116, 118–21, 123, 124, 196, 217
Nordhoff, Charles, 44
North American Phalanx, 71–73
Northampton Association, 54
Noyes, George, 56
Noyes, Harriet Holton, 56, 57
Noyes, John Humphrey, 39, 41, 47, 48, 55–60, 63, 64, 75
Noyes, Theodore, 59

Oberlin College, 23, 153–54, 180
Odd Fellows, 145
Ohio Reform Farm, 205
Oneida community, 39, 40, 55–61, 69, 72
Owen, Robert, 43, 46, 47, 48, 60–69, 73–75, 202
Owen, Robert Dale, 171, 187, 189, 190
Owen, William, 65
Owenism, 62–67, 72–74

pacifism, see nonresistance; peace movement
Paine, Thomas, 13, 190, 198
Panic of 1837, 40, 93, 120, 153, 180, 191, 193
Parker, William, 97
Peabody, Elizabeth, 51, 52, 73
Peaceable Kingdom, The (Hicks), 115

peace movement, xiv, 103, 115–24, 203; communitarianism and, 49

penitentiaries, 202–3, 208, 211

Penn, William, 115

Pennington, J.W.C., 142

perfectionism, 28, 29, 34–35, 51, 55–59, 92, 119, 148, 172, 178

Perkins Institute, 211

phalanxes, Fourierist, 68–73

Phelps, Anson, 178

Phillips, Wendell, 18

phrenology, xviii, 14, 148, 149, 158–65, 167, 168, 171–73, 175, 182, 197, 215, 217, 221

Pierpont, John, 171

pietistic communities, 41–49, 60, 63, 72

politics, 6–9, 12; evangelicals and, 31, 34; labor reform and, 186–91

population growth, 4

Populists, 18

postmillennialism, 18, 25–26

poverty, 176–82, 199–203; insanity and, 209, 212; public education and, 215

premillennialism, 24–25

Presbyterians, 22, 23, 26–27, 30, 33, 93, 116, 117, 128

prisons, 103, 202–3, 207, 211, 213, 217

private property, communitarian attitudes toward, 42, 44, 50, 52–53, 64, 65

professionalization, 209–10

Progressivism, xiii, xiv, 18, 222

Prohibition, xiv, 125, 146

prohibitionists, 137–39

prostitution, 179, 180

Protestantism, 65, 172–73; abolitionism and, 80, 88, 92; charitable activities of, 176–82; public education and, 214–16; spiritualism versus, 167–68; temperance and, 135; see also evangelical Protestants

psychology, 164

public education, 8, 188, 213–17, 221

Puritans, 213

Quakers, 13, 24, 33, 82, 108, 109, 114–17, 121, 127, 177, 202

racism, 101; abolitionism and, 85, 86; communitarian opposition to, 74–75; scientific, 148

radicals, definition of, xvi–xvii

railroads, 5

Randolph, John, 212

Rapp, George, 42–44, 48

Rapp, John, 44

reformers, definition of, xvi–xvii

reform schools, 204, 205

Remond, Sarah Parker, 142

Republican Party, 7, 92, 101, 139, 193; formation of, 98–99

revivals, *see* evangelical
Protestants
Rhett, Robert Barnwell, 126
riots, *see* mob violence
Ripley, George, 51–53, 55, 63
Roosevelt, Theodore, 18
Rush, Benjamin, 127, 128, 135,
150
Rush, Stephen C., 74

St. Mary's Mutual Benevolent
Total Abstinence Society, 135
Saint Nazianz community, 44
Saint-Simon, Henri, Comte de,
68
Scott, Dred, 99
séances, 166, 168
Second Great Awakening, 21, 24
segregation, opposition to, *see*
civil rights movement
Senate, U.S., 96, 100
Seneca Falls Convention (1848),
109–11, 113, 115
Seventh-Day Adventists, 158
sexuality: communitarianism and,
42, 44, 45, 47, 50, 55–60;
health reform and, 150–51;
spiritualism and, 167
Shakers, 40, 44–49, 60, 63, 65,
67, 72, 73
Sizer, Nelson, 165
Skidmore, Thomas, 186–87, 189,
195
slavery, 131; opposition to, *see*

antislavery movement; support
for, 9, 10, 12
Smith, Adam, 200
Smith, Gerrit, 137, 141
*Social Destiny of Man* (Brisbane),
68
socialism, 122, 190; communitar-
ian, 39, 53, 59
Society for the Diffusion of Spiritual Knowledge, 167
Society for the Prevention of
Pauperism, 176, 203
Society for the Reformation of
Juvenile Delinquents, 203
Sons of Temperance, 136, 141,
145
spiritualism, 24, 148, 149, 165–
73, 190
Spurzheim, Johann, 160, 161,
164
Stanley, Abraham, 45
Stanton, Elizabeth Cady, 109–
10, 113
Stanton, Henry B., 91, 109
stirpiculture, 58
Stone, Lucy, 109
Stowe, Harriet Beecher, 98
strikes, 183–85; African Americans and, 195; by women
workers, 113–14
suffrage, 85; for African Americans, 111; for white men, 8;
for women, xiv, 110–11
Sumner, Charles, 99–102
Sunday schools, 8, 31

Supreme Court, U.S., 99, 138
Swedenborg, Emanuel, 168–70

Tappan, Arthur, 13, 34–36, 178, 190
Tappan, Lewis, 13, 34, 35, 80–81, 90, 92, 94, 141
teetotalism, 132
temperance movement, xiii, xiv, xviii, 17, 103, 125–49, 152, 167, 173, 175, 177, 217, 221; African Americans in, 136, 141–43; antebellum, 4, 8, 15, 16; communitarians in, 49; evangelicals in, 23, 28, 30, 31, 33, 35–37, 129–30; ex-drunkards in, 133–36; health reform and, 156; phrenology and, 163; political action in, 136–40; in South, 140–41; women in, 106; working class and, 130, 134, 143, 146, 182, 189, 192
Temperance Society of Moreau and Northumberland, 127–28
tenement houses, 180–81
Ten Nights in a Bar-Room (Arthur), 134–35
territorial expansion, 4
Texas, annexation of, 95, 121
Thompson; Samuel, 148–49
Thoreau, Henry David, 101
Tocqueville, Alexis de, 178, 203
Tracts on the Coming Millennium (Owen), 73

Trall, Russell, 14, 157
Transcendentalism, 51, 52, 55, 101, 112, 168
transportation, 5
Truth, Sojourner, 74, 81, 109
Tubman, Harriet, 81
Turner, Nat, 78, 86

Una (journal), 111
Uncle Tom's Cabin (Stowe), 98, 147
underground railroad, 82
unions, see labor reform
Unitarians, 22, 24, 30, 31, 33, 34, 36, 51, 55, 82, 116, 117
United States Temperance Union, 130
Universalists, 30, 31, 36, 49, 51, 55, 168
urbanization, 5, 6, 85, 196
Utopia community, 74
utopianism, see communitarianism

Van Buren, Martin, 7, 8, 96, 191
Van Rensselaer, Stephen, 130
vegetarianism, 155
Vindication of the Rights of Women (Wollstonecraft), 104
Voice of Industry, 194
voluntary associations, 175; female, 106; male, 145
voting rights, see suffrage

Walker, David, 78, 100
Ward, Samuel Ringgold, 142
War of 1812, 3, 5, 7, 116
Warren, Josiah, 49, 50, 61, 67, 74
Washington, George, 7
Washingtonians, 133–36, 139–41, 144, 145
water cure, *see* hydropathy
*Water-Cure Journal, The,* 156, 163
Weld, Theodore Dwight, 28–29, 35, 81, 90
Whig Party, 7, 91, 92, 98, 99, 191, 215
White, Ellen, 158
Whitman, Walt, 147
Wilkinson, Jemima, 48
William and Mary College, 9
Wilmot, David, 95–96
Wilmot Proviso, 96
Wilson, Henry, 99
Wollstonecraft, Mary, 104
*Woman in the Nineteenth Century* (Fuller), 112
Woman's Christian Temperance Union, 136
women: in antislavery movement, 85, 88–90, 103, 106–9, 111–12, 123; communitarianism and, 49, 64; health reform and, 152, 156; in labor movement, 113–14, 193; peace movement and, 120; in prison, 202; rights for, xiii, xiv, 17,

103–15, 118, 124, 148, 186, 189, 203, 221, 222; in temperance movement, 132, 140, 142–44
Woodson, Lewis, 142
Woodward, Samuel B., 206, 208
Woolman, John, 13
Worcester, Noah, 116–18
working class, 175, 182–83; public schools and, 214; temperance and, 130, 134, 143, 146, 182, 189, 192; *see also* labor reform
*Working Man's Advocate* (journal), 187, 189
Working Men's parties, 186–91, 195
World's Anti-Slavery Convention (1840), 109
World War I, xiv
World War II, xiv
Wright, Frances, 75, 106–7, 112, 189, 190
Wright, Henry C., 118, 123
Wright, Lucy, 46

Yale University, 122, 154; Divinity School, 55
Young, William Field, 194

Zoar community, 41, 44

CPSIA information can be obtained
at www.ICGtesting.com
Printed in the USA
LVOW11s1931260418
574993LV00001B/2/P